# Usable Web Menus

*Andy Beaumont*

*Dave Gibbons*

*Jody Kerr*

*Jon Stephens*

Published by glasshaus Ltd,
Arden House,
1102 Warwick Road,
Acocks Green,
Birmingham,
B27 6BH, UK

Printed in the United States
ISBN 1-904151-02-7

# Usable Web Menus

**web professional to web professional**

© 2002 glasshaus

# Trademark Acknowledgements

# Credits

**Authors**
Andy Beaumont
Dave Gibbons
Jody Kerr
Jon Stephens

**Technical Reviewers**
Kapil Apshankar
Justin Everett-Church
Jon Duckett
Damien Foggon
Martin Honnen
Dan Maharry
Alex Shiell
Imar Spaanjaars
Stephen M Williams

**Proof Readers**
Dan Walker
Agnes Wiggers

**Technical Editor**
Chris Mills

**Commissioning Editor**
Chris Mills

**Managing Editor**
Liz Toy

**Project Manager**
Sophie Edwards

**Production Coordinator**
Pip Wonson

**Cover**
Dawn Chellingworth

**Indexers**
Adrian Axinte
Alessandro Ansa

# Cover Image

hunting-island-light-3 – from the *Carolina Lighthouses* series (for full series, go to *http://www.atpm.com/7.08/carolina-lighthouses/*). Photo taken by, and used by kind permission of A. Lee Bennett Jr (contact: lbennett@atpm.com).

We chose this image, not only for aesthetic pleasure, but also because the stairway signifies navigation within a site, and of course, navigation is what this book is all about!

"The historic Hunting Island lighthouse was originally constructed in 1859 and rebuilt in 1875 after it was destroyed during the Civil War. This is the only lighthouse in the state of South Carolina open to the public." "The Hunting Island lighthouse provided safe passage for ships until it was deactivated in June of 1933. A unique feature of this lighthouse is that it was constructed using cast iron plates and designed to be dismantled in case it ever needed to be relocated. As fate would have it, due to erosion of the beach in 1889, the lighthouse was moved inland 1 1/4 miles from its original site to where it presently stands."

Excerpts taken from the Hunting Island tourism page, *http://www.huntingisland.com/*.

# About the Authors

## Andy Beaumont

Andy Beaumont is a freelance interactive developer/designer based in central London. As a firm believer in the "sharing of knowledge" ethos that has made the Flash community so strong, Andy writes Flash tutorials for the likes of *pixelsurgeon.com* and Computer Arts magazine, teaches Flash and ActionScript at Mac Uni in London, and runs a personal Flash help site at *http://www.eviltwin.co.uk*. As something of an ActionScript mercenary Andy has worked with many top design agencies including magneticNorth, Conkerco, and Broadsnout.

*First and foremost I would like to thank my beautiful partner Kelli for belief and support beyond the call of duty. Professionally I need to thank the brilliant Brendan Dawes, Pete Barr-Watson, the BD4D people and the pixelsurgeons. Finally, thanks to everyone that contributes to the online Flash communities at were-here.com, ultrashock.com and the Flashcoders list, without whom I would know half as much as I do today.*

## Dave Gibbons

Dave Gibbons is a writer and web designer from Beaverton, Oregon, US. He recently worked for five years as a writer, Web/Intranet Designer and programmer, and usability tester at Intel.

When not losing sleep over proper menu design, Dave writes humor ("humour" in the rest of the English-speaking world), novels, and screenplays.

## Jon Stephens

A site developer, writer, and consultant living and working in Scottsdale, Arizona, Jon Stephens works with JavaScript, PHP, and in producing technical documentation for area firms. He's an original member of CNET's Builder Buzz developers' site, and has served there as a Community Leader since 1998. Jon has co-authored two books on HTML and JavaScript for Wrox Press.

*Acknowledgements: Chris Mills and Sophie Edwards at glasshaus – for encouraging me to participate in this project, and for putting up with my somewhat erratic and eccentric ways! My reviewers, including Martin Honnen – who helped make this a much better book; Ed Lonergan and colleagues at Corporate Architects and associated companies – for moral and other support; my friend and co-author Jody Kerr – whose fault it is that I wound up in Arizona; my parents; and Sionwyn – who took my hand from half a world away.*

# Table of Contents

# Introduction

Just menus?

Yes. This book focuses on a single, vitally important task that confronts everyone who builds web sites for use by people: how to code and present menus that are easy to understand and use, that convey what users need to know about the many paths they can take to get to the information they want, in a variety of technologies.

Every web site has a menu (trust us – we looked for a professional site without a menu, and came up empty). Some sites have two, three, or more menus on the same page. Menus give users a simple way to deal with the dozens, hundreds, even thousands of options (or more), ideally sorting those options into understandable divisions people can choose with some confidence that they'll end up more or less where they intended to go.

In this book, we'll show you how professional sites organize content, present options, and use a wide array of technologies for navigation. Sometimes these approaches work well and serve as excellent models for your own navigation systems. Sometimes? Well – nobody's perfect!

We'll walk you through an extensive range of different menu code that can be easily downloaded from *http://www.glasshaus.com/*, and adapted to your own needs, taking all the hassle out of menu coding. Because of the large choice of browsers available to surf the Web, our code has been extensively tested, and designed to work in:

- IE 4+, Netscape 4+, and Opera 5+ for PC

- IE 4+, Netscape 6+, and Opera 5+ for Mac

Unless specifically stated. We can't absolutely guarantee that it will all work in every browser, but you should be able to get some use out of it in just about any browser you care to mention.

In glasshaus books, we aim to keep the concepts clear and have a little fun along the way. Don't look for too much academic posturing. This book is about getting real work done in the real world for the benefit of real users. If there is anything mentioned in this book that has been gone over quickly for brevity, but which you would like to know more about, you can probably find something in the *Resources* section at the end of this book.

# Who is This Book for?

It is fair to say that this book is for Intermediate to Advanced Web Professionals – it isn't essential, but a reasonable grounding in HTML, JavaScript, Flash (for the Flash chapter, obviously), and at least the principles of server side scripting (for the more advanced dynamic menus later on) is definitely advised to get the most out of this book.

Developers will make great use of the examples as time savers, negating the need to code such mundane functionality themselves.

The book also includes essential menu design chapters – what you need to look into before you even get to the code, including usability and accessibility hints for menu design, and Information Architecture advice in the context of menus (including how to identify who your target audience are, and what they will want from a menu).

# What's Covered/Chapter Synopsis

This book basically looks at three fairly distinct areas – menu design principles, coding basic menus, and coding more advanced menus with dynamic server-side functionality. Without wasting anymore time, let's have a quick look at what each chapter goes into:

### Chapter 1: Rules of Good Menu Design

This chapter provides a set of general rules to follow when designing menus, to give you some parameters for creating well thought-out, usable menus that are accessible, extensible, and easy to use. It also shows examples from the real world, both of good menus and not so good menus.

### Chapter 2: Information Architecture for Menus

This chapter delves deeper into some of the issues you need to consider when designing the navigation for your site, some of which were touched upon in *Chapter 1*. We look at Information Architecture for menus, including choosing the right information hierarchy and granularity of your information, and looking at and making informed decisions based upon the target audience for your site. Here, we also look further at accessibility options for menus. We also show you how – and why – to test your assumptions on real users.

### Chapter 3: Basic JavaScript Menus

The first technology chapter, here we look at the more simple types of menu that are commonly utilized in web pages, including hyperlinked text menus, button menus, image rollover effects for menu options, check-box and radio-button menus, menus with separate corresponding image rollovers, and one- and two-level "jump menus".

### Chapter 4: Menus with Advanced Scripting and DHTML

This is a follow-on from the last chapter, in which we explore using CSS to enhance the look and feel of your menus, and DHTML to provide some advanced features. First, we look at providing a menu with a function to select a different stylesheet, providing a different look and feel for the navigation, and saving the user's preference in a cookie. Next, we look at using image maps in menus, including coding a floating menu design that travels with you as you scroll and resize the browser window. Finally, we walk you though the creation of some expanding/collapsing menus.

### Chapter 5: Flash Menus

This chapter first discusses creating site navigations in Flash, and the associated usability issues. We then go on to show a 3-stage menu development process. First, we see a flat expanding menu. Next, we show how to dynamically populate this menu with options contained in an XML file. Lastly, we show how to dynamically populate this menu with options contained within a MySQL database, using PHP (the code download also includes code that mirrors this functionality, using ASP and MS Access).

### Chapter 6: Dynamic Server-Side Menus

The final step in our journey through the world of web menus – this chapter shows how to take some of the menus from *Chapter 4*, and add dynamic server-side functionality to them. We will look at creating breadcrumb trails, and dynamically populating a menu using ASP/XML, ASP/SQL Server, and PHP/MySQL. We will also dip into menu creation using ASP.NET.

# Conventions

In this book, you will come across a number of conventions that help to outline certain types of information, to help with your comprehension of the subject matter. These are explained below.

## Styles

When new subjects are introduced, or important words and phrases are talked about, we use the `important words` style. For example: "We can also control their appearance to some degree in the newer browsers using `Cascading Style Sheets` (CSS)."

*This style* is used when discussing keyboard shortcuts, URLs, and text that you will see on your screen:

- To select the top option, press *Ctrl-z*.

- Go to *http://www.glasshaus.com/* for more information.

- When the site has loaded, press the button marked *Submit*.

When introducing a new block of code, we use the code foreground style:

```
<body bgcolor="#FFFFFF" text="#000000">
   <table width="150" border="0" cellspacing="0" cellpadding="5"
          bgcolor="#CCFFCC">
      <tr>
         <td align="center" valign="middle">
            <a href="contact.html" class="menu">CONTACT</a>
```

```
          </td>
        </tr>
    </table>
</body>
```

When we have seen code before, but wish to show it again, for example, when we are adding functionality to an existing piece of code, we use the code background style (see below). This can lead to a mixture of styles, like so:

```
<body bgcolor="#FFFFFF" text="#000000">
    <table width="150" border="0" cellspacing="0" cellpadding="5"
           bgcolor="#CCFFCC">
        <tr>
            <td align="center" valign="middle">
                <a href="about.html" class="menu">ABOUT US</a>
            </td>
        </tr>
        <tr>
            <td align="center" valign="middle">
                <a href="contact.html" class="menu">CONTACT</a>
            </td>
        </tr>
    </table>
</body>
```

When we want to talk about something that appears in code during a paragraph, it is presented like this: The `bgcolor` attribute of the `<body>` element sets the background color of your page. In this case, its value is `#FFFFFF` (the hexadecimal value for white). This style is also used for filenames, for example: `menu.html`.

---

Really important, not-to-be-missed points are encapsulated in boxes, like this.

---

*Asides to the current discussion are presented like this.*

## A Note About Code Formatting

In this book, the code formatting on the page is optimized for ease of comprehension. However, some of the whitespace added to achieve this would break the code if it were to be used as printed. For example, the following piece of JavaScript code:

```
        output+="<a href=\""+getPageName(pages[i][j])+".html\" class=\"page\"
title=\""+pages[i][j]+"\">";
```

would be changed to this:

```
        output+="<a href=\""+getPageName(pages[i][j])+".html\" class=\"page\"
                title=\""+pages[i][j]+"\">";
```

All of the examples in the code download are presented without this excess whitespace.

# Support/Feedback

At glasshaus, we aim to make our books as helpful and informative as possible. However, no matter how many edits we subject our chapters too, a few errors are bound to slip through. We would like to apologize for any errors that reach the published version in advance. However, all is not lost. If you spot an error in this book, please submit it to us by e-mailing it to support@glasshaus.com. We will then check out the error, and put it up on the Usable Web Menus errata page if it is something that will help out other readers too. The errata page can be found on *http://www.glasshaus.com*.

This address can also be used to access our support network. We are dedicated to helping your career at every stage, not just up until the book hits the shelves. If you have trouble running any of the code in this book, or have a related question that you feel that the book didn't answer, please mail your problem to the above address, in addition quoting the title of the book, the last 4 digits of its ISBN, and the chapter/page number your query relates to.

# Web Support

Feel free to go and visit our web-site, at *http://www.glasshaus.com/*. Here, you will find a wealth of useful resources:

- **Code Downloads**: The example code for this, and every other glasshaus book, can be downloaded from our site.

- **Site Gallery**: You will find a Usable Web Menus Site Gallery to complement this book on our site. There you will be able to find all the examples contained within the book, plus lots more, to give you ideas and inspiration. The examples are each presented as a functioning menu, plus a scroll box where you can view (and copy) the code, side by side – here's an illustration of this:

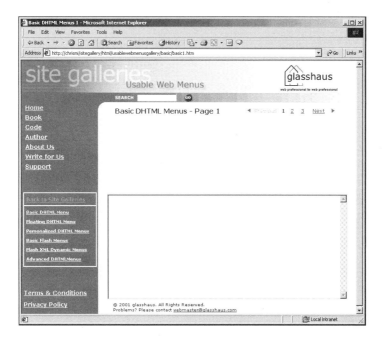

- **On-line Resource Center**: As a future endeavor, in the interests of you, the reader, we have decided to refrain from weighing down our books with appendices full of installation instructions, HTML tags, CSS properties, JavaScript functions etc. etc. Instead, we will be building up a definitive reference on the Web, to suit all such needs. This will be added to over time, so if there is anything you feel isn't up there but should be, just tell us!

# 1

- 12 rules to follow for designing usable menus

**Author: Dave Gibbons**

# Rules for Good Menu Design

As a Web Designer/Developer, you're constantly dealing with an amazingly unpredictable element: **the user**. Users (surfers, customers, etc.) rely on your help and judgment to guide them through your site, frequently taking turns you can't anticipate. This chapter looks at the ways in which many sites have approached the Herculean task of helping users find what they're seeking – often, unfortunately, losing their way themselves.

In this chapter, you will see:

- What we mean by "Usable Web Menus".

- Twelve key rules, illustrated by real examples, to help you design usable web menus.

We will also include many examples to further illustrate the points we make in this chapter, focusing not only on menus that we can see ways to improve, but also on well-designed menus. The principles in this chapter hold true regardless of the technology used, from plain HTML to DHTML to Flash. Specific technologies are discussed in detail in later chapters.

> Before we go any further, we'd just like to say that in no way do we wish to advocate that the example sites included in these chapters are badly designed, or that they have no value. Far from it – our aim is to promote better usability amongst web professionals, whether your site is featured here or not. We're not trying to suggest that we know best; we just want to help you to make your sites even better. Usability isn't measured against a Boolean ideal (bad usability vs. good usability), or even a point scale. Like the atmosphere of a restaurant, the measure (and, indeed, the value) of web site usability is subjective. It is difficult to state in concrete terms, but at the same time it is vitally important.

# Usable Web Menus

This book focuses almost exclusively on navigation menus, which show you how to get around a web site. We won't worry too much about esoteric distinctions like Internet/intranet/extranet or how to handle multiple sites or subsites. We will also stay away from discussing other types of menus, like the choice selection menus you sometimes find on fill-in forms.

We need to start by getting a couple of definitions out of the way, just to make sure we're all working with the same ideas:

- **Menu**: A navigational method that enables a user to go directly to specific, known parts of a web site. Almost every good web site has at least one menu, plus a search feature for finding information people couldn't figure out from the menu.

> Though it may seem like we're knocking "Search" as a bail-out throughout the introductory chapters, we're certainly not. A search feature obviously has many useful applications that don't necessarily mean your menu has confused or otherwise failed the user. For example, visitors to a CD shopping site who know what they want to buy will go straight to the search feature, rather than "drill down" through a menu system.

- **Usability**: How easily and quickly a device can be learned and put to work. If it takes two minutes to figure out a menu, it probably suffers from poor usability. If its purpose and use is immediately clear, a menu has very good usability.

> If you want more technical discussions of these topics, see one of the many books and courses on Human-Computer Interaction (HCI) or Human Factors. For our purposes, we'll work with much less formal definitions than you'd get from a PhD.

Note that the definition of usability we use incorporates the word "quickly," but not the word "beautifully." One of the first things learnt in usability testing is that fast, simple usage is more important than aesthetic splendour. Design and corporate branding are often at odds with usability. (We'll see many examples of ignorance in this area throughout this chapter.) Time savings are also often the most quantifiable measures of a particular design's success over its alternatives. For example, if you give a user the task of finding a particular piece of information with your menu, you may discover that it takes extra time when the menu includes branding or other overhead. You may also find that it makes no difference. See *Chapter 2* for information about testing your menus with users.

We're also looking at *how easily* users can use a menu. For example, if your menu is immediately readable and understandable, but the user has to position their mouse pointer in tiny squares to operate it, the menu is still not very usable, as we can see from the example opposite. This menu has many problems, including bad contrast and mysterious wording, but its biggest usability problem is that you have to click the little, dark squares to navigate to any subsection. (The excellent new version of *michaeljrosen.com* is scheduled for upload by the time this book comes out.)

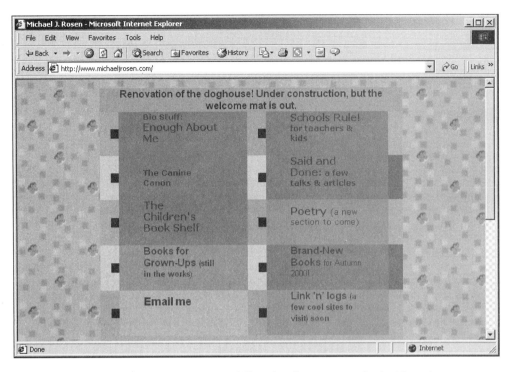

So, when we lay out guidelines for good usability of web menus, we're looking at ways your users – often, but not always, your customers – can get to work on your web site quickly and easily.

# 12 Rules for Web Menu Usability

While this is not an exhaustive list of menu design rules, these are certainly all factors designers need to keep in mind when designing (or redesigning) web menus. The guidelines in this list are detailed and illustrated throughout the rest of this chapter.

**1.** Menus must be considerate of the user's main task.

**2.** Menus must be distinct from content.

**3.** Menus must be clearly readable (this includes visual contrast and text and icon size).

**4.** Menus must be easily scanned for information.

**5.** Menus must be easily operated.

**6.** Menus must behave as your target user would expect.

**7.** Menus must load as quickly as possible.

**8.** Menus must be consistent across a site.

**9.** Menus must put a higher premium on usability than branding.

**10.** Menus must be localizable.

**11.** Menus must be accessible to the handicapped.

**12.** Menus must work on multiple browsers.

As you can probably immediately tell, almost all of these guidelines apply to web pages as well as menus. For example, number 7 tells you your menus should load as quickly as possible, but in most cases the menu loads at the same speed as the rest of the page. In these cases, where the concepts of "web page" and "menu" are inseparable, assume the guideline means your menu system shouldn't negatively affect the usability (including readability, speed, etc.) of the web page any more than necessary.

> Obeying all 12 of these guidelines would be a tall order, and of course rules are made to be broken – we certainly do not advocate that you should stick to every one religiously. However, this list should guide your web designs, even if you decide to shatter one or more of its tenets.

# Rule 1: Menus Must Be Considerate of the User's Main Task

A common mistake made by Web Designers and other interface designers is forgetting what the user really wants. If you go to Amazon, you probably want to buy a book, DVD, or one of the bazillion other things they sell. But you almost certainly **don't** want to read about what a great entrepreneur Jeff Bezos is, or how the web site works, or how cool things will be once you finally get a chance to buy something. Splash screens (or "Intro" screens) are a prime violator of this principle (see *http://www.artisandesigngroup.com/* below), but some menus are equally inconsiderate of the user's task. As we'll discuss in *Chapter 2*, you have to know why your user is visiting, what their primary task is, then build everything they see around making that task easier.

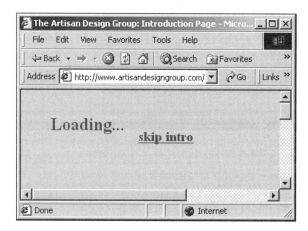

As much as possible, the web site should get out of the way and let the user get on with doing what they want to do. The user usually wants to bounce in, buy something or get some information, and bounce away again as quickly as possible. In an ideal world, they don't even notice the web site around their activity. Back to *Amazon.com* – one of the secrets to their success (in addition to very good Customer Relationship Management) is that you can go there, find what you want, buy it, and get on with your life with a minimum of interruption.

Even "destination sites" (and there aren't nearly as many destination sites as some would like to think) have something the user wants to do. A site where you play games online, for example, may capture a user's attention for hours at a time. But we can't forget that playing the game, **not** using the web site, is the user's goal. It's the same with information/news sites. The user wants to get the information; they don't want to use the site. If we lose sight of the user's goals, we may as well simply redirect them to other, more usable sites – they'll go anyway.

# Rule 2: Menus Must Be Distinct from Content

Because menus are so important to a user's navigation of a web site, they have to be immediately identifiable as menus. Some ways to set the menu apart from the rest of the content on a page:

- Use a different font size for the menu

- Use different line spacing (double-spacing works well in plain HTML)

- Make a visual cue to separate the menu from its surroundings, like a line or box

- Leave "whitespace" around the menu

> Another issue in distinguishing menus from content relates to your search functions. Menu elements should be excluded from text searches as much as possible. If your global menu includes the words "Kitchen Items," for example, you don't want a search for "Kitchen" to match every page on the site.

The example overleaf (*http://searchwebservices.techtarget.com/*) contains a lot of very useful information, but unfortunately, the layout makes it very hard to work out where to go to find anything. It certainly takes a while to work out where the menu is (the actual navigation menu is at the top) – it blends into the main logo, almost like a decorative underline. White on gray text adds to the effect, not catching the eye like a higher-contrast color scheme would.

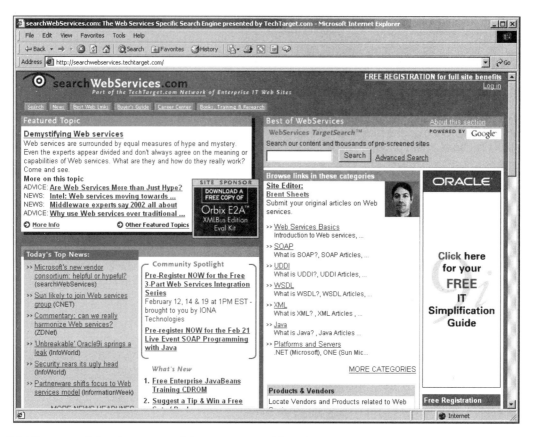

iBizKit, a portal development tool, has come up with an innovative way to separate the menu from its surrounding content (see *http://www.ibizkit.se/* – the site is in Swedish, so click the Union Jack on the menu to get the English version). The menu (see opposite) floats above the page, and can be positioned anywhere in the browser and expanded or contracted for more flexibility (as the diagram opposite shows). Unfortunately, this innovation introduces many usability problems. For one thing, the menu exists inside the browser window, so if you resize the window you may "lose" the menu entirely. It is also unexpected for a web menu to be a tear-off like this – users can easily get confused about how to use it. For most users, tear-off menus aren't even very usable in desktop applications, so putting them on the Web isn't likely to make your site more usable.

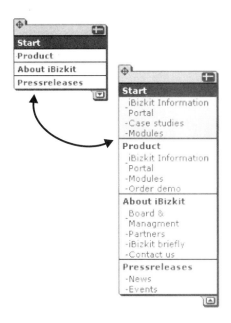

*For a working example of a floating menu that doesn't get lost off-screen, see the third Image Map example of Chapter 4.*

It's easy to fail to distinguish between menus and content. In the following figure (*http://www.coupdefoudre.com/*), the designer uses what looks like plain HTML but turns off the underline for links. Since web users largely expect to see links underlined (a number of sites these days also go against this rule), this page of links just looks like a bunch of text. Well, more accurately, the *Bookmark us!* link is underlined, but none of the other links are. More confusingly, the large headings like "*Questions*" aren't hyperlinks, but the text under them is.

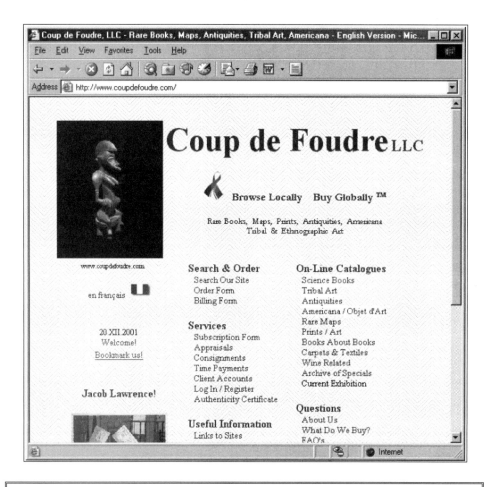

To underline or not to underline? Many sites now work around the browser defaults, turning off underlines for links and sometimes implementing HTML tricks to highlight links if the user happens to mouse over them. While there is a growing body of opinion that says links don't have to be underlined, you should only go with that crowd if your user testing bears out the alternative approach. Usability suffers whenever you go off the path people have learned to tread. When in doubt, check out the most successful sites on the Web. *Yahoo.com*, *Amazon.com*, and *CNN.com*, for example, use the browser defaults (usually blue underlined links which turn purple after they're visited).

There's a very cool and derogatory term for the way some artsy sites fail to be usable: **mystery meat** (think of those really cheap "meat" pies you got for dinner at school). These sites are so named because you have to poke around a long time to figure out what they are. In the figure opposite (*http://www.zcsterling.com/homepage.html*), a site celebrated by the famous web design site "Web Pages that Suck" (*http://www.webpagesthatsuck.com/*), a user would have to prod several of the beautifully designed but mysterious icons to find out what the site was about.

Of course, it is possible to go the other way, and take the division between menu and content too far – much too far, in the following example from car company Skoda (see below for an illustration of the site's menu section, or browse to *http://www.skoda.cz/info_index.htm*). This page of the site appears to have no menu at all, unless you happen to glance at the upper right corner and notice the word *menu*. Clicking this opens a menu that is too small to be useful, though not many users would get far enough to figure that out:

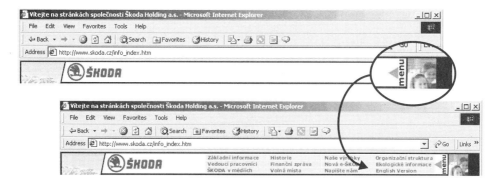

# Rule 3: Menus Must Be Clearly Readable

This rule is not about choosing words or symbols (that's rule 4), but about making the words and symbols visible to the user. This means:

- Text and graphics must contrast significantly with the background.

- Text and graphics must be large enough to be understood and operated even at high resolution.

- Never hide text or graphics that might be usable.

The figure below (*http://www.bluesky.com/*) shows a site that uses relatively clear graphics in an interesting design, but fails to give users a search feature. As the diagram illustrates, lucky users who happen to mouse over the box toward the lower right will find the search feature hidden there, in black-on-dark blue text until you mouse over it – in which case it lights up. There is no apparent point to this mouseover magic; it only serves to make the user experience less sensible.

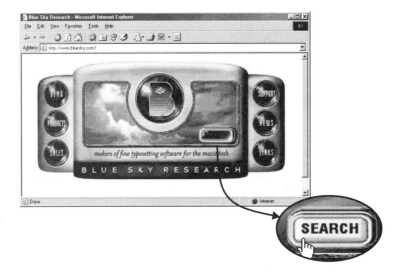

# Rule 4: Menus Must Be Easily Scanned for Information

One of the cardinal rules in design is that people don't read – they scan. Bold words in a long block of text (or indeed, underlined links in a long block of text) draw their attention. Menus, as we've already discussed, must be separate from the surrounding content, but they are still subject to the no-reading rule.

When a user sees a button that says "*Search*," they recognize it immediately. If they see the same button marked "*This is a good button to press if you want to search for information on this web site because it opens the page that searches for things*," they will not recognize it for what it is so easily, and also won't bother to read the text, so it is a useless button. This is obviously an extremely exaggerated example, but the principle applies to many common elements a user might scan for:

- *Search*

- *Print*

- *Products*

- Contacts

- A printer icon

- A shopping cart icon

- A telephone number

- An e-mail address

- An e-mail icon (typically an envelope)

- Their own name

Did you notice that "*Search*" shows up in that list even though it is mentioned in the previous paragraph? That's because many readers will only see the bulleted list, not the text above it. Remember that, despite the best efforts of writers, people don't read in these circumstances.

The "no reading" idea goes back to the first principle: consider the user's primary task. When trying to find something on their site, the primary task is not to read about how the site works, or even to read the navigation. They'll scan the navigation for familiar cues, but if they don't find what they're looking for right away, they'll dive straight into the *Search* feature.

Keep the following ideas in mind when designing a menu:

- Words are very important *even if you also use icons*, because there are so few pictures that are universally recognized.

- Use one simple word for an option if at all possible.

- Put the key word first if you must use multiple words. For example, "*Articles by me*" not "*Some articles*".

- Two or three simple words are better than one arcane word.

- For icons: explanations in tool tips are no substitute for labels right on or near the icon. Tool tips or `<alt>` tags should be used, certainly, if only for accessibility's sake, but don't count on them to make mysterious icons clear. People really aren't that curious.

- List options in order of their usefulness to your target customer. You will be able to find this order through testing and/or surveying. Arbitrary lists are not very useful as menus. Don't fall back on alphabetical or alphanumeric order unless the content dictates it. For example, a list of options with equal "weight" (like people's names or part numbers) should be in alphanumeric order, but lists of features or products are more usable if listed by other criteria like popularity. Also remember that your list may change when translated to other languages, making what you see as an ordered list into an arbitrary list for your foreign customers.

This chapter includes several examples of good design from Microsoft, so see the following example (*http://www.microsoft.com/jobs/design/*) for one that's both bad and ironic. It's bad because it's incomprehensible. It's ironic because it's a page of opportunities **for designers** to work at Microsoft.

The following site from Volkswagen (*http://www.vw.com/#/*) is not easily scan-able. The icons are nicely labeled, but by themselves they're incomprehensible – if you clicked the barely readable "*Icons only*" option at the left, would you know that the smiley face was the *MyVW* customer and fan portal? (Fortunately however, the default setting is "*Icons and Text*".) The second menu, the three buttons below the colored bar at the top, includes the bizarre option *VW etc*. Is that Volkswagen and other brands? Or is the label being dictated by the size of the button? With more space, the button could say "*Merchandise and Events*", which is what's really behind that button.

The site in the figure below (*http://www.digiwis.com/*) has a clear text link menu, but it also has an image map. If you happen to mouse over one of the cryptic images, a label pops up under it.

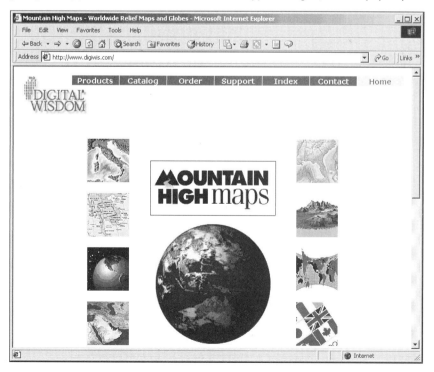

Bugatti's European site (*http://www.bugatti-cars.de/*, see below) looks like an intro screen, like something else will happen on its own. Once you realize that nothing is happening, you can try to figure out which of the options in this four-item menu will take you to useful information. Another strange point to add is that this page includes JavaScript that forces the browser window to be maximized, and disables the button that demaximizes the browser window – hence the unusual screenshot.

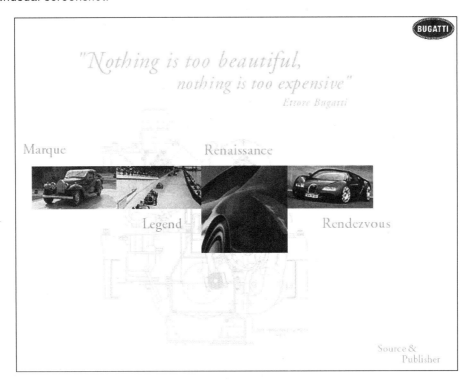

# Rule 5: Menus Must Be Easily Operated

It must be possible to use the menu with a normal degree of patience and dexterity. Menus on a graphical user interface are going to be used with a mouse or similar pointing device (leaving out special considerations for accessibility for the moment). The smaller the target for the mouse, the more likely you are to miss it, instead clicking on a non-active part of the page or, much more frustratingly, on the wrong link. This shows up as a problem with dynamic HTML, where you can highlight an entire line in the menu by mousing over it but be unable to click the highlighted option unless you're pointing precisely at the text itself.

> Make your mouse targets big enough to be hit easily. Wherever possible, keep the targets static even though Flash, JavaScript, and other technologies enable you to make them bounce around.

Also, if you are using text and graphics in combination, make both hot. It is very frustrating to assume the text is a link when the real link is the icon (see the chapter's first example, *http://michaeljrosen.com/*, for example) and vice versa.

In this next example from Microsoft, there isn't much air between links, so there's some danger that you'll hit the wrong one. However, the expanding/collapsing feature works very neatly, operating whether you click on the plus sign beside a label or on the label itself – as you can see, after clicking *Product Information*, the subsections expand elegantly, and even though the links in the menu aren't underlined the menu is fairly easy to use – so long as you use IE.

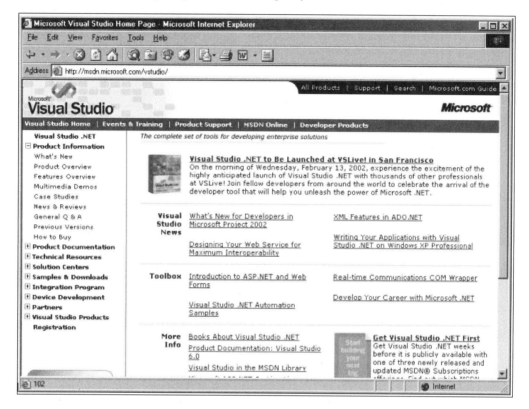

# Rule 6: Menus Must Behave As Your Target User Would Expect

One of the many rules of thumb in usability, in addition to "people don't read, they skim" and "icons are almost always better with text", is "there is no such word as **intuitive**". (Indeed, more scholarly works refer to the technical truth of this statement, since 'intuition' means knowing things without being taught them.) What this means for you as a designer is that no design you ever come up with will be instantly usable by everyone. The best you can shoot for is a design that is very easy for your target audience to learn, and the easiest things to learn are those that are familiar to us – in other words, we've learned them already.

A printer icon, though it looks like a fax machine, a sailboat, a hovercraft, or a hundred other things, looks like a printer to us because we've already learned that it's a printer icon. The Web has fewer pre-learned conventions to work with, but there are some.

For example, people expect every web page to give them a sense of place and purpose: "Tell me where I am and what I can do.", If your menu doesn't indicate these things, users will be confused.

In the increasingly prevalent left-hand-menu design, with or without frames, people expect that when they click on the left, the right will change to show what they clicked. The TRIO site (see below, *http://www.trioprograms.org/home.html*) has a confusing way of handling this, which changes only the left side (actually loading a new page in the left frame) when you first click there – in the diagram below, the left-hand menu is the menu before a menu option has been clicked, while the right hand one shows the state of the menu afterwards. The right-hand frame stays the same throughout.

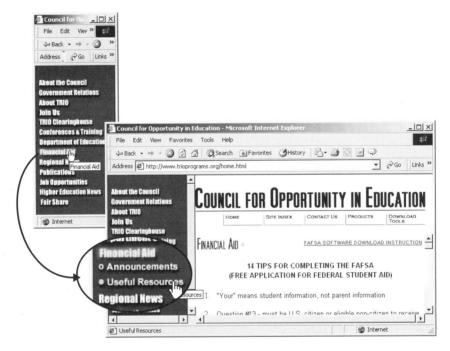

To make this kind of set up less confusing, you should certainly use visual cues like arrows that tell a user that something they do will exclusively affect the menu. Also, using DHTML or similar technologies where available, makes the menu respond to the user's input almost immediately, as opposed to the round trip to the server required for the approach shown above.

Some conventions are somewhat destructive. For example, users are so used to seeing ads in pop-up windows that it's now almost impossible to use pop-up windows for any other purpose – site navigation, for example. Another example based on users' learned response to ads shows up on *http://www.alistapart.com/*, seen opposite, where the bold text menu in the upper right could be ignored easily because, among other things, it could be mistaken for a square banner ad. In this design, factors that drive users' eyes away from the menu include visual cues like the large, out-of-place text and the choice of words. For example, *THIS WEEK* sounds more like an advert than a menu choice. As a user pointed out, swapping the left and right sides might have alleviated this problem, since users have learned to look for menus on the top and left.

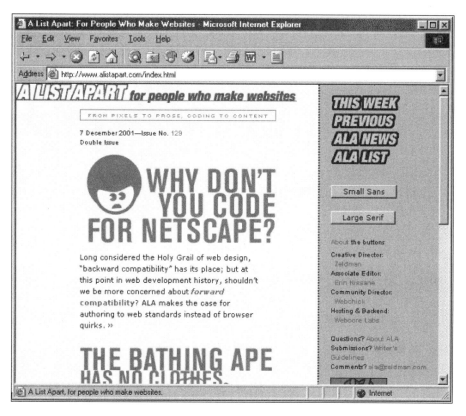

Depending on your audience, you may be able to get away with stealing conventions from the world of desktop applications. For a general web audience, this is very bad usability, but if your audience is composed of developers, like the visitors to Microsoft's Developer Network (see *http://msdn.microsoft.com/*, overleaf), you can use their experience with desktop applications to pull off some neat tricks. The arrows beside some of the options in this menu are identical to the ones used in pull-down menus in Windows. This is a perfect (learned) visual cue that another menu will open up to the right if you click (or, in this case, mouseover) that option. In Netscape and other non-IE browsers, Microsoft strips away the dynamic content, as well as the associated visual cues, leaving a menu of plain links.

## Rule 7: Menus Must Load Quickly

Don't make the mistake of thinking this rule only applies to users of the slowly dying dial-up lines – this rule is universal, even if you are working in a closed system like an intranet where you know everyone has high-speed access. Guaranteed high-speed access (if there was such a thing) wouldn't justify elaborate Flash or Java menus – even complicated DHTML menus – that take 10 or 15 seconds to load. Users get frustrated after about 2 seconds, and at 8-10 seconds they are likely to think their browser is locked up. This is when they hit the *Back* button or, worse, reload the page to try to fix the problem, before giving up.

Some clever web designers, like game designer David Brackeen (*http://www.brackeen.com/*), who know the user will have to wait for a minute or more have gone beyond the "*Please wait*" message and actually created interactive "*Please wait*" screens to distract the user. (Brackeen's is a Pong game – to see it in action, try loading a game.) This type of bandage is only for emergency use, though. As a rule, keep your menus simple and useful and your users will thank you. As a test, check the time it takes to load your page and Amazon's home page. Amazon's is likely to include much more information than yours, but it will probably load faster anyway because it is simple and optimized for speed.

Of course, it is possible to take simplicity too far. The usability site Alertbox (*http://useit.com/alertbox/*), home of usability guru Jakob Nielsen, is notoriously hard to use until you sit down and pay attention to it – not things you can count on from the average web user. The problem with Alertbox isn't just that it's too simple, even though it does eschew basic web navigation tools like menus. It also goes against some of the "learned behavior" common to web users. For example, the home page features a classic, centered text-entry/button combination that we've all learned to associate with the *Search* feature (see below). On this page, however, that combination is used to subscribe to Nielsen's e-mail newsletter. Of course, if you *read* the material around the box it's perfectly clear how this works, but you know the rule about web surfers and reading...

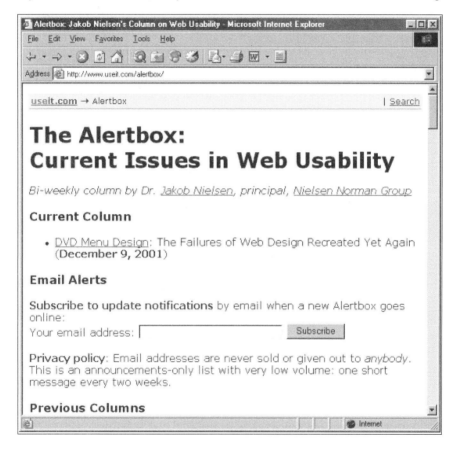

# Rule 8: Menus Must Be Consistent Across a Site

This rule is hard to observe, particularly if your site's pages are coded individually. As a user gets further into your site they are learning a little bit about what to expect. As soon as their expectations aren't met, they're confused. "Confused" is exactly what you're trying to avoid.

The example overleaf (*http://www.mindbird.com/raised_relief_maps.htm*) is not terribly confusing, but it is irritating. On the first page, the menu fits on this screen because the text is normal. On the second screen, the menu no longer fits and looks out of place because the text is bold (for no reason).

## Rule 9: Menus Must Put a Higher Premium On Usability Than Branding

This may be the toughest rule to sell to your Marketing department, particularly if they've already come up with a "corporate font" that they insist you use on the web site.

It's entirely possible that your corporate colors, fonts, and other branding elements are not usable on the Web. It's a completely different medium than packaging and print advertisements (the classic homes of branding). The most eye-catching colors (bright yellow for most things – particularly outside; silver and blue on packages) are perfectly hideous on the screen, but they're likely to be your corporate standards. This is where you may have to put a bad design against a good one head-to-head in usability tests.

Or, of course, you may lose the battle and be forced to put a bad design on a public site, as we see opposite, on *http://www.lamborghini.com/*. Here, Lamborghini is trying to convey the dark intensity of a legendary black bull by making as many elements as possible dark. Unfortunately, this includes the text, which is too small. It may work wonderfully on a slick page, but on a light-emitting device like a computer monitor, it's mud.

In the figure below (*http://www.xara.com/*), Xara takes a design that would be great in print, and tries to utilize it on the Web. The circles with labels end up looking like a menu, though they're actually not – if you click on *and more*? it takes you to the same place as *buttons*, *rollover bars*, and *$69*.

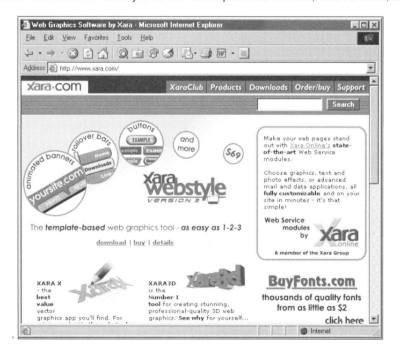

# Rule 10: Menus Must Be Localizable

It is beyond the scope of this book to explain everything that goes into internationalization (or I18n for short) and localization (I10n for short), but there are many volumes on this complicated subject.

The least you need to know is that it will cost at least 10 times as much to localize a word in a graphic or multimedia presentation as it will to localize the same word in plain text. That cost can be 100 times as much, depending on the project. If you know your site will be translated, stick to text as much as possible. (Note: Newer technologies like **Scalable Vector Graphics (SVG)** may reduce designers' dependence on static GIF and JPEG graphics, with the added benefit of being easier to localize.) Think about using a text menu with pipes (the I character) or brackets between the options instead of a graphic with the same words. Automatic translation sites like AltaVista's Babelfish (*http://babelfish.altavista.com/*) also leave your graphics intact, so if your navigation is graphical or multimedia, international users will be out of luck.

If you do have alternative versions of your site for other languages, there are a number of approaches to cluing in your international users to the fact that they can view the site in their own language. One that has become something of a standard is the use of flags, which can be a problem for widely used languages like French, English, and Spanish. Does everyone in America identify with the Union Jack? Probably not any more than Venezuelans identify with the flag of Spain. A simpler approach is to call out the language by name (in that language, if possible – for example, "*français*" instead of "*French*"). It is important to remember that people don't read, particularly if they're thrown by seeing a page in a foreign language. They might stumble across the name of their language simply because it's the only familiar thing on the page, particularly if it's in their language. An Italian site that listed the languages in Italian would show English as "Inglesi" – hardly something that would visually pop out of a menu viewed by, for example, an Australian user. A more usable option is to call out the languages more boldly, like the high-contrast color scheme used in the figure opposite (*http://www.nasasrbija.com/*). Here, the links to other languages are right at the top of the menu in a higher contrast color (if you go and look at the actual site, you'll see that it's gold on black).

# Rule 11: Menus Must Be Accessible To the Handicapped

This is an area where XML/XSL(T) and CSS can come in very handy, and where Flash and other multimedia often make things very difficult.

It's all right to use the most visually stimulating color scheme you can come up with (remembering to keep the contrast high), but you have to remember that many users won't ever "see" it. Blind and otherwise visually impaired users may "see" your site through a voice system or an electronic Braille reader. This doesn't mean you have to stick to plain HTML, but it does mean you must have a way for your site to make sense in plain text, either through an alternative address or through stylesheets. The added benefits here include the ability to have your site indexed by spiders (HotBot, for example) and having them available to WAP and other non-standard Internet devices.

Stylesheets for your site are a good idea anyway, but particularly with regard to accessibility. Many users who rely on special equipment to navigate through your site, also rely wherever possible on device-specific stylesheets (usually CSS, but increasingly XSL(T) on the server). You don't have to create those stylesheets, simply identify your site in its code as relying on a stylesheet, and let the user's device substitute its own stylesheet as needed.

Use meaningful `<alt>` tags on all important graphics, particularly those that are hot. For an option like "*Home*," for example, an `<alt>` tag that simply says "home" is meaningful. At the same time, an `<alt>` tag that is designed for fun or strictly to jazz up your site's tool tips ("Click here!" or "I don't know what I want.") is much less useful.

To find more about web accessibility, go to the homepage of the W3C Web Accessibility Initiative (*http://www.w3.org/WAI/*), and the Section 508 page of the US Access board (*http://www.access-board.gov/508.htm*). In addition, an excellent eye-opener for accessibility issues is Bobby (*http://www.cast.org/bobby/*). Bobby is a tool that analyzes your site and points out potential difficulties with text, graphics, styles, and much more.

# Rule 12: Menus Must Work On Multiple Browsers

Now that everything – from PDAs to sewing machines – is Internet-ready, it's next to impossible to assume a set of capabilities that your audience brings to the site. Their browser of choice might be a text-only phone browser, throwing your thousand-hour Java navigation project out the window.

The simple way to approach this contingency is to offer a text-only link near the beginning of your page – as long as you remember why you offer that link. In the following figure (see *http://www.worldsat.ca/* on the right), the graphics on the home page include a "text only option," but there is, ironically, no text version of that link. If you visit this site with a text-only browser, you won't see the "*Text-based Navigation*" link! However, alternative browsers will display it, and you can present them with a usable site specific to their needs. XML/XSL and CSS are obviously more complicated ways to address this, but they are far superior if you can afford them (see *Chapter 4* for CSS in action).

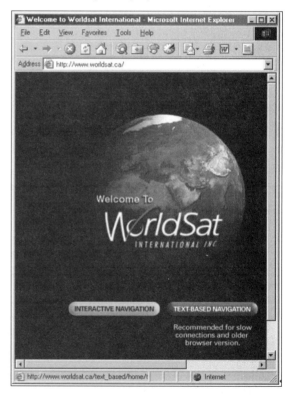

Even on the desktop, IE, Netscape, and Opera each handle things like stylesheets, Java, multimedia, and other fairly mainstream issues in unique ways. Test your designs on the browsers you expect your target audience to have, and include a cursory check with at least two other browsers: Lynx (a text-only desktop browser – see opposite) and a phone emulator like the one available at *http://www.openwave.com/products/developer_products/index.html* (see *Chapter 2* for an example of this in action).

```
LYNX                                                          _ □ ✕
Auto  ▼  ☐ ▣ 🖹 ⊞ 🖺🖺 A

                                    Welcome to Worldsat International

         [spacer.gif] [spacer.gif] [spacer.gif] [spacer.gif] [spacer.gif]
              [spacer.gif] [spacer.gif] [spacer.gif] [spacer.gif]
                        [indexr1_c1.jpg] [spacer.gif]
         [indexr2_c1.jpg] [globe_slice.jpg] [indexr2_c7.jpg] [spacer.gif]
              [web_award.gif] [indexr3_c8.jpg] [spacer.gif]
                        [indexr4_c7.jpg] [spacer.gif]
                        [indexr5_c2.jpg] [spacer.gif]
    [indexr6_c2.jpg] [indexr6_c3.jpg] [indexr6_c4.jpg] [indexr6_c5.jpg]
                        [indexr6_c6.jpg] [spacer.gif]
              [indexr7_c3.jpg] [indexr7_c5.jpg] [spacer.gif]
                   [inter.jpg] [text.jpg] [spacer.gif]
              [indexr9_c3.jpg] [indexr9_c5.jpg] [spacer.gif]




Commands: Use arrow keys to move, '?' for help, 'q' to quit, '<-' to go back.
 Arrow keys: Up and Down to move.  Right to follow a link; Left to go back.
 H)elp O)ptions P)rint G)o M)ain screen Q)uit /=search [delete]=history list
```

The above screenshot shows the WorldSat page in a text-only browser, Lynx – can you find the link for "*Text-based navigation*" on this page? Note that Lynx is available from *http://www.trill-home.com/lynx/binaries.html*.

# Summary

That's a lot to keep in mind, but every point we made in this chapter has been (and likely will be again) a headache for real-world Web Designers. Slap a Post-it note on the 12 rules page and review it whenever you build a new site.

The key thing to keep in mind is that everything you publish on the Web is intended for a user, and every one of those users has a unique background and real-world demands. Everything you can do to make their web use easier and faster is valuable to them and, ultimately, to you.

In *Chapter 2*, we'll dig into deciding how you should structure a site's navigation from the ground up for maximum usability, including information architecture principles and testing your assumptions with real users.

# 2

- Information Architecture for menus

- Identifying your target audience

- Choosing the correct hierarchy and granularity for your menus

- Menu Accessibility

- User testing

**Author: Dave Gibbons**

# Information Architecture for Menus

At this point in the book, you've already seen several real-world examples of menus incorporating good and bad features, and some general guidelines for creating usable menus. The rules and guidelines we've covered so far apply to how a good menu works, but not so much what it says. In other words, you now know how to provide good, readable, usable navigation, but we haven't yet talked about where you're navigating people to.

In this chapter, you will see:

- The challenges of presenting information for easy access to your target user.

- The challenges of organizing information in menus.

- How **Information Architecture (IA)** addresses those challenges.

- How you can apply IA concepts to your web content.

- How to make sure your design is usable before and after it goes live.

- Examples of different approaches, focusing, as with the previous chapter, not only on the missteps but also on menus that are well done.

*Information Architecture is basically the practice of looking at the needs of a web site's users, and the information to be contained within that site, and organizing that data, and the means of navigating said data to make it as usable as possible. For a more detailed discussion of IA, go to http://hotwired.lycos.com/webmonkey/design/site_building/tutorials/tutorial1.html for a useful tutorial on the basics of IA.*

# Challenges in Making Menus Meaningful

In the previous chapter, we defined a menu as "A navigational method that enables a user to go directly to specific, known parts of a web site.".

We distinguish this from another popular method of navigation: a **search feature**, which enables users to bypass (or otherwise give up on) your menu scheme and simply guess how you might have classified the information they need. In very complex environments, for example, Google (*http://www.google.com/*, see below), which indexes almost everything on the Web, searching is the primary navigation device. In these cases, a navigation menu would likely be more trouble than it's worth. Google includes such a menu, but it is more or less hidden behind the *Directory* link, clearly secondary to the search.

For a contrasting example, see opposite – HotBot (*http://hotbot.lycos.com/*), another search engine. It immediately provides an extensive menu that enables users to drill down to what they need, but the desired information can be 2, 5, or 10 menus away from the home page. Users are more likely to find what they need on HotBot by simply using the search feature. (HotBot implicitly nods to this reality by automatically moving your text cursor to the *Search* field when you enter the site.)

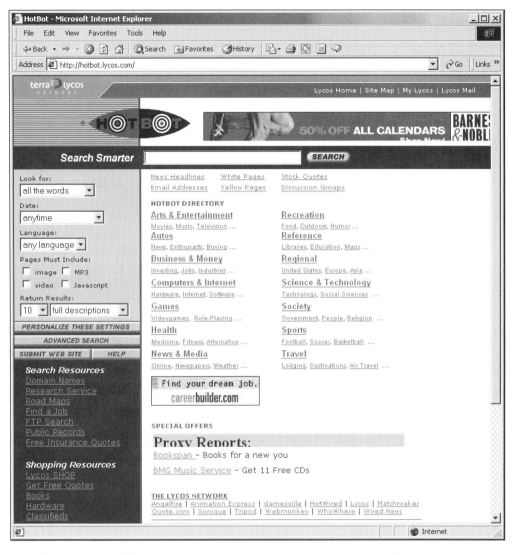

But for the purposes of this book, we're assuming you're not indexing 2 billion pages. On a simple 50-, 500-, or 5000-page site, users should be able to find what they want easily and quickly using your menu scheme, supplementing this menu scheme with a search feature for those who know exactly what they want. This is where time spent on design and testing really pays off. If your menu system is technically wonderful, stunning visually (or aurally, or whatever), but terribly incomprehensible to your target user, it is still not usable – in other words, it's useless (for example, look at the *http://www.zcsterling.com/homepage.html* site we saw in *Chapter 1*).

So, in addition to the technical and usability goals set out in the previous chapter, your menu system must strive to be meaningful to your target user. Challenges in making a menu system meaningful include:

- Setting company priorities (often marketing-driven).

- Understanding the target user.

- Existing material.

- Technical limitations.

# Setting Your Priorities

The first priority in menu design, as in virtually all design, should be the end user. This consideration obviously has to harmonize with concerns like budget, schedule, and technical issues. For example, the most user-friendly approach might be to fly an engineer to each user's house and have the engineer do everything for them, but that absurd scheme is hardly likely to fit into the reality of a small e-commerce site.

The actual first priority of most for-profit companies, however, is the user's money. What one has to understand is that the money doesn't flow without the user's permission. Conversely, the more considerate your site is to the user, the more likely you are to see their money, so the end user is once again the first priority.

A mistake made by some marketing departments is to try to trick the web user into going somewhere they don't want to go. The corporate thought process goes like this: "We know everyone comes to this site for car batteries but the profit margin is better on steering wheel covers. Let's downplay the batteries, hiding them later in the menu in a tiny font, and put steering wheel covers right at the top in big, bold, flashing, animated letters!". To take a more realistic example, imagine a software company rolling out a new product line. They may want this new initiative to take priority over everything else in a web page, including coming first in basic navigational menus.

This approach, obviously, is counterproductive. It is likely to confuse or frustrate the user, which is as good as redirecting them to a competitor's site.

Such shuffling of navigation menus to meet purely internal goals breaks two important rules in navigation:

1. Navigation is not the same as advertising – the marketing department isn't the target user.

2. Users don't read, they skim and simplify.

The belief that putting something first on a menu means everyone visiting a site will read it is contrary to the way real people handle navigation. It's like assuming that as soon as anyone looks at a map of Africa, they are going to notice Senegal because it's furthest left or Morocco because it's in the upper-left corner. (Either of these last examples would be true with screen-reading software for the visually impaired, which we discussed in *Chapter 1*.)

Faced with a large amount of information, and even a 10-item menu could qualify as a large amount of information, users will skim it to find a pattern and simplify it into smaller, more manageable units. Skimming doesn't equal reading. Tests have shown that a person can subconsciously spot pieces of important data (their own name, for example, a dollar or other currency symbol, the word "free," or "Mercedes" if they have a particular interest in or need for that item) on a busy page of dense text flashed in front of their eyes for less than 500 milliseconds.

They may have subconsciously "read" the page, but for practical purposes they skimmed it, simplified and clarified it as much is possible (checking to see if it was in their native language, and maybe getting so far as checking whether it was an alphabetical list, for example), and caught the most important element, all without consciously reading anything.

This is exactly the way users will approach your menus: they'll scan, simplify, and focus on what's important to them (or what is interesting to them). If this process fails to find what they're looking for, they'll bail out, either to your search function (as a last-ditch attempt to find what they're after), by clicking the "*back*" button to go to the previous page, or, worst of all, by leaving your site altogether.

Always prioritize your menus based on what the user needs. As you'll see in the "*Information Architecture for Menus*" section later in this chapter, you can model your menu on their natural information processing functions and meet their needs quickly and easily.

# Understanding Your Target User

To design a menu for this target user, you'll need to get something of a mental picture of that user. Some designers go so far as to name users (real or imagined) and put pictures of them with experiential profiles on the wall. From experience, we can say this approach is very successful as long as the descriptions are detailed enough and everyone working on a design knows and understands the same things about these users. Broad definitions, even with rudimentary personalization, can bring confusing and counter-productive preconceptions to light – be specific! For example, if you say your target user is "a shopper named Melinda who normally buys electronic components", one designer might want to present her with a menu focusing on engineering electronic components (such as capacitors, diodes, and whatnot) while another will present her with consumer electronic components (for example, video recorders and CD players).

Here are four things to consider when thinking about your target user:

- The user's role/behavior (shopper, researcher, reader, etc.).

- Your assumptions about the user's technology (desktop browser, WAP phone, Java).

- Your assumptions about the user's experience (very experienced web user, novice, busy vs. interested).

- Important exceptions (accessibility and localization, among other issues).

Brainstorm these issues, and make sure the entire design team agrees (or agrees to disagree) with the user assumptions before you start the technical design phase of your development. If you can agree on who the user is and what they want, members of the team can develop their individual pieces, comfortable in the knowledge that they're thinking about the same user as other team members.

## *Why Is the User Here?*

How you decide to present choices in a menu depends on what you expect your primary user to do with those choices. At this stage of the discussion, it is vital to know who your primary users are. Other types of users will have their chance at the table, but at the beginning you really must think about that one, ideal, typical visitor to your web site and what he or she wants.

For example, if you are designing a shopping site, you know the primary user's goal is to find things they want and/or need and, hopefully, buy them. While other users will visit to find out about return policies, find a job with your company, or profile your board of directors, "The Shopper" is the primary user.

Flesh out these primary users to the highest practical degree. (This is a good place for the pictures/profiles exercise mentioned previously.) If your site specializes in academics, are your primary users university professors or kindergarten students? Do they want information, interaction with peers, or some other resource?

At this point, you will almost always find that the "one, ideal, typical visitor" has more than one *behavioral* profile. Some users who fit the label "shoppers" are looking for clothes while others are looking for music, candy, books, or carpenters' supplies. Some are more experienced with the Web than others. They're all at your web site to shop, though, so your home page menu can make some assumptions about common behaviors among your various shoppers:

- Find the section I'm interested in.

- Find the products I want.

- Get information about those products.

- Order the products (including checking the status of orders, canceling orders, etc.).

The profiles you generate tell you how to present your menu options. If your target user is very experienced with the Web, you have more leeway to "break the rules" of usable web design. Microsoft, for example, uses simple links on its home page (for a general audience – see the below left-hand screenshot, *http://www.microsoft.com/*) but incorporates more advanced options like fly-out menus in its developer-oriented sections (see the below right-hand screenshot, *http://msdn.microsoft.com/*).

 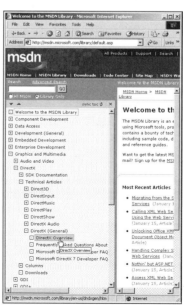

If you find that your target user is likely to access your site through a text-based handheld device like a mobile phone, you can account for that in your menu presentation and the technology you choose for designing and presenting the pages.

*Amazon.com*'s main menu, for example, enables various types of shoppers to go immediately to the section that suits their needs, including items like "*Books*", "*Electronics*", and "*DVDs*":

What about huge conglomerates like Fujitsu, though? Who are the ideal visitors to *fujitsu.com*? Potential corporate customers, perhaps? Current small office/home office customers? Investors? The site map lists over 80 individual companies (on six continents) within Fujitsu, each of which has one, four, or a dozen target users. In a case like this, where a site is divided into dozens of subsites (hundreds, in this example), the menu on the home page must be usable for a myriad of users. Since "myriad" isn't a good place to start profiling users, you must still make some assumptions about the ideal users of that home page. For example:

- They are interested in technology.

- They are likely or very likely to speak a language other than English.

- They are visiting to interact with a very small portion of your site.

For a site with such diverse users, the main menu typically has very broad options like "*Products*", "*Services*", and "*Support*" (see below, *http://www.fujitsu.com/*). As users get closer to the area they need, menus start to become more specific to them and their needs.

## What Technology Does the User Have?

The basic assumption for most web sites is that the typical visitor uses a relatively up-to-date, graphical desktop browser on a color display with a relatively high-speed connection (a 56K dialup or faster, for example). "Up-to-date" browsers (such as IE 5+/Netscape 6, etc.) presumably include support for advanced markup (frames, fonts) and scripting languages (DHTML, JavaScript, CSS, potentially XML/XSL) and multimedia plug-ins like Flash. While it would be a mistake to assume that *every* user had these capabilities (unless, of course, you're running a site specifically for users or developers of that technology), it would similarly be a mistake to avoid all of these technologies out of fear that some users would be unable to use them. This is the "lowest common denominator" approach/mistake, assuming that you can't assume anything and therefore have to code for the barest minimum capabilities (some people still use 14" monitors, with Netscape 1.0 on 14.4K modems), but it almost always spawns very boring and surprisingly unusable sites. You're not going to alienate a significant proportion of your potential target audience by not supporting these technologies. That's what this whole book is about: making the most that you can of those technologies for navigation menus – hence the cross-browser compatible manner in which our menus are coded in later chapters.

This is not to say that you should ignore the users who bring limited technology to the party. There are important reasons to provide simpler (usually text-based) alternatives for those who need simpler presentation. Devices and software that help disabled users work with the Web often rely on a simple design, for example. Additionally, the fledgling "Wireless Web" is still largely limited to very slow transfers and small screens.

A better approach to dealing with the array of technical capabilities that users bring to your site is to put browser-aware intelligence on the server and present the appropriate content to each user.

One of the most common issues in making technology assumptions is screen real estate. While it is not a hard-and-fast rule, it is now generally accepted that desktop/laptop users use resolutions of 800x600 and above. Coding for plain VGA screens (640x480) is no longer a requirement for most applications. Of course, there are exceptions to this rule. Many handheld devices provide 320x240 resolution, also called "quarter VGA." If your target user accesses the site with such a device, an intranet for PDA-equipped sales people for example, you must naturally consider such real estate restrictions.

## What Does the User Know Already?

The experience (and patience, and inquisitiveness) of a web audience varies to a degree, but it is surprisingly consistent in a few areas. There are two generally accepted skills you can count on, regardless of your web audience:

**1.** They can click on underlined links, which they expect to be blue before they've been clicked and purple afterward (depending on the browser settings – in any case, they expect the default that they're used to).

**2.** They will click the "*Back*" button if a page doesn't immediately appear useful.

Beyond that, you're introducing complication and potential confusion – the enemies of usability. For usability's sake, keep your links underlined. Even changing the behavior of underlined links (making them red instead of blue, for example) reduces the usability of your site. While many sites you've visited break these simple rules and seem quite usable to you, you must concede that if you're reading this book you are unlikely to be the "typical web user".

*Amazon.com*, an example we use frequently because of its excellent usability, has an advanced, attractive design. Its left-hand navigation links are underlined in blue (the browser's default), and once you've clicked a link the link turns purple (again, the browser's default). The same is true of *Yahoo.com*, another very usable site. These link behaviors date back to the earliest web browsers, and they have become the fundamental rules in text-based web navigation. *Slashdot.org*, a popular developers' site whose target audience is very experienced in using the Web, underlines its links, though it uses a slightly different color scheme than the standard blue-new/purple-visited format. Despite the many variations in approaches to links that crop up all the time, a site that aims for good usability and a general audience should let the browser decide the link color.

Image maps and other clickable images come with their own set of expectations. If a user hovers over a link on an image map, particularly a link they're unsure of, they have learned to expect some direction on the browser's status bar. This "direction" is usually a URL (hopefully a meaningful URL like *products.html* rather than *file003.html*), but could alternatively be a short text explanation of the link. Server-side image maps, which provide X/Y coordinates instead of direction, are less usable than client-side image maps. This same expectation of direction can make Flash less usable than HTML, though it can be overcome by providing immediate in-context help and other assistance, which we'll get on to in *Chapter 5*.

In general, users expect menus to be at the top of the screen, or on the left side. Menus at the bottom of a short screen are also acceptable, and in many cases more usable than the popular left-side navigation menus. This is especially true in framed layouts, where the bottom-of-screen navigation stays in place even though any navigation on the page itself would scroll past the top of the screen. If the screen is usually taller than one browser window, however, you should avoid end-of-page navigation simply because the user won't see it when they initially try to understand the page.

Right-side menus are generally not expected, but can have useful applications. For example, in text-heavy pages, right-side navigation can aid readers who might otherwise be distracted by out-of-place text at the beginning of the line. Still, as one researcher pointed out, the expectation that the menu will be at the top or on the left has become a standard, for better or worse. Right-side menus also have difficulties with issues like fly-out menus (appearing to the left rather than the right) and resized windows, where the menu might seem to disappear completely.

If your target user is a web developer, an artist, or someone else who you believe is likely to intuit alternative approaches to navigation (links that aren't underlined, obscure or clever tooltips, etc.), you should still avoid these alternatives if you want your site to be usable. Make your navigation straightforward in all cases. If you need to spread your wings creatively, do it in the body of the page, not the navigation. Navigation should be as transparent as possible – after all, you want people focusing on the page content, not the menu.

## *Who Else Will See This Site?*

Important exceptions to your target user profile are usually based on one or more of these factors:

- Language

- Accessibility

- Technology

As you define your target user and choose technologies for implementation, you will realize that your assumptions, by their very nature, can't cover all contingencies. Consider the important users who fall outside of your assumptions.

Important exceptions are distinct from "corner cases," a term that usually means "possible but highly unlikely." An example of a corner case would be the person who puts cheese in their printer's paper tray. Possible? Yes. Plausible? Not really. So designing a warning label about cheese in the paper tray is not a good use of one's time.

However, receiving a web visit from a user who doesn't speak your language is much more of a likelihood. If you have the resources to translate your site into other popular languages that might be used by your target audience, by all means do so. If not, refer to the tips in *Chapter 1* on making your navigation compatible with automatic translation tools (see Rule 10).

Similarly, as we have already discussed here and in *Chapter 1*, devices like Braille screen readers and text-to-speech translators rely on plain text navigation. That doesn't have to be your primary design, but if your site could be useful for disabled users, you should provide it as an option. Assuming you don't have access to a text-to-speech browser, try loading your page in Lynx to see how your site would appear to a text-only tool (for more on Lynx, see Rule 12 in *Chapter 1*).

The technology being used to surf the Web is becoming more diverse, a trend that will hopefully reverse itself as wireless devices become less proprietary. For now, providing alternative text-based navigation is the easiest option. A more usable but also more complex option is leveraging stylesheets and device-aware servers to serve up appropriate content.

For example, this simulator from *openwave.com* shows how Google's menu is simplified for presentation on a wireless phone. Compare this with the desktop version seen earlier!

# Dealing with Existing Content

Organizing existing web content presents several challenges that should **not** inform your menu design:

- Pre-existing technical structure

- Pre-existing interface

- File/record organization

- Internal company naming conventions

Users don't care what goes on behind the scenes, what department at your company made which page, or how the original web designer put it all together. Users care about exactly one thing with regard to navigation: finding the content they want.

In the Information Architecture sections that follow, you'll see how to organize content effectively. The key thing to remember is that no matter where or how your content is stored or presented right now, your goal is to present it in a usable fashion. If that means pointing to the same page from fifteen different places throughout the site, so be it. Keep presentation separate from content creation wherever possible so you don't get locked into a structure that aims for department or company expediency, rather than users' needs.

# Information Architecture for Menus

Information Architecture is the practice of structuring information for easy access. A commonly used example is a library's card catalog (if you can remember when libraries had card catalogs). Information in card catalogs is organized according to the ways people look for books:

- By author

- By title

- By subject

Since author and title are static, the information architect's job in a library would be to work with the variable element: **subject**. Naming a book's subject is more challenging than it might seem. A book on Japan, for example, would be naturally filed under the subject of Japan. But the information architect has to figure out what additional subjects a user might search for to find the information in this book. For example, if the book has significant information about the somewhat mysterious Ainu tribe (*http://www.dromo.com/fusionanomaly/ainu.html*), it might be filed under the subject "Ainu" as well. People might search for specific cities, islands, or regions, any of which should point back to the book on Japan.

This concept carries over to the Web in the form of search engines, including the online versions of card catalogs. For our purposes it also carries over into menus.

If you have a page on your site listing contact information for the executives and departments, for example, you have to consider how visitors might recognize that option on your menu. Obviously, visitors with different goals have different ideas on which menu item would take them to information on that page. For example:

- Contacts

- Company Information

- Important numbers

- Info

- Departments

- About Us

- Phone Numbers

- Staff

- Executives

- Folks who work here

- Investor Information

Any of those labels would be logical to someone. One of your challenges in architecting a menu is to find labels that are meaningful to the broadest cross-section of your target user population.

# Putting IA To Work On Your Menus

Information Architecture in its broadest sense deals with organizing information, titling pages and sections, dividing sites into subsites and many other elements that are beyond the scope of usable web menus. For our purposes, Information Architecture is much simpler: it means choosing effective labels and putting them in usable menus.

We've already discussed what makes menus *technically* usable. Another consideration is making them *practically* usable. A menu of links to a thousand pages is likely to be technically usable, but it may or may not be practically usable.

Usable menus take into account everything we can know about the target user and what they expect. For example, if your menu is a site map, users expect it to list the pages available on all the sections of your site, grouped by section. If your menu is a main navigation menu, users might expect it to show departments (like the *Amazon.com* example) or company functions (like the *Fujitsu.com* example), and they will always expect it to be able to get them back home.

Some things that make menus less usable are:

- Arbitrary organization

- Alphabetical/alphanumeric organization (this varies by content)

- Informal or slang labels

- Extraneous words

When a user sees something they can identify as a menu, they expect it to offer some kind of order that makes sense to them. A restaurant's menu, for example, might group dishes together by their primary ingredients (beef, chicken, vegetables) or the appropriate course (appetizers, soups, main dishes, desserts). If a restaurant menu simply listed every item arbitrarily or even alphabetically, it would be much less useful and less usable.

Earlier in the chapter we discussed how people scan information (remembering that people don't really read on the Web). They look for patterns and simplify. In a menu, people look at the size first to make the subconscious decision whether they need to simplify. This is where the vaunted `Magic Number` 7 comes into play.

There is a psychological theory dating back to at least the 1950s (see "The Magical Number Seven, Plus or Minus Two: Some Limits on Our Capacity for Processing Information" by George A. Miller, 1956, at *http://www.well.com/user/smalin/miller.html*) that says the memory's magic number is 7. People can remember 7 things, and they can quickly discern the meaning of and reorganize groups of 7 items. In IA terms, this has mutated into a simple rule:

> A list should have 7 items, plus or minus 2.

While there is some controversy about whether "memory" should relate to menus (which you don't have to remember), this rule has become a de facto standard for the Web. Less than five items doesn't look like a list, and more than nine is too complicated, depending on the content. This concept has some elasticity, however. It might apply to columns in a list rather than entire lists. Yahoo currently lists 14 main topics on its home page, dividing them neatly into two columns of seven. HotBot does exactly the same thing. The magic number might apply to groups within a list as well. For example:

| | | |
|---|---|---|
| Apples | Bouillon | Beef |
| Bananas | Chowder | Chicken |
| Oranges | Consommé | Lamb |
| Pears | Stew | Pork |
| Carrots | Vegetable Soup | Halibut |
| Peas | Caesar Salad | Snapper |
| Potatoes | Fruit Salad | Tuna |
| | Waldorf Salad | |
| | Rye Bread | |
| | Wheat Bread | |
| | White Bread | |

The theme in this list is obviously food or groceries, but it illustrates the "magic number 7" concept in a couple of ways. First, there are seven major divisions in this list (fruit, vegetables, soup, salad, bread, meat, fish), so even though there are 25 items in this list it is easily simplified and understood. The left and right column follow the "7 plus or minus 2" rule, each with seven items. The center column seems to violate the rule, with 11 items, but it is easily simplified into three major divisions: soup, salad, and bread, so the column is easily sorted out, into 3 subcategories. An even more usable approach to a menu like this would be to label the natural divisions, like this:

| Fruit | Soup | Meat |
|---|---|---|
| Apples | Bouillon | Beef |
| Bananas | Chowder | Chicken |
| Oranges | Consommé | Lamb |
| Pears | Stew | Pork |
| | Vegetable Soup | |
| **Vegetables** | **Salad** | **Fish** |
| Carrots | Caesar Salad | Halibut |
| Peas | Fruit Salad | Snapper |
| Potatoes | Waldorf Salad | Tuna |
| | **Bread** | |
| | Rye Bread | |
| | Wheat Bread | |
| | White Bread | |

Even apparently arbitrary lists often imply some kind of order. Looking at Amazon's menu, we see the following items:

- Books
- Electronics
- Toys & Games
- Music
- Health & Beauty
- DVD
- Software
- ...other departments

The list is clearly not alphabetical, listing Music after Toys, for example. We could argue that it is an arbitrary list of departments because the items don't fit any kind of pattern. The factor that influenced this list's order is probably popularity, but it might include other issues like profit margin. Still, it looks to the user like there's an order to this long list: **popularity**. If Amazon, which will probably forever be associated with books in users' minds, put "*Books*" at the bottom of its menu, it would simply look out of place. Using "*Books*" in the primary position gives this menu an intuitive order because of the context.

Extraneous words can make it very difficult to scan a menu. Look at this list:

- Several Things I did on Vacation
- Some of the Photos I Took
- The Things I Wore
- Great Buys at the Gift Shop
- Stuff we Ate

This menu would be simpler like this:

- Vacation Activities
- Photos
- Clothes for the Trip
- Souvenirs
- Food/Restaurants

In the revised list, the first word in the item is now a meaningful word, rather than an extraneous word like "some" or "the." However, if the items in a list are very consistent, it can still be easily scanned, even with certain extraneous words. For example:

- How to Fish

- How to Fix a Scratched CD

- How to Make a Banjo

- How to Row a Boat

- How to Edit a Movie

In this case, the mind tells the eye to filter out the "How to" at the beginning of each item and jump either to the next word (fish, fix, make, row, edit) or the last word (fish, CD, banjo, boat, movie), whichever appears more meaningful. However, one comment to be made here is that an even better way to deal with this kind of list is to take the common extraneous word (in this case, "How") from each list entry, and add it as a title for the group, like so:

**How to:**

- Fish

- Fix a Scratched CD

- Row a Boat

- Edit a Movie

Meaning is obviously very important to menus. Many personal web pages use slang, intentional misspellings, or obscure words in their navigation. This is fine for personal web pages, assuming your only visitors will be your friends. But for professional sites, you need to keep your language simple and clear. Remember that some of your visitors will have limited knowledge of your language, and that many words have several meanings. Obscure acronyms and initialisms are rarely helpful in a menu, since they limit the menu's utility to people who already know these terms.

# Depth in Navigation

Depth of content is a very important consideration in organization. In some ways, it is the heart of Information Architecture, because depth is determined by how well or efficiently you organize your content. "Depth," in this context, means the number of levels a user must traverse to get to the information they want. For example, if your home page has no content, only a menu, then all information is at least one level away from the home page.

In very deep sites, the content people are looking for maybe several levels away. In "narrow" sites, content is never very far away – as little as one click – but the number of links on a page can be enormous. News/opinion sites (particularly "blog" sites, which exist more or less exclusively to link to stories on other sites) often take the narrow approach, sometimes putting hundreds of links on their home pages.

As to which approach is more effective, usability tests are split along lines of focus and audience. For sites with ultra-specialized content, like finance sites or the blog sites mentioned earlier, narrowness is very effective. The scope of the information is already so tightly focused that categorizing the content might be ineffective or counterproductive. The target user for these sites is typically very experienced and engaged, looking for stories related to their interest, not necessarily *categories* of content dreamed up by someone else. These narrow sites usually have longer, more descriptive link names, which look like headlines – for example, look at some of the headings on *http://www.nuzee.com*, below:

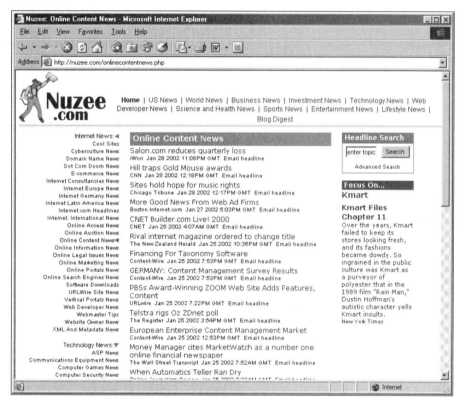

For general-use, public sites, however, a reasonable amount of depth is probably better than the narrow approach. In the excellent book "*Web Site Usability*", by Jared Spool et al (ISBN: 155860569X), they observe, "In general, the more links on a page that led to other pages, the harder it was for users to [find the information they sought]". For a broader audience, stick with smaller menus (5-9 items, generally) and try not to make the content so deep that finding it is more tedious than it's worth.

It is not uncommon in practice for designers to set a "target depth" for their sites. For example, "A user should be able to get to the correct section within three clicks" or "Never more than four clicks". Targets like this can bring up an issue with very large sites: if your target depth is three clicks and your maximum menu size is 9 items, simple math says you can only have 729 pages (9 links on the home page, each of which can link to 9 pages, each of which can link to 9 more pages; 9 x 9 x 9 = 729). Obviously, if your site has 5,000 or 50,000 pages, you'll either raise the target depth or the maximum menu size. The optimistic view of this formula, of course, tells you that within three clicks you can make over 700 pages available to your audience – enough to enable users to focus on a very extensive amount of content.

# Testing to Verify Your Design Decisions

There can hardly be a more valuable tool for a designer or developer than a usability test. Watching a real user interact with your design invariably throws questionable decisions and incorrect assumptions into sharp relief. You will quickly learn, through the one-way glass of a testing booth or simply by watching over someone's shoulder, that no design can be considered usable until it has been tested.

Testing methodology can be complicated or simple, and indeed the field is very complicated – you can get a doctorate degree in Human-Computer Interaction or Human Factors Engineering. In its simplest form, however, a usability test can be done quickly, inexpensively, and informally.

One common misconception about usability is that you need many different opinions to make a valid test. In practice, you'll find that five or six subjects will provide just about all the useful data you'd get from 20, 40, or 1000 tests.

Another issue is expense. Do you need a fully equipped usability lab with a soundproof booth, one-way glass, eye-movement monitors, and video cameras? No. Those things are nice, and very useful, especially for enabling multiple observers to oversee a test. Taking the simple route, however, you can ask five or six volunteers to let you watch them tour your site and find a few items using your menus. Even friends and family can be good informal usability testers, assuming they approximate the audience for the content. If you can afford it, you might consider hiring usability testers (also called **Human Factors Engineers**, or **HFEs**) for short contracts or turning to an online usability tester, like Vividence for example (*http://www.vividence.com/*). Such formal testing is usually reserved for projects that are relatively mature, however, because it can get quite expensive.

If the site isn't "live" to be tested, you can get good data by showing users printouts or mockups of a design and having them pretend to interact with it. For example, show them a printout of a menu and ask them where they would click to find a specific bit of information, or what they would expect to happen if they clicked a particular option. While interaction is obviously the key to success on the Web, the data you get from paper tests is statistically about the same as what you get with "live" tests.

It is important in testing to put people (test subjects) at ease. They should understand that they aren't being tested; they're simply giving you valuable information about how well a design works. Depending on your relationship with the subject, you may also need to point out that no one's ego will be damaged by anything they tell you.

Always keep your tests consistent. For example, if you ask one person to perform 10 tasks, make sure you ask the other four or five people to go through exactly the same tasks with the same prompting. There is a temptation in testing to refine your presentation as you go along, but this can adversely affect your data. If you offer people too much guidance, they will always "succeed," but you won't learn anything about how people with no guidance in the real world will interact with your design. Don't be so strict, however, that you frustrate your subject. If a subject "locks up" (stares at the screen wondering what the heck to do – very common in usability tests), ask them to tell you what they're wondering about and feel free to give them the answer. You still have a data point to record: at this point in the test, the subject got lost and required prompting to continue.

And of course, you want to quantify results as much as possible. Whether you're measuring time savings, number of mistakes, number of clicks, or any other data, measurement will give you a good gage to tell you how a design is progressing through subsequent tests.

# Summary

Organizing web content is a challenge, but one that pays off immensely if done right. Always look to the target audience, testing with real members of that audience wherever possible.

Some things from this chapter to keep in mind:

- Make your menu items meaningful but not verbose.

- Keep the target audience in mind at all stages.

- Make sure your development team agrees on what the target user wants and expects.

- Know the distinction between "corner cases" (unrealistic situations that may come up one time in a thousand – these you can ignore) and "important exceptions" (users with the same needs as your target user but different technology, abilities, etc. – ignore these at your peril).

- Don't force users to read your navigation carefully – it is more natural for them to skim over the detail quickly, rather than read all the information.

- As much as possible, stick to the expected browser defaults for common features like link colors.

- Try your site on different desktop browsers and different types of browsers, like phone simulators and text-only browsers.

- Organization should look like it falls into sensible groups, never arbitrary ones – only use alphanumeric organization when the items you're organizing have equal weight (names, part numbers, etc.).

- 7 items, plus or minus 2, is a good target for easy understanding.

- Always test your assumptions with real people, even if you have to borrow a co-worker or family member to play with your site navigation.

In the chapters that follow, we'll show you how to put your chosen technologies to work building your menus.

# 3

- Menus with JavaScript

- Simple text link and button menus

- Rollover effects, check box and radio button menus, jump menus

**Author: Jon Stephens**

# Basic JavaScript Menus

In this chapter we're going to look at creating and using some basic menus, using JavaScript and a bit of CSS. We'll concentrate on using three common sorts of elements, which can be used in nearly any graphical web browser: text, images, and form elements such as input buttons and dropdowns (HTML `<select>` and `<option>` elements). The examples we use in this chapter will be compatible with the more recent and common browsers supporting JavaScript, so unless otherwise stated, they should work in version 3+ browsers.

We assume at least a basic familiarity with these technologies. If you're completely new to either, or both, we strongly encourage you to get up to speed with the help of the resources listed in the *Resources* section at the end of the book. However, you should still be able to adapt these examples for your own use with a minimum of trouble.

## A Brief Aside into JavaScript, DHTML, and CSS

Just in case it's been a while since you've used JavaScript, let's review quickly the issues we're likely to encounter in its use. **JavaScript** is a scripting language that can be embedded into any number of different applications. As used in web browsers, where we refer to it as a *client-side* technology, it can't access files on either the client or the server, with very few exceptions. (Using it in this manner is also referred to as "embedding JavaScript into a web page".) Nor can we access the user's operating system or other applications aside from the web browser itself. However, we can:

- Load new URLs into the browser.

- Store script functions in separate files and load those into multiple pages, so that we can use the same functions in separate pages (but we can't write to these files).

- Read and write cookies on the client and thus store and access a very limited amount of data (4K of text) between sessions – note that this is the *only* way, using cross-browser, client-side JavaScript alone, in which we can write to files of any sort on either the client or the server. There are additional limitations on the number of cookies that we can use – see *Chapter 4* for the specifics.

- We can access elements of pages in other windows and frames, so long as we created the windows originally, and the pages in those windows originate from the same domain as the page containing or referencing our script.

What about **Dynamic HTML (DHTML)**, and how is it different from JavaScript? JavaScript itself is just a scripting language that doesn't do anything terribly interesting without an environment to work in and application-specific objects to work upon. "DHTML" came about more or less as a marketing term coined to describe the then-new capabilities of version 4 (and higher) browsers. Prior to this, the elements accessible to scripting were quite limited – as the **Document Object Model (DOM)** became standardized and browsers developed to match, it became possible to access nearly any page element and its properties. It also became possible to do a lot more with event handling, which in the older browsers was quite limited in terms of *what events could be associated with which elements*. So, as a matter of convenience more than anything else, when we say "JavaScript" we'll be referring to this older paradigm with its limited object collections and event handling, and when we refer to "Dynamic HTML" later on, and especially in *Chapter 4*, we'll be talking about the ability to access (nearly) all page elements and their properties, including styles, as well as increased event-handling capabilities and even the ability to assign event handlers on the fly. Again, for more in-depth information, we direct the reader to the references indicated above.

So how can the use of JavaScript help us create more effective menus for our web sites? In a nutshell, it's because we can offer real-time interaction with the users of our sites. In particular, we can provide visual cues to let the user know that the interface is active and that he or she can expect something to happen when they're used. For instance, when the user moves his or her mouse pointer over an image link and it changes color, we've made it more obvious that clicking there will cause something interesting and/or useful to happen. It's also a very handy way to pass a bit of information along to the users about what's waiting for them on the next page, either by means of those visual cues or (as we'll see towards the end of this chapter) by displaying some extra text without mangling the layout of our menu or the page it's in.

Of course, we must also take into account that some users may be visiting our sites with browsers that don't support JavaScript, or that they may have client-side scripting disabled, so we need to be careful that our menus don't "break" for those users, or to provide an alternative for them.

In addition to using basic JavaScript to make our menus responsive to user actions, we can also control their appearance to some degree in the newer browsers using `Cascading Style Sheets` (`CSS`). There are some limitations: IE 3.0 does boast some CSS support, but it is extremely poor. Netscape introduced CSS support in Netscape 4.0, but the `:hover` pseudoclass wasn't implemented until Netscape 6.0/Mozilla. (`a:hover` allows us to change the appearance of a link on a mouseover without resorting to script.) In the case of Netscape 4.X browsers, we have 2 choices regarding the provision of equivalent functionality: we can use Netscape 4 Layers, or we can employ image rollovers to display changing text. We'll include a working example of the former in our final example of the chapter, and examine it in greater detail in *Chapter 4*. The latter is a poor choice, since for Netscape 4 users it adds download time and requires added work to produce the required images whenever the site is updated – if we're going to be forced to do so for a limited subset of our users, we might as well just use the images for all browsers, which means we've lost the economy achieved by the use of CSS. We also have the option of simply allowing CSS text hovering to fail silently in Netscape 4.X; fortunately, browsers that don't understand CSS or certain CSS features will do this with no special effort on our part.

# Example 1: Text Link Example with CSS

The most basic element available for a web navigation menu is the venerable text link. In itself, it's not terribly exciting, although we can dress it up somewhat in the newest browsers using CSS. For most older user agents, we can set fonts, colours, and sizes for our link text using the now-deprecated <font> tag, but we won't clutter things up with these here. Let's look at a very simple and straightforward example, which we've included as the file ch3_ex1.html, in the code download for this book, available from *http://www.glasshaus.com*:

```html
<html>
<head>
  <title>Chapter 3, Example 1</title>
  <meta http-equiv="Content-Type" content="text/html; charset=iso-8859-1">
  <style type="text/css">
<!--
a.menu {font-family: Arial, Helvetica, sans-serif; font-size: 14px;
        font-weight: bold; color: #FF6600; text-decoration: none;
        background-color: #FFFF99}
a.menu:hover {color: #336600; background-color: #FFFF00}
-->
  </style>
</head>

<body bgcolor="#FFFFFF" text="#000000">
  <table width="150" border="0" cellspacing="0" cellpadding="5" bgcolor="#CCFFCC">
    <tr>
      <td align="center" valign="middle">
        <a href="index.html" class="menu">HOME</a>
      </td>
    </tr>
    <tr>
      <td align="center" valign="middle">
        <a href="products.html" class="menu">PRODUCTS</a>
      </td>
    </tr>
    <tr>
      <td align="center" valign="middle">
        <a href="services.html" class="menu">SERVICES</a>
      </td>
    </tr>
    <tr>
      <td align="center" valign="middle">
        <a href="about.html" class="menu">ABOUT US</a>
      </td>
    </tr>
    <tr>
      <td align="center" valign="middle">
        <a href="contact.html" class="menu">CONTACT</a>
      </td>
    </tr>
  </table>
</body>
</html>
```

We've used two styles in this example affecting links in menus (both of which are applied using <a class="menu" ...>), one for their "normal" state, and one for their "hover" (or mouseover) state. While it is probably best not to remove underlines from links that occur in content, in this case we're applying the styles only to links within the menu, which exhibits a tabular or list-like layout that's distinct from the content of the page itself. This is why we've created a **menu** style class and pseudoclass rather than applying the styles to the <a> element itself. HTML and CSS purists will also likely note that we've used a couple of deprecated attributes (most notably the align attribute for tables and table cells and valign for table cells) in order to supply easy compatibility with older browsers that don't support the latest versions of these. At any rate, in IE 4+, Opera 5+, and Netscape 6+, the user will see something like the image on the left when they load the page, and the one on the right when he or she mouses over the topmost link:

Netscape 4 users won't see any change on a mouseover but won't encounter any problems in using the links. Earlier browsers will simply display the text links in their default fonts and colours. By declaring and assigning multiple style classes, we can set apart different text menus in the same page. For instance, on a large site with many sections each containing a number of pages, we might use a row of text links at or near the top of each page to provide access to sections, with a column of text links down one side linking to the various pages within the current section.

# Example 2: An Image Rollover Menu

We'll return to and expand upon something quite similar to this later in the chapter, but for now let's move on and see what we can do to make our menus more visually appealing using images and JavaScript. First, we should consider some of the pros and cons of using images instead of text. Of course, one of the disadvantages is that images take longer to download. This can be alleviated somewhat by optimizing our images as much as possible using an application designed for the purpose such as Macromedia Fireworks or Adobe ImageReady. In addition, we should consider the fact that once our images are downloaded, repeated instances of them on succeeding pages will be pulled from the user's browser cache (providing that the cache has not been disabled) and not from the server, so we only have to be concerned about the extra time and bandwidth once for each image we use in our menu.

Another disadvantage of using images is that users of text-only clients such as Lynx won't be able to view them, so we must be careful to provide alternatives such as text links, or to employ the HTML `alt` and `title` attributes to let these users know what to expect when they follow our image links, or both. We also need to take into account that there may be users of browsers that can't or don't support JavaScript, or that don't support image swaps (Netscape 2 and IE 3 being cases in point), so we don't want to make our design completely dependent on them. Rather, we should remember that we're providing something extra to enhance the user experience for those visitors who can take advantage of it, while not causing problems in the form of scripting errors or insufficient information for those who can't.

Of course, there are some advantages to using images – else why even bother? We can easily control the size and appearance of our links without worrying about CSS support, fonts available on the user's system, browser and system settings, etc. And while CSS has come a long way in a very short time, there is still quite a lot that it can't do with regard to our presentation. Eventually we'll be able to make use of **Scalable Vector Graphics (SVG)** or something similar that will obviate the need for the many types of images we now use regularly on our sites, but implementation of this standard is as yet incomplete and built-in support for it is at least a full browser generation away from where we are now. So – enough with the chatter, let's get back on track with the examples and take a look at a basic menu using JavaScript image rollovers:

In this figure, we show in our browser window a basic table layout containing a set of image links. On the left is the "default" view; on the right, we can see what happens when the user mouses over the "*HOME*" image link, for which the HTML code is:

```
<a href="index.html" onmouseover="rollOn(0);" onmouseout="rollOff(0);">
    <img name="home" src="images/home_off.jpg" width="100" height="35"
        alt="Home Page" border="0">
</a>
```

We've omitted the code for the table itself here, as it's not particularly remarkable, but the curious can see it in the file `ch3_ex2.html`. Also in this file is the JavaScript code used to power the rollovers. This is a little bit more interesting, so we'll examine it in its entirety here:

```
<script type="text/javascript" language="JavaScript">
<!--
  var imgNames,numImgs,imgsOff,imgsOn;
```

Above, we declare some variable to hold, in order, the name attributes of the `<img>` elements – the number of images, the Image objects for the "on" states, and the Image objects for the "off" states. Below, we check for browser support of the `image` object; it so happens that all browsers that support this object also support JavaScript arrays, so we can avoid causing script errors in browsers that don't support either feature. If the browser supports both, we create the arrays.

```
if(document.images)
{
  // arrays for image names/objects
  imgNames=new Array("home","products","services","about","contact");

  numImgs=imgNames.length;

  imgsOff=new Array(numImgs);
  imgsOn=new Array(numImgs);
```

We store the names of the images in the `imgNames` array – these are also used for the filenames of the "on" and "off" versions of the images as well as for the `name` attributes of the corresponding `<img>` tags. (For HTML 4.01 compliance it's permissible to use the same values for `id` attributes at the same time.) By storing the Image objects in a couple of arrays, we can make our code very compact; rather than using a couple of lines each to define and instantiate ten different Image objects, we can do the same thing with two lines of script contained in a loop. By preloading the images, we make sure that all of the image files have been cached by the browser before we try to make use of them in our image-swapping functions, as some browsers can give us scripting errors, "hang", or even crash if we try to call upon objects which haven't yet been completely created and populated, particularly if the user is on a slow Internet connection.

```
  // preload images

  for(var i=0;i<numImgs;i++)
  {
```

Each time through the loop, we populate the next element of the `imgsOff` array with an instance of the `Image` object, and then we assign its `src` property to an image file on the server.

```
    imgsOff[i]=new Image(100,35);
    imgsOff[i].src="images/"+imgNames[i]+"_off.jpg";
```

Then we do the same with the next element of the `imgsOn` array.

```
    imgsOn[i]=new Image(100,35);
    imgsOn[i].src="images/"+imgNames[i]+"_on.jpg";
  }
}
```

```
function rollOn(index)
{
  if(document.images)
  document.images[imgNames[index]].src=imgsOn[index].src;
}

function rollOff(index)
{
  if(document.images)
  document.images[imgNames[index]].src=imgsOff[index].src;
}
//-->
</script>
```

We also check for `Image` object support in our preload code as well as the image-swapping functions themselves in order to make sure that the browser understands what we're telling it to do and doesn't throw errors or warnings at the user in the event it doesn't. We always want to do our best to ensure that our menus remain usable and don't cause problems for those visitors who can't take advantage of all the functionality we offer them, so in addition to the defensive scripting techniques we use here, we also include `alt` attributes for the images; in a production setting, it might also be wise to employ the `title` attribute for each of the `<a>` or `<img>` elements, or both, depending on the circumstances.

Another advantage to using the arrays is that it makes our code easier to maintain. Suppose our client decides to start offering company press releases and links to news items involving the company, and so requests that we add a new "Press" page or section to the site – and along with it, a new "*Press*" link in our menu pointing to the page `press.html`. We add the following to our menu:

- A new table row/cell containing an image in the `images` subdirectory whose filename is `press_off.jpg` which is linked to the corresponding page, and whose `name` attribute also has the value `"press"`.

- A second image whose filename is `press_on.jpg` to the same subdirectory.

- An element to the `imgNames` array, consisting of the string `"press"`.

- The appropriate calls to the two image-swapping functions in the link's `onmouseover` and `onmouseout` event handlers.

We don't even have to worry about the numbers passed as arguments to the function when they're called, so long as we're consistent; we can add the "*PRESS*" link to the middle of the menu and the string `"press"` to the end of our array of image names, so long as we remember that it's the last element in our array, and use the corresponding index in our function calls:

```
<a href="index.html" onmouseover="rollOn(5);" onmouseout="rollOff(5);">
  <img name="press" src="images/press_off.jpg" width="100" height="35"
      alt="Press Releases" border="0"></a>
```

Other than adding the new `Array` element, we need make no changes to the JavaScript preload code or functions. Additional advantages to organizing our menu code in this way will become apparent, when in *Chapter 6* we'll look at creating menus like this one using server-side techniques where we'll generate the HTML and JavaScript using a couple of loops of ASP or PHP code acting on values obtained from a database. Here's a quick example using PHP and MySQL to generate the table, link, and image code:

```
<table width="100" border="0" cellspacing="0" cellpadding="0">
  <?php
    $count=0;
    $my_query="SELECT name,alt FROM menu_images ORDER BY id";
    $my_result=mysql_query($my_query);
    while( $my_row=mysql_fetch_row($my_result) )
    {
      $my_link=$my_row[0];
      $my_alt=$my_row[1];
      echo "<tr><td><a href=\"$my_link.html\" onmouseover=\"rollOn($count);\" ";
      echo "onmouseout=\"rollOff($count);\"><img name=\"$my_link\" ";
      echo "src=\"images/$my_link_off.jpg\" width=\"100\" height=\"35\"";
      echo "border=\"0\" alt=\"$my_alt\">";
      echo "</a></td></tr>\n";
      $count++;
    }
  ?>
</table>
```

But we're getting a bit ahead of ourselves, aren't we? Let's see how we can enhance our rollover menu with a couple of minor additions to our layout and JavaScript code.

# Example 3A: Using a Sidebar Rollover Image

Now we'll add a sidebar image to our menu. This image will change as each link is moused over, in order to provide additional information or visual cues to the user, as shown in *ch3_ex3.html*).

As in our previous examples, the view on the left is the default one, when the mouse pointer is not positioned over any of the menu's image links; on the right, we see what happens when the user mouses over the "PRODUCTS" link.

In order to accomplish this, we add a second column to the table, span all its cells together and add a default "placeholder" image to the resulting cell:

```
<td rowspan="5">
  <img name="sidebar" src="images/side_off.jpg" width="100" height="175"
      border="0">
</td>
```

No link or event handler code is required here, only that we give the sidebar image a `name` attribute so that we may identify it readily in our JavaScript code. Of course, we could refer to this image – and to each of the other images used in this menu, for that matter – by its index in the `document.images` collection, but using distinct `name` attributes instead makes it much easier for us to recognize which image we're working with. In addition, should we change the layout of our page by adding or removing other images in it? We might well change the indexing of our menu images, which would require a change in how we refer to them in our script. Turning our attention back to the scripting code itself, we need to accomplish two objectives:

**1.** Preload the six sidebar images – one for each link in the menu plus an "off" image that's displayed when no menu links are being moused over.

**2.** Update the image swapping functions so that the appropriate sidebar image will be swapped in when a menu link is moused over.

Even though we're now using six images, five of them fit the pattern we've already established, so there's no reason why we can't give those images filenames that follow the pattern (`home_side.jpg`, `products_side.jpg`, etc.) so that we can employ the same loops for the sake of economy and maintainability of the code. We define a new array,

```
var sideOn=new Array(numImgs);
```

then in the preload section of the code we populate this array with `Image` objects and instantiate them in a manner quite similar to how we did it above:

```
sideOn[i]=new Image(100,175);
sideOn[i].src="images/"+imgNames[i]+"_side.jpg";
```

Of course, we'll need to preload the default image separately:

```
var sideOff=new Image(100,175);
sideOff.src="images/side_off.jpg";
```

Then we add a line to the `rollOn()` function to swap the source of the sidebar image when one of the menu links is moused over:

```
document.sidebar.src=sideOn[index].src;
```

We also need to add a similar, complementary line to the `rollOff()` function to swap it back to the default image source:

```
document.sidebar.src=sideOff.src;
```

Of course, since there's only one "off" image for the sidebar, there's no need to reference any arrays here.

A couple of caveats before we proceed:

**1.** The first potential source of trouble has to do with CSS positioning and Netscape browsers of the Netscape 4.X series. This is on account of the fact that Netscape 4 considers positioned elements to be Layer objects and introduces an additional kink into its DOM hierarchy. We won't do a full-blown example here, but let's suppose we take our menu and place it inside an absolutely-positioned <div> whose id or name attribute is "menu". Because each Netscape Layer contains its own Document object with all elements within descending from that object, our original rollOn() function might wind up looking something like this:

```
function rollOn(index,layerId)
{
   if(document.images)
   {
      var imgRef=document.images[imgNames[index]];
      if(document.layers&&layerId)
      imgRef=document.layers[layerId]imgRef;
      imgRef.src=imgsOn[index].src;
   }
}
```

If we aren't using absolute positioning for the image, the second argument – the id attribute of a Netscape Layer – can be safely omitted. We'll be visiting this issue again in the next chapter, when we discuss some techniques for creating menus with advanced JavaScript, CSS, and Dynamic HTML.

**2.** This example won't work as written in Netscape 2.X or IE 3.0, since they don't support the Image object. Nor will it fail gracefully in those browsers – this is because they have no native support for user-created arrays. If backward-compatibility with these browsers is of concern (and it hasn't been to this author for at least two years at the time of writing), it will be necessary to take additional precautions. One way to accomplish this is to define a custom Array object. Another is to use a browser check. We've included the same one in the example files as we used before.

# Example 3B: An "Intelligent" Menu

For now, let's take the example just discussed and make it more useful and informative by turning it into an **intelligent menu**. By the term "intelligent" we mean very simply a menu or other navigational interface that detects what page it's being used in and alters its own appearance and behavior accordingly. For example, when this menu appears on the "*HOME*" page, there really isn't any need for a link to index.html, is there, since we're already there, right? However, we can use this image to remind the visitor which page is being viewed. For this example, we've created another set of images, one of which we'll use to indicate the current page, if it's one of our predefined set of pages.

We've named these images `home_here.jpg`, `products_here.jpg`, and so on. If this seems confusing, let's take a look at how this example works to clear things up. On the left in the figure below is how the *HOME* page appears when it's first loaded. Notice that we've used a heading and the `home_here.jpg` image file to show that the user has landed on that page; in addition, the default sidebar image also corresponds to the *HOME* page. If you load this page into a browser, you'll see that the left-hand image is static and it's not linked to anything, since the user, already being on `index.html`, has no need for a way to get there. However, as you can see on the right, the remaining images still function as rollover image links.

Here's the code for our revised example, `ch3_ex3B.html`:

```html
<html>
<head>
  <title>Chapter 3, Example 3-B</title>
  <meta http-equiv="Content-Type" content="text/html; charset=iso-8859-1">
```

We should note that we've changed the `language` attribute of the `<script>` tag to `JavaScript1.1` – this is because we'll be making use of the `String` object's `split()` method, which isn't available in JavaScript 1.0.

```html
<script type="text/javascript" language="JavaScript1.1">
<!--
var imgNames,imgAlts,numImgs,imgsOff,imgsOn,sideOn;

if(document.images)
{
//  arrays for image names/objects

  imgNames=new Array("home","products","services","about","contact");
```

```
imgAlts=new Array("HOME PAGE","OUR PRODUCTS","OUR SERVICES",
                  "ABOUT OURCO.COM","CONTACT");

numImgs=imgNames.length;

imgsOff=new Array(numImgs);
imgsOn=new Array(numImgs);
sideOn=new Array(numImgs);
}
```

Note the presence of the new `imgAlts` array. As the observant reader may have guessed from seeing this, we're going to be generating the HTML code for the menu using JavaScript, and having the `alt` attributes for our menu images in this array will make it easier for us to do so using a compact loop rather than writing each row in our table separately.

Here's where we detect which page the browser is currently loading. First we separate the complete URL into pieces, using the slash character as a delimiter; we know from the way in which our URLs are put together that the last of these will be the filename *xxxxx*.html. Since each of our filenames ends with .html, we don't really need that either in order to identify the file uniquely, so we split the filename again, this time using the period as our delimiter so we can cast off the file extension. We don't have any image filenames containing the string "index" but we do have several corresponding to the index page that contains "home", so if we're loading the index page, we change this value to the latter.

```
//  what is the current URL?
var URLbits=self.location.href.split ("/");
```

The `split()` method returns an array whose elements are the substrings left after we remove all instances of the delimiter from the original string. For example, let's define a string named `myString` containing some occurrences of the latter **a**, then split that string using **a** as a delimiter character:

```
var myString="Crusty is a bad cat.";
var pieces=myString.split("a");
//  pieces[0] is equal to "Crusty is "
//  pieces[1] is equal to " b"
//  pieces[2] is equal to "d c"
//  pieces[3] is equal to "t."
```

(Note that spaces count!) The number of substrings or elements of the resulting array is equal to the array's `length` property, so the first substring in the `pieces` array is `pieces[0]` and the last one is `pieces[pieces.length-1]`. Incidentally, we can reverse the process by calling the array's `join()` method like so:

```
var yourString=pieces.join("a");
```

and `yourString` will contain exactly the same value as the original `myString`.

```
var currPageName=currPage.split(".")[0];
```

We need to take care of what happens if we try to use the menu if it isn't in one of the predefined pages, so we'll initialize a `flag` variable to `false`, then set it to `true` if the current page is one of those. Since we already have a loop a bit further on that iterates through all of the page names, we'll test this condition in the same loop.

```
var flag=false;
```

In addition, if the current page is the index page, we'll want the page heading and the `alt` tag for the "*HOME*" image to read "*HOME*".

```
    if(currPageName=="index")
        currPageName="home";

//  preload images
if(document.images)
{
    for(var i=0;i<numImgs;i++)
    {
        imgsOff[i]=new Image(100,35);
        imgsOff[i].src="images/"+imgNames[i]+"_off.jpg";
        imgsOn[i]=new Image(100,35);
        imgsOn[i].src="images/"+imgNames[i]+"_on.jpg";
        sideOn[i]=new Image(100,175);
        sideOn[i].src="images/"+imgNames[i]+"_side.jpg";
```

Here's where we perform the test to determine whether or not to set the flag to `true`. If the current page name is any one of the predefined page names, we'll do so; if we get through all of the predefined values without obtaining a match, then the flag's value will remain `false`.

```
        if(currPageName==imgNames[i])
            flag=true;
    }
```

Here's where we make use of the flag. If the flag's value is `true`, we know that the current page is one of our predefined pages, and we'll set the default or "`off`" sidebar image to match. Otherwise, we'll use the generic "`off`" sidebar image from the previous example.

```
    var sideOff=new Image(100,175);
    if(flag)
        sideOff.src="images/"+currPageName+"_side.jpg";
    else
        sideOff.src="images/side_off.jpg";
}
```

There's one small change made to our image preloading code. We want the default sidebar image to match the page we're presently viewing, so we make the source of that image point to it, instead of to the "*Welcome*" image we used in the previous example.

```
var sideOff=new Image(100,175);
sideOff.src="images/"+currPageName+"_side.jpg";
```

Note that our image-swapping functions remain unchanged:

```
function rollOn(index)
  {
    if(document.images)
    {
      document.images[imgNames[index]].src=imgsOn[index].src;
      document.sidebar.src=sideOn[index].src;
    }
  }

function rollOff(index)
  {
    if(document.images)
    {
      document.images[imgNames[index]].src=imgsOff[index].src;
      document.sidebar.src=sideOff.src;
    }
  }
//-->
</script>
</head>
```

Here's where things get even more interesting. Instead of the HTML table we used in Example 3, we've got a `<script>` block in which we'll write the code for the complete table at load time. The reason we're writing the entire table instead of only the rows or cells containing the images is to maintain backwards compatibility with Netscape 3, which doesn't like `document.write()` statements in the middle of static tables. Depending on the circumstances, trying to do so will cause the dynamically-written markup to be garbled or not appear at all, and may cause scripting errors. While we're on the subject of older browsers, it should be noted that this example, like the one before, is not particularly safe to use with Netscape 2 or IE 3 either, the first reason being the same as before: no native support for the `Array` object. There's another problem with this script and earlier browsers as well, which we'll mention shortly.

```
<body bgcolor="#000099" text="#FFFFFF">
<script type="text/javascript" language="JavaScript1.1">
<!--
```

This `document.write()` statement really has nothing to do with the menu itself, and could easily be removed or replaced with something else. However, it does help demonstrate how we can generate content based on the page URL, so we've left it in our example.

```
document.write("<h1>"+currPageName.toUpperCase()+"</h1>");
```

Here's where we start assembling the code for the table. It requires much less space to assemble all the markup into a single string then write it all to the page at once, rather than use numerous `document.write()`s. It's also less demanding on the user's system resources.

```
var output="<table width=\"100\" border=\"0\" cellspacing=\"0\"
            cellpadding=\"0\">\n";
```

This `for` loop adds the markup for the table rows to our output string.

```
for(var j=0;j<numImgs;j++)
{
```

We check to see if the current row/image corresponds to the current page. If it does, we don't make the image in this cell into a link.

```
var fileName=imgNames[j];
output+="<tr><td>";
currFileName=(j==0)?"index":fileName;
```

Each time through the loop we insert the correct filename to which the link should point, as well as the parameter values for the calls to our image-swapping functions. For those who may have wondered if it's possible to use JavaScript to write more JavaScript, it's now apparent that the answer is in the affirmative.

```
if(fileName!=currPageName)
{
  output+="<a href=\""+currFileName+".html\"";
  output+=" onmouseover=\"rollOn("+j+");\"
onmouseout=\"rollOff("+j+");\">";
}
```

Next, we write the `<img>` tag for this row:

```
output+="<img name=\""+imgNames[j]+"\" src=\"images/"+imgNames[j];
output+=(fileName!=currPageName)?"_off":"_on";
output+=".jpg\" width=\"100\" height=\"35\" alt=\""+imgAlts[j]+"\"
        border=\"0\">";
```

Then we close the `<a>` tag if we started one, prior to writing the `<img>` element. In other words, the image is either a link, or isn't, and in the former case, we need to write both opening and closing tags for the link.

```
if(fileName!=currPageName)
output+="</a>";
output+="</td>\n";
```

Once we've closed the cell, we check to see if we're currently assembling the markup for the first row of the table; if we are, we need to write a second cell containing the sidebar image. We write the HTML code for this second cell just once because, as you might recall, it spans the remaining rows of the table.

```
if(j==0)
{
  output+="<td rowspan=\"5\"><img name=\"sidebar\"
          src=\"images/"+sideOff.src+"\"";
  output+=" width=\"100\" height=\"175\" border=\"0\"
          alt=\""+currPageName.toUpperCase()+
          " -- YOU ARE HERE\"></td>";
}
```

Then we close the row.

```
    output+="</tr>\n";
}
```

Having finished all our rows, we close the table,

```
output+="</table>\n";
```

and write the resulting string to the page.

```
output.write(output);

//-->
</script>
```

For browsers that don't do JavaScript, we've included a static version of the table, enclosed in a `<noscript>` element. Here's where the other problem with Netscape 2 and IE 3 arises. User agents that support JavaScript are supposed to ignore any content inside a `<noscript>` block. However, these two browsers ignore the rule itself, instead of ignoring the `<noscript>` content. In other words, both of these browsers will display the contents of a `<noscript>` block whether or not JavaScript is enabled or not. (This tag wasn't formalized until HTML 4.0 came out, and both Netscape 2 and IE 3 were released prior to that time.) So, if this is an issue, appropriate measures will need to be taken. In this particular case, we can solve the problem by placing all of the code in the second `<script>` element inside a single `if(document.images){ ... }` block. To see the table, check out `ch3_ex3_B.html`, in the code download.

We'll examine and provide some more sophisticated examples of "intelligent" menus in the next chapter when we discuss advanced client-side scripting techniques. For now, let's turn our attention to what can be done to create some more basic web menus using common form elements powered by a little JavaScript.

# Menus Using Form Elements

Generally speaking there are at least two definite advantages to using forms and basic form elements in web page design, particularly when we're creating user interfaces such as menus. First and foremost, they're universal: all web browsers support them in one way or another, even text-based ones such as Lynx. For this reason, users will most likely recognize them easily as being controls. Second, their behavior is highly consistent across user agents and platforms. There are a few instances (but not many) where browsers deviate from one another in this regard, and we'll indicate where and when these differences come into play.

There are also some disadvantages from a designer's point of view: the way in which form elements are rendered vary considerably between different operating systems and even user agents on the same platform can display the same ones differently. Also, form elements tend to be rather utilitarian in appearance, although some browsers allow for a small amount of control over the appearance of form element text using `<font>` tags. The most recent browsers support CSS styling of form elements; however their rendering of these can vary with the browser and its level of CSS support.

For similar reasons, it's probably wise at present to restrict oneself to the use of HTML 3.2 `<form>` elements in application-critical settings, at least on the open web, as support for the newest ones from HTML 4.0 and 4.01, such as `<fieldset>` and `<optgroup>`, is still not widespread. However, there's still quite a bit to be said for the use of `<form>` elements, as the site designer or developer doesn't have to worry about creating his or her own controls, nor about said controls being recognized as such by users.

It's difficult to imagine anyone who's used a computer not recognizing or feeling comfortable with on-screen push button controls. In a web context, these would most likely be `<input>` elements of type `button`, `submit,` or `reset`. (The latest browsers also support the HTML 4 `<button>` element, but for backward-compatibility, we won't be using it here.) In fact, it would probably be a real challenge to find any but the most trivial software application that doesn't make use of them! Since we're not providing any fields to be completed by the user, nor are we actually going to be submitting any information to a web server, we won't worry about the latter two here – just `button`.

# Example 4: A Basic Button Menu

This kind of menu is very simple, very basic, and when dressed up with a little CSS for those browsers that support it, not entirely unaesthetic. Users of browsers that aren't CSS-conformant will see something that's not quite so pleasing to the eye – for instance, the buttons will be of varying widths, but the menu will still be quite usable so long as the browser supports JavaScript. (If those browsers that don't support JavaScript are likely to be making use of this menu, it's a good idea to provide text or image links encased in `<noscript>` tags.) Let's see how our example looks in three different browsers, starting with Netscape 4 (left), and IE 5.5 (right):

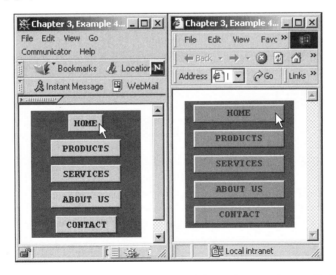

As you can see, Netscape 4's support for CSS styling of form elements is very limited – it renders the button text using the Courier New font specified in the stylesheet we'll see shortly, but that's about it. Internet Explorer supports a much wider range of CSS properties for these, including color, background color, and size. Overleaf, we show how Netscape 6.2 supports all the styles on these elements that IE does, as well as the `:hover` pseudoclass, not just for links, but for other elements as well, including the `<input>` tag. On the left, we show the menu as initially loaded; on the right, you can see how the menu appears when the user's mouse is over the "*HOME*" button:

Now here's the source code for our example, `ch3_ex4.html`:

```
<html>
<head>
    <title>Chapter 3, Example 4</title>
    <meta http-equiv="Content-Type" content="text/html; charset=iso-8859-1">
```

We define a pair of styles for the `<input>` element in order to enhance the menu's appearance in those browsers that support CSS for form elements.

```
<style type="text/css">
<!--
input {font:normal bold 14px 'Courier New',monospace; color:#990000;
width:125px;
        background-color:#CC9900;}
```

This is the `:hover` pseudoclass for the `<input>` element that we spoke of above. As with most other CSS attributes, it's simply ignored by those browsers that don't render it, so it's safe to include this for the benefit of Netscape 6 users, without causing any problems for visitors reaching the site with other browsers.

```
input:hover {color:#669900; background-color:#FFCC00;}
-->
</style>
<script type="text/javascript" language="JavaScript">
<!--
```

This relatively simple JavaScript function is used to power the menu buttons. The argument passed to it is a string, to which ".html" is appended. The browser is then redirected to the resulting URL.

```
    function goThere(destination)
    {
      self.location.href=destination+".html";
    }

    //-->
    </script>
</head>

<body bgcolor="#FFFFCC" text="#FFFFCC">
    <form>
        <table align="center" width="150" bgcolor="#666600" border="0" cellspacing="0"
               cellpadding="5">
```

Each button input has the `goThere()` function defined above attached to its `onclick` event handler. The first button calls the function with the string `"index"` as its argument, so the user will be redirected to the page `index.html`. Note that we surround the string with single quotes, since the function call itself is already double-quoted. If we attempted to use two sets of double quotes, like so,

```
onclick="goThere("index");"
```

the browser would see only `onclick="goThere("` which would result in a script error.

```
        <tr><td align="center">
          <input type="button" value="HOME" onclick="goThere('index');">
        </td></tr>
        <tr><td align="center">
          <input type="button" value="PRODUCTS" onclick="goThere('products');">
        </td></tr>
        <tr><td align="center">
          <input type="button" value="SERVICES" onclick="goThere('services');">
        </td></tr>
        <tr><td align="center">
          <input type="button" value="ABOUT US" onclick="goThere('about');">
        </td></tr>
        <tr><td align="center">
          <input type="button" value="CONTACT" onclick="goThere('contact');">
        </td></tr>
    </table>
  </form>
</body>
</html>
```

# Example 5: Radiobutton Menus

We can also do something quite similar using radiobuttons (left) or checkboxes (right):

The code used to drive each of these menus is quite similar. We've written a function, goThere(), which loops through the form's elements, finds the one that was checked, and uses that element's value in assembling a URL. In Example 5A (ch3_ex5A.html), the radiobuttons example, the function looks like this:

```
function goThere(form)
  {
    var destination="";
    for(var i=0;i<form.elements.menu.length;i++)
      if(form.elements.menu[i].checked)
        destination=form.elements[i].value.toLowerCase();
      if(destination!="")
        self.location.href=destination+".html";
  }
```

and in Example 5B (ch3_ex5B.html) like this:

```
function goThere(form)
{
  var destination="";
  for(var i=0;i<form.elements.length;i++)
    if(form.elements[i].type=="checkbox"&&form.elements[i].checked)
      destination=form.elements[i].value.toLowerCase();
    if(destination!="")
  self.location.href=destination+".html";
}
```

In both of these examples, `goThere()` is called from the radiobuttons' or checkboxes' `onclick` event handlers like so:

```
<input type="checkbox" value="INDEX" onclick="goThere(this.form);">
```

Or we could add a button input to the same form and use its `onclick` handler instead. The argument `this.form` passed to the function stands for the containing form of the `<input>` element from which it's called, so the function receives a JavaScript `Form` object, and it is this form's properties that are referenced therein.

Time for another caveat here with regard to using radiobuttons. As can be seen from the figure on the right, Netscape 4 has a slight problem displaying radiobuttons in tables:

When the table background colour and that of the page itself are different, Netscape 4 shows the radiobuttons with the latter rather than the former. Fortunately, we can set the `background-color` style property of the `<input>` element to take care of this, and we've done so in the actual example files.

# Example 6A: A Basic "Jump Menu"

We'll complete our look at scripted form elements for navigation interfaces with what is commonly referred to as the "jump menu". This consists of a `<select>` containing a group of `<option>` elements; the user selects one of the options, and is redirected to a corresponding page. It also seems to be an endless source of problems for those trying to implement it for the first time. This is due both to a poor understanding of the DOM as it relates to these elements, and to the fact that Internet Explorer permits the use of non-standard, browser-specific shortcuts in referring to `<option>` elements. This can be confusing for developers who use IE as their primary browser, employ these shortcuts in their code, and then find that they encounter scripting errors in non-Microsoft browsers.

To avoid such problems, we will employ the standard object references to `<form>` elements in the example that follows, which are recognized by all browsers, including IE. Overleaf is our basic jump menu (*ch3_ex6A*):

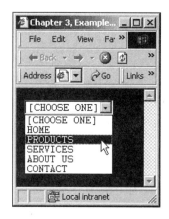

And here's the code for it:

```
<html>
<head>
  <title>Chapter 3, Example 6-A</title>
  <meta http-equiv="Content-Type" content="text/html; charset=iso-8859-1">
  <style type="text/css">
  <!--
    select, option {font:normal normal 14px 'Courier',monospace;
                    text-align:center;}
  -->
  </style>
  <script type="text/javascript" language="JavaScript">
  <!--

  function goThere(select)
  {
```

So long as the user employs the menu for navigating around the site, they can't select the "*CHOOSE ONE*" option because it's already selected when the page is loaded. However, if they use the browser's *Back* or *Forward* buttons, they'll return to a page that's as it was when they left it before, with a different option selected than the usual default, in which case it would be possible to select "*CHOOSE ONE*" – and this would result in the browser trying to load a non-existent page named ".html". Since we want to preclude such an occurrence, we insert the following line:

```
    if(select.selectedIndex)
    self.location.href=select.options[select.selectedIndex].value+".html";
  }
```

This will keep anything from happening when "*CHOOSE ONE*" is selected. If you think your users might still not get the message, you can provide them one by adding:

```
else
  alert("Please select a page from the menu.");
```

which should make it absolutely clear to the user why they've not gone anywhere!

```
    //-->
    </script>
</head>

<body bgcolor="#000099" text="#000033">
  <table border="0" cellpadding="0" cellspacing="0">
    <tr>
      <td>
        <form>
          <select name="menu" size="1" onchange="goThere(this);">
            <option value="" selected>[CHOOSE ONE]</option>
            <option value="index">HOME</option>
            <option value="products">PRODUCTS</option>
            <option value="services">SERVICES</option>
            <option value="about">ABOUT US</option>
            <option value="contact">CONTACT</option>
          </select>
        </form>
      </td>
    </tr>
  </table>
</body>
</html>
```

There's nothing terribly remarkable about the HTML markup: just a `<form>` with a typical dropdown-style `<select>` with six options, the first of which is the default and which has an empty string as its value. The other five options have for their `value` attributes the same filenames of the five pages (less the `.html` extension) we're using all along in this chapter for our example site. We use the `<select>` element's `onchange` event handler to call the `goThere()` function that sends the browser to its destination.

The right-hand side of the single line of code in this event handler is a lot less mysterious than it might look. Let's take it apart from the inside out. The `this` keyword in JavaScript stands for "the current object". The parameter passed to the function is the `select` object from which it is called – so what we refer to as `select` within the function itself is the `select` object whose name is "menu". The index of the option, (starting with zero in the same order in which the `<option>` tags appear in the page) that was selected by the user is `select.selectedIndex`. The options themselves are elements in the array `select.options` – the selected option is thus `select.options[select.selectedIndex]` and its value is `select.options[select.selectedIndex].value`.

So, if the user selects the third option (labelled *PRODUCTS*), the script gets the value of that option, in this case the string `"products"`, tacks the string ".html" onto the end of it, and sends the browser to the page with that filename.

Before we continue, we should make a couple of points regarding usability:

- This menu is unusable by browsers that don't support JavaScript. If this is an issue, then you should provide alternative navigation such as hyperlinks, possibly within a `<noscript>` element.

- Some older JavaScript-capable user agents don't support the `onchange` event handler. A suggested workaround is to add a button input to this same form and use the button's `onclick` handler instead: `onclick="goThere(this.form.menu);"`.

- In addition, users who need to employ keyboard navigation will need to be accommodated. In this case, if JavaScript is known to be enabled, removing the `onchange` handler from the `<select>` tag and using the button input should resolve the issue. If JavaScript is not an option, then hyperlink navigation should be provided, as in point 1.

# Example 6B: A Jump Menu with Intelligence

If you run through the previous example a few times and travel to various pages in our example "mini-site", you might notice that, as with the original rollover menus we created earlier in the chapter, there's a superfluous option in the menu on each page we go to, which corresponds to the current page. Not only is this unnecessary, but users on a slow connection could waste valuable time on our site by simply reloading the same page if they accidentally select it. Let's do as we did in Example 3B, and help the user out by making sure that this never happens! It would also be a good idea to do this as unobtrusively as possible, by simply not displaying that option. We could write the HTML on the fly using a loop to assemble the markup, and `document.write()`ing the result to the page as it loads like we did before. However, with form elements there's another technique that can be used, involving JavaScript objects. We'll employ this now because we're going to need it in Example 7, very shortly. Here's the menu as rendered on two different pages of our example site, `index.html` on the left, and `services.html` on the right:

Notice that this version of the jump menu, unlike the previous one, omits the option corresponding to the page in which it appears. Now let's take a walk through the code that makes this happen (`ch3_ex6b.html`); we'll explain what's new and how it works along the way:

```
<html>
<head>
  <title>Chapter 3, Example 6-B</title>
  <meta http-equiv="Content-Type" content="text/html; charset=iso-8859-1">
```

Note that we've included a style rule for the `<select>` and `<option>` elements, the same as in the previous example, that will make our menu look a bit nicer in those browsers that support it without causing problems in those that don't.

```
<style type="text/css">
  <!--
    select, option {font:normal normal 14px 'Courier',monospace;
                    text-align:center;}
  -->
</style>

<script type="text/javascript" language="JavaScript">
  <!--
```

The `fillSelect()` function does all the work of customizing the menu to whichever page it's used in. We define two arrays, one of which contains the unique portions of the URLs we want the menu to point to, just as we've done in several previous examples in this chapter. These will serve as the `value` attributes of the `<option>` elements we're about to create. The other array contains the text that we wish to have displayed in each option (and correspond to the `text` property of each one).

```
function fillSelect()
{
  var pageNames=new Array("index","products","services",
                          "about","contact");
  var pageTitles=new Array("HOME PAGE","OURCO PRODUCTS", "OURCO SERVICES"
                          ,"ABOUT OURCO.COM","CONTACT US");

  var numPages=pageNames.length;
  var j=1;
```

This next bit should look familiar, as it's exactly the same code as we've used before to parse out the unique portion of the current page's URL.

```
  var URLbits=self.location.href.split("/");
  var currPage=URLbits[URLbits.length-1];
  var currPageName=currPage.split(".")[0];
```

In browsers that support JavaScript1.1 and above, we should be able to create new options for an existing `<select>` element dynamically, using the `new Option()` constructor. However, Netscape 4 doesn't allow us to do this as neatly as we'd like; in that browser, we can change the properties of existing `<option>` elements, but not create new ones from scratch.

In any case, we loop through the elements of the arrays we defined above. For each element in the `pageNames` array, we check to see if it's the same as `currPageName`; if it's not, we call the `new Option()` constructor using the $i^{th}$ elements of the `pageTitles` and `pageNames` arrays as the arguments corresponding to that option's `text` and `value` attributes, then assign it as the next option belonging to our select.

```
  for(var i=0;i<numPages;i++)
  {
    if(currPageName!=pageNames[i])
    {
      document.navForm.menu.options[j]=new Option(pageTitles[i],
```

```
                                                          pageNames[i]);
               j++;
            }
         }
      }
   }
```

Once our dropdown menu is complete, it acts precisely as though we'd hard-coded the necessary values and text into the corresponding HTML; our users can interact with it in exactly the same fashion as they would with any other `<select>` elements, and we can use exactly the same `goThere()` function as we did for Example 6A:

```
function goThere(select)
{
  self.location.href=select.options[select.selectedIndex].value+".html";
}

//-->
</script>
</head>
```

We can't manipulate page elements that don't yet exist, so we ensure that they do by explicitly calling the `fillSelect()` function after the page has finished loading using the `onload` attribute of the `<body>` tag.

```
<body bgcolor="#000099" text="#000033" onload="fillSelect();">
  <table border="0" cellpadding="0" cellspacing="0">
    <tr>
      <td>
        <form name="navForm">
```

Nothing special about the HTML markup we're using here, except that all of the `<option>` elements inside our `<select>` contain no values or descriptive text (except for the first one) – these are created programmatically.

```
        <select name="menu" size="1" onchange="goThere(this);">
          <option value="" selected>---------[CHOOSE ONE]--------</option>
          <option></option>
          <option></option>
          <option></option>
          <option></option>
        </select>
      </form>
    </td>
  </tr>
</table>
</body>
</html>
```

In IE 4+ and Netscape 6, there's no need to hard-code any of the `<option>` tags, and we could take care of the default option by calling its constructor first, with an additional argument: `document.navForm.menu.options[0]=new Option("","[CHOOSE ONE]",true);`. The third argument sets the corresponding option's `selected` attribute.

If it's desirable to use a listbox-style menu rather than a dropdown, all that needs to be done with our example is to change the `size` attribute of the select. We should note also that, for Netscape 4, we need to make sure that the default option is long enough to accommodate the text of the longest option in the `<select>` group, otherwise the text for one or more of the options may get cut off. Fortunately, this doesn't happen when we use the dropdown-style menu. We've included an example among our sample files as `ch3_ex6B_2.html`.

A typical page from this set looks like this:

# Example 7: A Double Jump Menu

Now let's build a more sophisticated version of our jump menu using the same technique. This time we'll actually make use of **two** dropdown menus in order to accommodate the sudden growth of our site: it seems that OurCo's business is up and there's a demand for expanded company information and services online. Instead of giving the user the ability to visit one of four other pages than the current one, we need to give him or her the ability to choose, first between five different sections of the site (six if we include a main "home" page), and then between a number of pages within each section. Also, we'll want to make this an intelligent menu that doesn't bother the user with an option to visit the current page.

Here's a chart of the sections and pages belonging to each section:

| SECTIONS | PAGES |
|---|---|
| Home | Main (`index.html`) |
| Offices | Aurora<br>Birmingham<br>Buenos Aires<br>Cartagena<br>Kempsey<br>Pune<br>Scottsdale<br>Stavanger |
| Products | Gizmos<br>Somesuches<br>Thingoes<br>Whatsi*<br>Widgets |

*Table continued on following page*

| SECTIONS | PAGES |
|---|---|
| Services | Deliveries<br>Estimates<br>Exchanges<br>Specifications |
| About Us | Company History<br>Corporate Profile<br>Management<br>Mission Statement |
| Contact | Customer Service<br>Sales Enquiries<br>General Information<br>Telephone Numbers |

[*The plural of *whatsits*, of course!]

Now let's walk through the code:

```
<html>
<head>
  <title>Chapter 3, Example 7</title>
  <meta http-equiv="Content-Type" content="text/html; charset=iso-8859-1">
  <style type="text/css">
  <!--
    select, option {font:normal normal 14px 'Courier',monospace;
                    text-align:center;}
  -->
  </style>

  <script type="text/javascript" language="JavaScript">
  <!--
```

First we store the names we wish to have appear in the first dropdown in an array named `sectionNames`, then an array of the same length named `pages`.

```
var sectionNames=new Array("HOME PAGE","OFFICES","OURCO PRODUCTS","OURCO
                           SERVICES","ABOUT OURCO.COM","CONTACT US");
var numSections=sectionNames.length;
var pages=new Array(numSections);
```

Each of this second array's elements is actually an array of its own save for the first, which contains the names of the pages falling under each section name.

```
pages[0]="";
pages[1]=new Array("Aurora","Birmingham","Buenos Aires","Cartagena",
                   "Kempsey","Pune","Scottsdale","Stavanger");
pages[2]=new Array("Gizmos","Somesuches","Thingoes",
```

```
                             "Whatsi","Widgets");
        pages[3]=new Array("Deliveries","Estimates","Exchanges","Specifications");
        pages[4]=new Array("Company History","Corporate Profile",
                           "Management","Mission Statement");
        pages[5]=new Array("Customer Service","Sales Enquiries",
                           "General Information","Telephone Numbers");
```

This is the same snippet of code we've been using to parse out the unique portion of the current page's URL.

```
        var URLbits=self.location.href.split("/");
        var currPage=URLbits[URLbits.length-1];
        var currPageName=currPage.split(".")[0];
```

We need to make sure the user has actually selected a section to navigate to before trying to redirect the browser, so we declare a `flag` variable we'll use to keep track of whether or not this selection has taken place, and initialize its value to `false`.

```
        var flag=false;
```

This is the function that builds the first dropdown. It works in a very similar fashion to that used in the previous example, except that it's always the same on every page save for the main index page – where we don't want to display the "*HOME*" option. It's triggered by the page's `Load` event.

```
        function fillSections()
        {
          var j=1;

          for(var i=0;i<numSections;i++)
          {
            if(i!=0||currPageName!="index")
            {
              document.navForm.sectionMenu.options[j]=new Option
              (sectionNames[i],i);
              j++;
            }
          }
        }
```

When the user selects an option from the *Sections* dropdown, we check to see if it's the option containing the text "*HOME*"; if so, we immediately send the user back to `index.html`. Otherwise, we get the index of the selected option and display the corresponding pages as options in the *Navigate* dropdown. Notice that if the "*HOME*" option is displayed, we need to subtract 1 from the `selectedIndex` so that we're pulling the page titles in from the correct array.

```
        function fillPages(form)
        {
          var mySelectedIndex=form.sectionMenu.selectedIndex;
          if(form.sectionMenu.options[mySelectedIndex].text=="HOME PAGE")
             self.location.href="index.html";
```

```
    else
    {
      var m=1;
      selectedSection=mySelectedIndex;
      if(currPageName!="index")
        selectedSection-=1;

      for(var k=0;k<pages[selectedSection].length;k++)
      {
        var selectedPageName=pages[selectedSection][k];
        var selectedFile=selectedPageName;
```

We've used a very simple naming scheme for the pages themselves: we just use the title, and if it contains two words rather than one, we toss out the first word, for example the filename for the page containing information about the company's Buenos Aires office is `aires.html` (we convert the value to lowercase below).

```
        if(selectedPageName.indexOf(" ")!=-1)
          selectedPageName=selectedPageName.split(" ")[1];
```

Now we set each option's `text` and `value` properties appropriately:

```
        form.pageMenu.options[m]=new Option(selectedFile,selectedPageName);
        m++;
      }
```

For Netscape 4 compatibility, we need to display the maximum possible number of option spaces, and "blank out" those that aren't needed, should we not require that many options.

```
        for(n=pages[selectedSection].length+1;n<9;n++)
          form.pageMenu.options[n]=new Option("","");
```

Finally, we set our flag to `true`, indicating that the second dropdown is ready for use:

```
        flag=true;
      }
    }
```

Here's our now-familiar `goThere()` function, which we've modified slightly.

```
    function goThere(form)
    {
```

If the `flag` variable's value is `false`, we know that the user hasn't yet made a selection from the Section's dropdown. In this case, we notify the user of this with a standard JavaScript `alert()` dialogue, reset the Navigation dropdown to its default state, and set focus on the Selections menu to help make the point clear.

```
    if(!flag)
    {
      form.pageMenu.options[0].selected=true;
      alert("Please select a section of the site.");
      form.sectionMenu.focus();
    }
```

Otherwise, we get the value of the selected option, convert it to lowercase, tack the string ".html" onto the end, and send the user to the page bearing that filename.

```
    else
    {
      var myValue=form.pageMenu.options
      [form.pageMenu.selectedIndex].value;
      if(myValue!="")
      self.location.href=myValue.toLowerCase()+".html";
    }
  }

  //-->
  </script>
</head>
```

Here's a split-screen view of both sides of the menu expanded, before a selection has actually taken place:

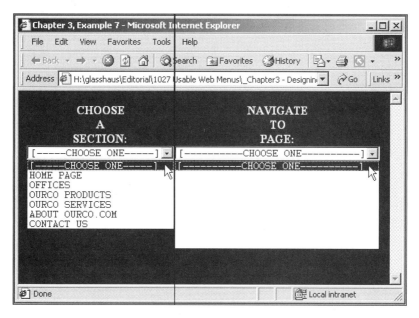

This is how the menu appears once the user has clicked on the "*OFFICES*" option:

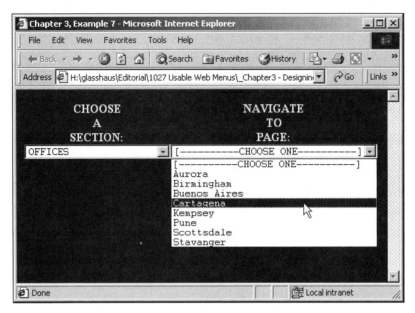

As in the previous examples of this type, there's nothing particularly special or different about the HTML we've used here to build the dropdowns, except that this time there are two `<select>` elements: the one named `sectionMenu` is used to choose a section of the site, and the other one, named `pageMenu,` is the one from which a page will be selected to navigate to once it has been populated by choosing a section from the first one.

```
<body bgcolor="#000099" text="#FFFFCC" onload="fillSections();">
  <form name="navForm">
    <table border="0" cellpadding="0" cellspacing="0">
      <tr>
        <th>CHOOSE<br>A<br>SECTION:</th>
        <th>NAVIGATE<br>TO<br>PAGE:</th>
      </tr>
      <tr>
        <td>
          <select name="sectionMenu" size="1"
                  onchange="fillPages(this.form);">
            <option value="" selected>[-----CHOOSE ONE-----]</option>
            <option></option>
            <option></option>
            <option></option>
            <option></option>
            <option></option>
          </select>
        </td>
        <td>
          <select name="pageMenu" size="1" onchange="goThere(this.form);">
```

```
                <option value="" selected>[----------CHOOSE ONE----------]
                </option>
                <option></option>
                <option></option>
                <option></option>
                <option></option>
                <option></option>
                <option></option>
                <option></option>
                <option></option>
              </select>
            </td>
          </tr>
        </table>
      </form>
    </body>
  </html>
```

This completes our look at some uses of forms and form elements for constructing navigation menus.

# Summary

In this chapter, we've examined the most common HTML elements for creating menus in web pages: text and image links, along with forms and form elements. We've touched on using CSS to control their appearance in a manner that enhances their aesthetic appeal in more advanced browsers, without impairing usability in older user agents. We've given a quick lesson in creating JavaScript image rollovers, which can aid in drawing attention to important navigational elements and demonstrated how to create a very basic example of an often-requested enhancement, the off-image rollover. This is where we provide a secondary image that changes as each navigation link is moused over, in order to provide additional visual cues or other information to the user as to what the link is to be used for, or where it leads.

We've shown several different ways in which various form elements, such as pushbuttons, radiobuttons, and checkboxes, also powered with client-side JavaScript, can be used to create navigational or other interfaces for our pages. Also discussed and demonstrated were basic as well as more advanced "jump menus", created with <select> and <option> elements.

Along the way, we slipped in a lesson or two about "intelligent" menus that "sense" which page they occur in, and display their options accordingly. We also hinted at how server-side programming such as PHP and ASP can be used to build and customize these menus to make them even more powerful and flexible, a topic which we'll examine in much greater depth in *Chapters 5* and *6*. Finally, we discussed many of the compatibility issues that arise when it's necessary to support older browsers back to the third generations of Netscape and IE, and provided some fixes and suggestions to help handle these situations.

# What's Ahead

Coming up in *Chapter 4*, we'll discuss more sophisticated menus created with image maps, CSS styling and positioning, and advanced client-side scripting techniques, including the saving of user preferences using cookies. We'll look at some common and popular DHTML techniques for menus, including expanding/collapsing menus, and provide some scripts that you can adapt for your own purposes. After a time-out in *Chapter 5* to explore some Flash techniques for creating menus, we'll be re-using and expanding upon one of the examples from *Chapter 4* in our discussion of server-side techniques for dynamic menu creation and deployment in *Chapter 6*.

# 4

- Advanced DHTML menus

- CSS, including pages with different stylesheet selectors

- Saving preferences with cookies

- Image maps and floating menus

- Expanding/Collapsing menus

**Author: Jon Stephens**

# Menus with Advanced
# Scripting and DHTML

In the previous chapter, we looked at some ways in which basic HTML elements such as text and image links can be used to create web menus, and then looked at how we can also make use of form elements plus JavaScript. Now we'll build on these concepts and techniques to make our menus even more useful, attractive, and responsive to the needs and preferences of our users. In this chapter, we'll:

- Start out by offering a basic refresher on what CSS is, and how to use CSS to control the appearance of our menus and other content. We'll demonstrate the power of CSS and a little scripting, with a couple of examples. One is fairly basic and backwards compatible with the version 4 browsers, while the other is somewhat more involved, and makes use of some basic CSS and HTML **Document Object Model** (**DOM**) scripting.

- Take a look at image maps, and some examples of how they can be used in creating menus, including one with a tabbed interface.

- Explore the powerful combination of CSS and advanced DOM scripting (DHTML), which can be used to change the content and appearance of pages in real time. We'll demonstrate some additional ways to make use of this combination to create dynamic menus that are both useful and eye-catching. In all the remaining examples in this chapter, we'll take those concepts in conjunction with the DOM to produce a number of really cool and useful menu enhancements for web pages, including:

- Text rollovers and tooltips

- A floating menu

- Expanding & collapsing menus

Along the way, we'll talk about the concept of **modularity** and the advantages of separating content, style, and scripting code. And of course, we'll offer examples or suggestions on how to make our code compatible between different web browsers and browser versions, or alternatives where they simply aren't compatible.

By the time you've reached the end of this chapter, you'll have learned about a number of techniques for menus and hopefully be inspired to adapt them in many different ways to suit the needs of your own projects and their users. Let's begin with a short refresher on CSS, as an understanding of it is crucial to most of what follows.

# CSS Basics

Stylesheets are a very powerful yet simple tool for controlling the appearance of web page content. In the "bad old days" before CSS, the use of fonts, colours, and sizing of text was accomplished through the use of the `<font>` tag:

```
<b><font face="Helvetica,Arial,sans-serif"
     color="#CC0033" size="+1">Pay attention to this -- it's
important.</font></b>
```

As the size and complexity of pages and sites grew, there came to be less and less that was right with doing things in this way. There were at least three major reasons for this:

**1.** Maintainability: Suppose that, in building a site, we use a certain custom style, scattered liberally in different places, to add emphasis. Then someone decides that the background being used isn't what was really wanted and mandates a change. The designer or developer is directed to change all instances of #CC0033 to #003366 – all 197 of them. "Oh, and while you're at it, make them all a size larger, too." Search-and-replace is a viable option, but it turns out that one member of the team consistently used the order `face`, `color`, `size`, while another preferred `face`, `size`, `color`, and a third member of the team didn't use any particular order at all, crossed the bold and font tags in numerous places, and used `size="3"` because it looked the same to him. Wouldn't it be nice if we had a way to control the appearance of all these instances of text from one central point? CSS lets us do just that: we define a style,

```
<style type="text/css">
.payAttentionToThis {font:normal bold 110% Helvetica,Arial,sans-serif;
                     color:#CC0033;}
</style>
```

Then, wherever we need to use this style, we can write:

```
<b class="payAttentionToThis">Pay attention to this -- it's important.</b>
```

Later, if we need to change the appearance of all these important bits of information, all we need to do is change the appropriate style rules in the class definition – once – and we're ready to move on.

**2.** Economy: Now let's suppose that we're displaying information in an HTML table that contains 12 columns and 45 rows, and that we'd like to make all the text in the 528 cells that aren't header cells look like our custom style. That means we're adding about 40K to the file size of the page. If we use the `.payAttentionToThis` class on the `<td>` tags instead, we can save about 30K of that. Better still, by using a CSS selector for the tag itself (td {font:normal bold 110% Helvetica,Arial,sans-serif; color:#CC0033;}) we add less than 100 bytes to the page (or 0 bytes to the HTML file if we're using a separate CSS file), which makes for even less bloat. While the availability of broadband connections is increasing, it's by no means universal, and not likely to be for some time - the majority of web users are still using dialup modems, so you should try to save on file size wherever possible.

**3.** Separation of Content from Appearance: Very simply, this means we can re-use the same information in different settings without either taking its appearance along for the ride, or having to stop and unravel the two. As we'll see shortly, this allows us to easily present the same content to different users in different ways, conferring both aesthetic and practical benefits. The converse is also true – we can use the same set of styles to give a uniform presentation to different documents, or other pieces of data.

Additional benefits of using CSS are that the range of style information that we can set for page elements (and not just text elements) is greatly enhanced. In the newest browsers, we can apply CSS to just about any HTML tags, including tables, forms, and the elements they contain. Aspects of element display that we can control through CSS include:

- Background images and colors

- Borders, margins, and padding

- Clipping

- Visibility and display

- Positioning

We'll be making considerable use of the last two of these especially, later on in this chapter.

# CSS Example 1: Choosing a Stylesheet

In this example, we'll allow the user to choose between one of four different stylesheets to use for viewing a menu used throughout a site. In order to be backwards compatible to the version 4 browsers, this example will make use of a pop-up window with a form `<select>` control to display and choose among the different style options. This is because Netscape 4 doesn't support changing styles or stylesheets in real time.

We'll make use of a cookie to save that choice across pages, and to check the user's preference and write an appropriate `<link>` to the correct stylesheet at load time. We'll also share a couple of functions for reading and writing cookies, which you can reuse in your own scripts very easily.

Here's the listing for one of the stylesheets, `menu1.css`:

```
a.menu {font:normal normal 12px Arial,sans-serif; color:#CC0033;}

a.menu:hover {font-weight:bold; color:#CCCC00;}

td.menu {background-color:#000066; text-align:center;}

th.menu {font:normal bold 14px Arial,sans-serif; color:#0000CC; text-align:center;
        background-color:#666666;}

p.menu {font:normal bold 12px Arial,sans-serif; color:#FFFFFF;}
```

we apply this using `<link rel="stylesheet" type="text/css" href="styles/menu1.css">` in the `<head>` of a static page (note that the `href` attribute of this tag points to the stylesheet that is to be linked into the page). Our sample page, `ch4_ex1.html`, contains (among other things) the following table:

```
<table width="200" border="0" cellpadding="5" cellspacing="0">
  <tr>
    <th class="menu">OURCO.COM<br>SITE<br>NAVIGATION</th>
  </tr>
  <tr>
    <td class="menu">
      <p class="menu">The OurCo.com Main Entry Page:</p>
      <a class="menu" href="index.html">HOME</a>
    </td>
  </tr>
  <tr>
    <td class="menu">
      <p class="menu">Our Fabulous Line of Widgets, Gizmoes, Whatsi, and
More!:</p>
      <a class="menu" href="products.html">PRODUCTS</a>
    </td>
  </tr>
  <tr>
    <td class="menu">
      <p class="menu">How Can We Help You Today?:</p>
      <a class="menu" href="services.html">SERVICES</a>
    </td>
  </tr>
  <tr>
    <td class="menu">
      <p class="menu">More About OurCo Than You'll Ever Want To Know:</p>
      <a class="menu" href="about.html">ABOUT US</a>
    </td>
  </tr>
  <tr>
    <td class="menu">
      <p class="menu">Questions? Comments? Problems? Fill Out Our Contact
Form:</p>
      <a class="menu" href="contact.html">CONTACT</a>
    </td>
  </tr>

  <tr>
```

```
        <td class="menu">
          <p class="menu">
            Don't Like How Our Navigation Menu Looks? Do Something
            About It Here:
          </p>
          <a class="menu" href="javascript:setCustomMenu();">
            CUSTOMIZE
          </a>
        </td>
      </tr>
    </table>
```

Nothing particularly remarkable here, except for two things: the bottom table cell contains a `javascript:` link. When clicked, this calls a JavaScript function that allows the user to choose a preferred menu style; we'll walk you through that function shortly. You might also notice that we've used `class="menu"` for all the elements to which our stylesheet applies, which is also reflected in the stylesheet code above. This makes it easier to keep our style names straight, although you can choose to name them differently in your stylesheets.

We're going to use JavaScript to write the `<link>` to one of the four stylesheets `menu1.css`, `menu2.css`, `menu3.css`, or `menu4.css`. We'll do this based on the value of a cookie named `styleCookie` which, if set, will contain one of the values "1", "2", "3", or "4". Cookies have received a lot of bad press because of privacy concerns. While it's true that some unscrupulous developers have abused cookies for things like storing information that's best kept private, or for tracking user's surfing habits, cookies can also be quite useful. For example, TVGuide.com uses them to store the user's zip code or postal code and a code for the local cable system or satellite service so that returning visitors can go straight to the programme listings page without having to re-enter that information each time they want to know what's on. The alternative would be to maintain an account for each user, and require them to log in each time they want to check the listings, which is exactly what we're trying to avoid, at least in this case. We want the user's menu style preference to be chosen once, which is then implemented transparently. We can also store information that's useful to us, as well as to the user – for instance, how many times the user's visited our site or one or more given pages on that site.

However, we should **never** store sensitive, personal information such as credit card or Social Security numbers, address, telephone, etc., in a cookie – even if we're using secure cookies, there's still the possibility that this information could be obtained from our computer by a visitor to our site. Another unpleasant possibility would be someone hacking into the server and "eavesdropping" on the information being sent back and forth. At least one widely-used book on scripting suggests that storing addresses in cookies is an acceptable practice, but we strongly disagree – not only for the reasons we've already stated but also because there are bugs in some browsers that allow code from one domain to access cookie sets from another, even when this shouldn't otherwise be possible. For information about some additional browser cookie bugs, see http://www.zend.com/manual/function.setcookie.php. For more about cookies and privacy concerns from a user's point of view, a good place to start is http://www.junkbusters.com/cookies.html.

## *Generic Cookie Functions*

A cookie consists at a minimum of a name, which identifies the cookie, and a value, which contains the data we want to save in the cookie. Optionally we can add information about how long the cookie will be active, from what server and directory it can be accessed, and if we want to set and retrieve it via a secure (`https://`) connection. Here are some cookie utility functions that can be used independently of any other scripts we use in this example or this chapter. They're basically shortcuts to help us read and write an assignment of the form:

```
document.cookie="myCookieName=myCookieValue; expires=Mon, 14 Jan 2003 04:07:32
GMT; path=/; domain=ourco.com;";
```

Notice that this is a single JavaScript statement. We've placed these cookie utility functions in a separate file `cookie_utils.js`, in order to make them available to any page on our site – simply include a reference to it in the `src` attribute of a `<script>` tag. Since we're keeping all our standalone scripts in a **scripts** directory below our HTML files, we include the file (and thus all the functions and other script code in that file) in our pages using:

```
<script type="text/javascript" language="JavaScript"
src="scripts/cookie_utils.js">
</script>
```

Note that they appear here in a slightly different order from that in the file.

The first of our utility functions allows us to set a cookie.

```
function setCookie(name,value,expires,path,domain,secure)
```

The arguments passed to this function are all strings (except for `expires` and `secure` – see below), and all but the first two may be omitted. We'll make use of the `name`, `value`, and `expires` arguments in the scripts in this chapter. The default values for `path` and `domain` are the current path and domain of the page they're set from, that is, the current directory and domain. To make the cookie available from all directories in a domain, set the `path` value to `"/"`. The `secure` attribute is omitted unless we wish to set it to `true`. Note that, in order to make use of secure cookies, there must be a secure connection between the server and client; otherwise, setting this value does nothing. For more information on how to use these last three attributes, see references cited in the "Resources" section at the end of the book.

```
{
    document.cookie=name
```

The `name` of the cookie can be any string that is a legal JavaScript variable name, and the `value` can contain any characters except for semicolons, commas, or whitespace characters. Using JavaScript's `escape()` function on `value` before adding it to the cookie string converts these to their hexadecimal equivalents, so that we can safely store strings containing them.

```
+"="+escape(value)
```

If we don't set an expiry date for the cookie, it will expire at the end of the current browser session; the browser deletes it automatically. If we wish to save the data between sessions, then we need to specify an expiry date in the future. To do this, first we create a `Date` object corresponding to the current date and time, then use the appropriate `get()` and `set()` methods to modify it before passing it to the `setCookie()` function. The built-in `toGMTString()` method called in the function ensures that it's passed to the browser in the correct format:

```
+((expires)?"; expires="+expires.toGMTString():"")
```

Finally, the remaining three parameters are added onto the cookie string.

```
        +((path)?"; path="+path:"")
        +((domain)?"; domain="+domain:"")
        +((secure)?"; secure":"");
    }
```

Note that we can store up to 20 cookies from a single domain. Cookies do not contain any executable code; each cookie may contain up to 4K of character data, which includes the cookie's name and value. One further limitation is that a web browser is not required to store more than 300 cookies total – when we try to set a cookie that would cause either of the limits to be exceeded the cookie will in fact be set, but the browser may delete its least-recently used cookie in order to keep from going over the limit. Different browsers may possibly be able to store more cookies than these minimums, but since we can't guarantee this, it's best to assume that the limits are in effect for all user agents. To recall the value of a given cookie by name, we can use the getCookie() function, which takes the name of the cookie as its sole argument:

```
function getCookie(name)
{
  var cookieArg=name+"=";
  var argLength=cookieArg.length;
  var cookieLength=document.cookie.length;
  var i=0;
```

We search along the length of the cookie string for a portion of it containing name=; if we find it, we pass its position to the getCookieVal() function, which returns the actual value to the getCookie() function, which then passes it back to wherever we called that function in our script; otherwise, we return a null value.

```
  while(i<cookieLength)
  {
    var j=i+argLength;
    if(document.cookie.substring(i,j)==cookieArg)
      return getCookieVal(j);
    i=document.cookie.indexOf(" ",i)+1;
    if(!i)break;
  }
  return null;
}
```

The getCookieVal() function finds the portion of the cookie string between name= and the next semicolon, unescapes it, and returns it to getCookie():

```
function getCookieVal(offset)
{
  var end=document.cookie.indexOf(";",offset);

  if(end==-1)
    end=document.cookie.length;

  return unescape(document.cookie.substring(offset,end));
}
```

To delete a cookie, all we need to do is set the expiry date of the cookie to a date in the past.

```
function deleteCookie(name)
{
```

If the cookie with the indicated name exists,

```
if(getCookie(name))
{
```

we create a new `Date` object corresponding to the current date and time,

```
var killDate=new Date();
```

change the value stored in that `Date` to one corresponding to a date in the past (we chose 10*365*24*60*60 = 548,640,000 seconds, or ten years ago!):

```
killDate.setTime(killDate.getTime ()-10*365*24*60*60);
```

and then set the cookie's value to an empty string and its `expires` value to the past date value we just created:

```
setCookie(name,"",killDate);
}
}
```

Now that we've explained how our cookie utility functions work, let's put them to use in getting and saving a user's preferences.

## Using a Cookie To Set a Stylesheet Preference

When a user visits one of our pages for the first time, they'll see a very plain navigation menu, with a white background, just like the rest of the page, and default text and link colours. This is because the cookie we're using to write the `<link>` to a stylesheet hasn't been set yet, and we've set up the function not to write one at all in this case. So when the page first loads, the appearance of the menu will be controlled only by the `content.css` file. Let's look at the `writeStyle()` function, contained in the file `set_menu_style.js`, and included in each of our pages using the appropriate tag `<script ... src="...">` tag:

```
function writeStyle()
{
```

First we create an output variable whose initial value is an empty string, and set a convenience variable equal to the value of the cookie named `styleCookie`:

```
var output="";
var myCookie=getCookie("styleCookie");
```

We test to see if the cookie's been set by checking to see if it contains a non-empty, non-`null` value. If it doesn't, we return out of the function without doing anything else:

```
if(!myCookie||myCookie==null)
  return;
```

Otherwise we use the cookie's value (which, as we'll see shortly, should always be "1", "2", "3", or "4") in the output string as part of the name of the CSS file we wish to include, along with the rest of the `<link>` tag:

```
output="<link rel=\"stylesheet\" type=\"text/css\" ";
output+="href=\"styles/menu"+myCookie+".css\">\n";
```

We then write it to the page, like so:

```
document.writeln(output);
}
```

This will override any styles affecting the menu elements in the `content.css` file. Then we actually call the function:

```
writeStyle();
```

To get an idea of what we're trying to achieve here, look at the figure below. On the left is the menu's default appearance, while on the right we see how the menu appears once the user has selected one of the style options (#2 in this case):

Also in the `set_menu_style.js` file, we define the function `setCustom()` that's called by the "CUSTOMIZE" link that appears at the bottom of the menu. This is not a particularly complex function; all it does is create a small pop-up window that contains a page named `chooser.html`:

```
function setCustomMenu()
{
   var windowParams="width=425,height=200,toolbar=no";
   var myChoiceWin=window.open("chooser.html","myChoiceWin",windowParams);
}
```

The pop-up looks like this:

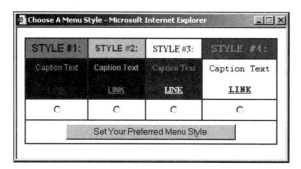

Now let's look at the source for the pop-up (`chooser.html`):

```
<html>
<head>
   <title>Choose A Menu Style (Chapter 4, Example 1)</title>
   <meta http-equiv="Content-Type" content="text/html; charset=iso-8859-1">
```

Here's a link to a stylesheet that contains all the styles for all four menus. If you look at `chooserwindow.css`, you'll see that we've copied the styles from `menu1.css` as `p.menu1`, `td.menu1`, and so on, and then done likewise for the styles from each of the other three CSS files to be applied to the pages containing the menu.

```
   <link rel="stylesheet" type="text/css" href="styles/chooserwindow.css">
```

Next, we include our cookie utility script, since we'll want to set the menu-preference cookie from this window.

```
   <script type="text/javascript" language="JavaScript"
           src="scripts/cookie_utils.js">
   </script>
```

Now let's get to the script function that actually gets the user's choice and sets the cookie accordingly. We've written this one inline since we don't need to access it from any other pages.

```
   <script type="text/javascript" language="JavaScript">
   <!--

   function setStyle()
   {
```

We declare a variable `myStyle` to hold the user's choice and initialize its value to 0, then declare a second variable `myChoice` and set its value to the array of radiobuttons named `choice`, which we'll see in the form below.

```
var myStyle=0;
var myChoice=document.myForm.choice;
```

Next, we loop through the individual radiobuttons, each of which has a Boolean `checked` property. In any group of radiobuttons sharing the same name, there can be at most one whose `checked` property is `true`; we set the `myStyle` variable equal to this radiobutton's value, and break out of the loop once we've found it:

```
for(var i=0;i<myChoice.length;i++)
{
  if(myChoice[i].checked)
  {
    myStyle=myChoice[i].value;
    break;
  }
}
```

Now we test the value of `myStyle` to see whether or not it's equal to zero – when performing a true/false test, JavaScript converts zero to `false`, and considers any non-zero value to be `true`.

```
if(myStyle)
{
```

If `myStyle` contains a non zero value, we create a new `Date` object named `expiryDate` and set it 30 days in the future:

```
expiryDate=new Date();
expiryDate.setDate(expiryDate.getDate()+30);
```

We then set a cookie named `"styleCookie"`, the value of which is the same as that of `myStyle` and which expires on `expiryDate`.

```
setCookie("styleCookie",myStyle,expiryDate);
```

Finally, we refresh the page that opened the current window so that the style choice takes effect immediately, then close this window, since it's served its purpose and is no longer needed.

```
opener.history.go(0);
self.close();
}
```

If `myStyle` is still equal to zero, then we know the user clicked the form button without selecting one of the style choices; in that instance, we present her with an `alert()` dialog which reminds her to choose one before doing so.

```
else
alert("Please select one of the four menu styles before clicking the
      button.");
```

```
    }

  //-->
  </script>
</head>
<body bgcolor="#FFFFFF" text="#000000">
```

The `<body>` of the page contains a form and the table whose content uses the styles we mentioned above to illustrate the available choices.

```
<form name="myForm">
  <table width="400" border="1" bordercolor="#CC0033" cellpadding="5"
       cellspacing="0" align="center">
   <tr>
     <th class="menu1">STYLE #1:</th>
     <th class="menu2">STYLE #2:</th>
     <th class="menu3">STYLE #3:</th>
     <th class="menu4">STYLE #4:</th>
   </tr>
   <tr>
     <td class="menu1">
       <p class="menu1">Caption Text</p>
       <a class="menu1" href="#">LINK</a></td>
     <td class="menu2">
       <p class="menu2">Caption Text</p>
       <a class="menu2" href="#">LINK</a></td>
     <td class="menu3">
       <p class="menu3">Caption Text</p>
       <a class="menu3" href="#">LINK</a></td>
     <td class="menu4">
       <p class="menu4">Caption Text</p>
       <a class="menu4" href="#">LINK</a></td>
   </tr>
   <tr>
     <td align="center" valign="middle">
       <input type="radio" name="choice" value="1"></td>
     <td align="center" valign="middle">
       <input type="radio" name="choice" value="2"></td>
     <td align="center" valign="middle">
       <input type="radio" name="choice" value="3"></td>
     <td align="center" valign="middle">
       <input type="radio" name="choice" value="4"></td>
   </tr>
```

The bottom row of the table contains a button input whose `onclick` event triggers the `setStyle()` function:

```
   <tr>
     <td colspan="4" align="center" valign="middle">
       <input type="button"
           value="Set Your Preferred Menu Style"
           onclick="setStyle();"></td>
   </tr>
  </table>
 </form>
</body>
</html>
```

It would be relatively simple to expand upon this example to include additional style choices, or even allow the user to choose between a menu with text links or one using images, different layouts, etc. We could also dispense with the "CUSTOMIZE" text and link in the menu itself, and just call the `setCustomMenu()` function from the page's `onload` event handler so the user would get the popup as soon as the page loads. However, you'll have to decide if you want to disable the popup once the cookie's been set, and how to allow the user to change their mind later on. For this reason, we've opted to stay with the link in the menu itself, so that the customization and the popup window remain completely under user control. Designers and developers are limited only by the requirements of the site and its users, and by their own imagination. While we didn't do so here, it could also be combined with one or more of the techniques we used in the previous chapter to create an "intelligent" menu whose appearance can also be changed in this manner. Some additional scripting might be desirable for usability reasons; for instance, you might want to `document.write()` the "CUSTOMIZE" text and link so that it won't show up for browsers that don't support JavaScript. For the same reason, you might want to employ one of the `.css` files as a default for browsers that support CSS but not JavaScript by writing a `<link>` element inside a `<noscript>` block in the head of the page, for example:

```
<noscript>
  <link rel="stylesheet" type="text/css" href="styles/menu1.css">
</noscript>
```

Finally, it's always a good idea to let the user know that you're using cookies, what information you're going to store in them, and why!

# CSS Example 2: Choosing a Stylesheet (Advanced Browsers)

In the previous example, we used a bit of a kludge (writing a `<link>` to a stylesheet into the page as the page loaded) in order to be backwards-compatible with older browsers (Netscape 4, IE 3) that provide some CSS support, but not for the scripting of styles. In this version we'll take advantage of features in the newest browsers (NS 6, MSIE 5.5+) to let the user change the stylesheet controlling the appearance of the page in real time (without a page refresh). When users decide which one they prefer, they'll be able to save that choice, again using a cookie (and the same cookie utility functions as above) to accomplish this. We'll also show you how to make this an "intelligent" menu by updating the table HTML appropriately after the page has loaded.

Let's start by taking a look at the complete source of the HTML file (`ch4_ex2.html`):

```
<html>
<head>
  <title>Chapter 4, Example 2B</title>
  <meta http-equiv="Content-Type" content="text/html; charset=iso-8859-1">
  <link rel="stylesheet" type="text/css" href="styles/content.css">
```

A few words of explanation here: CSS-2 allows us to specify alternative stylesheets by using `rel="alternative stylesheet"` in the `<link>` tag, the idea being that that the user can choose between several of these to suit her needs or preferences. We can also set one or more of these to be in effect by setting the `disabled` property to `true` or `false`. Here we've written four of these into the page, one for each stylesheet, from which we'll let the user choose.

```
    <link id="menuStyle1" title="Style #1" rel="alternative stylesheet"
type="text/css"
        href="styles/menu1.css" disabled="true">
    <link id="menuStyle2" title="Style #2" rel="alternative stylesheet"
type="text/css"
        href="styles/menu2.css" disabled="true">
    <link id="menuStyle3" title="Style #3" rel="alternative stylesheet"
type="text/css"
        href="styles/menu3.css" disabled="true">
    <link id="menuStyle4" title="Style #4" rel="alternative stylesheet"
type="text/css"
        href="styles/menu4.css" disabled="true">
```

Netscape 6 has a built-in mechanism for allowing the user to choose from among these stylesheets, even if JavaScript is disabled. Note in the figure below how Netscape 6 uses the `title` attributes that we've specified in the `<link>` elements to identify the linked stylesheets to the user:

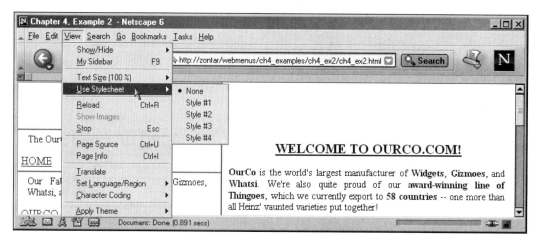

However, we can still use some client-side scripting to integrate this capability directly into our page for users of IE 5.5 and 6 so that they may select their preferred viewing style as well. Netscape 6 users will be able to take advantage of this added capability without losing what their browser already provides.

Back to the `ch4_ex2.html` code – here we have included two JavaScript files, the first of which contains the cookie utility functions we used in the previous example (`cookie_utils.js`). The second (`set_dyn_style.js`) contains the functions and other script necessary to build the menu itself, to set the viewer's style preference, and to save that preference to (and retrieve it from) a cookie. We'll look at its script code shortly.

```
    <script type="text/javascript" language="JavaScript"
            src="scripts/cookie_utils.js"></script>
    <script type="text/javascript" language="JavaScript"
            src="scripts/set_dyn_style.js"></script>
</head>
<body bgcolor="#FFFFFF" text="#000000" leftmargin="0" topmargin="0"
        marginwidth="0" marginheight="0">

    <table border="0" cellpadding="0" cellspacing="0">
        <tr>
```

```
      <td id="menuCell" align="top"></td>
      <td valign="center">
        <h1>WELCOME TO OURCO.COM!</h1>
        <p><b>OurCo</b> is the world's largest manufacturer of <b>Widgets</b>,
        <b>Gizmoes</b>, and <b>Whatsi</b>. We're also quite proud of our
        <b>award-winning line of Thingoes</b>, which we currently export to
        <b>58 countries</b> -- one more than all Heinz' vaunted varieties put
        together!</p>
        <p> </p>
        <p>On our site you'll be able to view all of those as well as our many
        other fine products, read <b>product specifications</b> for each, and see
        how <b>OurCo</b> can help you with all your <b>Widget and other needs</b>.
        We'll tell you about the many services we offer, and how you can contract
        those to help you in your <b>home</b>, <b>school</b>, or <b>business</b>.
        While you're here, you'll also have an opportunity to read the <b>OurCo
        Story</b> and learn how we grew from a <b>cottage industry</b> (founded in
        an actual cottage, no less) back in 1679 to one of the <b>great
        manufacturing behemoths of the 21st Century</b>. And you can use our handy
        <b>Contact Form</b> to ask <b>questions</b>, make <b>comments</b>, or
        inquire about <b>making an order</b>. Just use the handy <b>Navigation
        Menu</b> to your left to get about our site.</p>
        <p> </p>
        <p>We're terribly glad that you've come to visit our home on the World Wide
        Web, and we hope you'll enjoy your visit. And don't forget to come back
        soon, when we'll be unveiling our new <b>Virtual Tour</b> of an actual
        <b>Widget Production Facility</b>.</p>
      </td>
    </tr>
  </table>

</body>
</html>
```

The first thing you might ask after looking around a bit is, "But where's the menu? All I see is a single-row table with two cells – and one of them is empty, and there's not even any scripting inside it for us to write some content." Note that the empty cell has an `id` attribute whose value is `menuCell`; this is going to help us ensure that it doesn't remain empty for very long.

Before we go any farther, let's look at how the menu will appear and work once the Products example page (`products.html`) has been loaded into a compatible browser, in this case, IE 5.5 running on a Windows PC. On the left we show how the page appears when initially loaded. On the right, we can see what happens when the user has clicked the button labelled "Style #1". Not only does the appearance of the menu itself change, but so do those of the buttons used to select the styles; they reflect the style of the menu. In addition, you can see that Button #1 is "greyed out", and if you load the page into your own compatible browser, you'll discover that it's now inoperative. That's because we've set the corresponding `<input>` element's `disabled` property to `true`. This serves as a way to let the user know they're viewing the menu with Style #1 (`menu1.css`) enabled, while at the same time being prevented from wasting their time trying to re-select it. If we click on Button #2, the menu will be displayed using Style #2 (that is, `menu2.css` becomes the enabled stylesheet), Button #2 becomes disabled, and Button #1 is once again active.

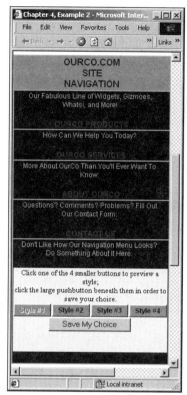

Now let's examine `set_dyn_style.js`. It may seem long and confusing at first glance, so we'll go through it bit by bit and help you make sense of everything that's going on.

First we declare a global variable `selectedStyle`, which we'll use later on to hold the value that's been saved in a cookie. We also declare a second global variable named `myChoice`, which we'll use to hold a value corresponding to the user's current choice of menu presentation style, before it's been saved to the cookie. We want these variables to be global because we're going to use them in several different functions throughout the script, and it's more economical to set their values once and keep them in single variables, rather than retrieving or recalculating those values several times.

```
var selectedStyle;
var myChoice=0;
```

Next we have a function that attempts to retrieve the value of a cookie named `dynStyleCookie`, using the `getCookie()` utility function we discussed in the previous example, and return it to wherever the `retrieveStyle()` function's been called from. If the cookie isn't found, it returns a zero instead.

```
function retrieveStyle()
{
   var myCookie=getCookie("dynStyleCookie");

   return (!myCookie||myCookie==null)?0:myCookie;
}
```

This is the function that sets the current style being used by the browser in viewing the menu. It's called by clicking any one of the four numbered buttons appearing at the bottom of the menu. We generate the HTML code for the buttons using JavaScript – we'll show you how that's done a bit further along.

```
function chooseStyle(button)
{
```

We know that each of the four button inputs has a value of "Style #1", "Style #2", and so on. In order to identify which button was clicked, we pass its value to the function, and use the split() method to obtain the number following the "#" sign, which we then assign as the value of buttonValue.

```
buttonValue=button.value.split("#")[1];
```

Now we loop through two sets of elements, the four stylesheet links whose id attributes are menuStyle1, menuStyle2, etc., and the four buttons with the ids choice1, choice2, etc. We set the disabled attribute of each stylesheet to true, and that of each button to false. This ensures that we've disabled the previously-active stylesheet and enabled the previously-inactive button input, no matter which those might be.

```
for(var i=1;i<5;i++)
{
   if(document.getElementById("choice"+i))
      document.getElementById("choice"+i).disabled=false;
   document.getElementById("menuStyle"+i).disabled=true;
}
```

Now we enable the stylesheet corresponding to the button that was just clicked, and disable that button input.

```
document.getElementById("menuStyle"+buttonValue).disabled=false;
document.getElementById("choice"+buttonValue).disabled=true;
```

Finally, we set the global variable myChoice equal to the value of buttonValue so we can use that value later on in other functions in this script.

```
myChoice=buttonValue;
}
```

Here's a **document** method you may or may not be familiar with, which is essential to DOM scripting in the version 5 and newer browsers: document.getElementById(). This does pretty much what it suggests – it takes the id attribute of an HTML element (quoted because it's a string value) as its argument, and returns an object reference to that element so that we can manipulate it using script.

> When authoring HTML documents, it's very important to ensure that an element's id attribute is unique (no other element shares it). Otherwise, attempting to retrieve an object reference to the element using document.getElementById() will cause script errors.

In this instance, we use `document.getElementById()` to obtain references to the `<link>` elements whose `id` attributes are `menuStyle1`, `menuStyle2`, etc. As for the `<link>` elements themselves, we could have created these programmatically using `document.write()` or more advanced DOM methods. For more information on the latter, consult the DOM references in the Resources section at the end of the book.

The `saveChoice()` function, called when the user clicks the Save My Choice button, is nearly identical to that used in the previous example, the only major difference being the name of the cookie:

```
function saveChoice(form)
{
```

If the user has made a choice, we set the `dynStyleCookie` accordingly and let them know that choice has been recorded. (Once again we make use of the fact that when JavaScript tries to perform a truth test on a number, it converts zero to `false` and any other number to `true`.)

```
if(myChoice)
{
  expiryDate=new Date();
  expiryDate.setDate(expiryDate.getDate()+30);
  setCookie("dynStyleCookie",myChoice,expiryDate);
  alert("You\'ve chosen Style #"+myChoice+",\nbut you can change it again at any
        time.");
}
```

Otherwise, we alert the user to make a choice before trying to save it.

```
else
{
  alert("Please select a menu style before clicking the \"Save\" button.");
  return;
}
}
```

By now you might be wondering when we're going to do something about the "missing" menu, not to mention the "missing" form whose elements we've been accessing. The following function takes care of these "omissions".

```
function buildMenu()
{
```

First we assemble the HTML for the first row of the table, which includes the header cell, common to all the pages:

```
var tableStart="<table width=\"200\" border=\"1\" bordercolor=\"#CCCC00\"
               cellpadding=\"1\" cellspacing=\"0\">";
tableStart+="<tr><th class=\"menu\">OURCO.COM<br>SITE<br>NAVIGATION</th></tr>";
```

Next, we write the HTML for the last row, which contains the controls we provide for the user to preview and then set a preferred style for the menu's appearance:

```
var tableEnd="<tr><td class=\"menu\"><p class=\"menu\">Don\'t Like How Our
        Navigation Menu Looks?";
tableEnd+=" Do Something About It Here:</p><form name=\"styleForm\">";
tableEnd+="<table border=\"0\" cellpadding=\"1\" cellspacing=\"0\"
        bgcolor=\"#EEEEEE\">";
tableEnd+="<tr><td colspan=\"4\" align=\"center\"><small>Click one of the 4
        smaller buttons to preview a style;<br>";
tableEnd+="click the large pushbutton beneath them in order to save your
        choice.</small></td></tr><tr>";
```

Now we put together the HTML for the four style selection buttons.

```
for(var i=1;i<5;i++)
    {
        tableEnd+="<td align=\"center\">";
        tableEnd+="<input class=\"menu\" type=\"button\" id=\"choice"+i+"\"
value=\"Style #";
```

Notice we call the `chooseStyle()` function with the `this` keyword as its argument; in effect, we're passing a reference to the button itself back to the function.

```
        tableEnd+=i+"\" onclick=\"chooseStyle(this);\"";
```

Each time through the loop, we check the value of `selectedStyle` against the loop counter; if it's the same, then we add `disabled="true"` to the string we're building. In other words, if the cookie's been set, we add the `disabled` attribute to the `<button>` element corresponding to the cookie's value.

```
        if(selectedStyle==i)
            tableEnd+=" disabled=\"true\""
        tableEnd+="></td>";
    }
```

We finish the `tableEnd` string by tacking on an additional button input and the tags necessary to close the form and the inner table it contains, as well as the table containing the menu itself.

```
tableEnd+="</tr><tr><td colspan=\"4\" align=\"center\">";
tableEnd+="<input type=\"button\" value=\"Save My Choice\"
        onclick=\"saveChoice();\">";
tableEnd+="<p> </p></td></tr></table></form>";
tableEnd+="</td></tr></table>";
```

Having stored the HTML making up the beginning and the end of the menu table in appropriately named variables, let's assemble the HTML for the menu table cells, captions, and links that go in the middle. We won't offer a blow-by-blow account here, as this is essentially the same thing we did in Chapter 3, where we created and populated arrays for the link text, captions, and filenames of what we're linking to.

```
var tableRowStart="<tr><td class=\"menu\"><p class=\"menu\">";
var tableRowEnd="</a></td></tr>";

var fileNames=["index","products","services","about","contact"];
var pageTitles=["HOME","OURCO PRODUCTS","OURCO SERVICES","ABOUT OURCO","CONTACT
            US"];
```

```
var captions=["The OurCo.com Main Entry Page:",
              "Our Fabulous Line of Widgets, Gizmoes, Whatsi, and More!",
              "How Can We Help You Today?",
              "More About OurCo Than You\'ll Ever Want To Know:",
              "Questions? Comments? Problems? Fill Out Our Contact Form:"];

var URLbits=self.location.href.split("/");
var currPage=URLbits[URLbits.length-1];
var currPageName=currPage.split(".")[0];
var numPages=fileNames.length;
```

We declare a new variable, `newHTML`, to store the HTML string in one place, skipping those that correspond to the current page as we run through our arrays in order, when adding the markup for the menu cells and links. Once we've got these in place, we concatenate `tableStart` and `tableEnd` onto the beginning and end of this string, respectively.

```
var newHTML="";

for(var j=0;j<numPages;j++)
{
  if(currPageName!=fileNames[j])
  {
    newHTML+=tableRowStart+captions[j]+"</p>";
    newHTML+="<a class=\"menu\" href=\""+fileNames[j]+".html\">";
    newHTML+=pageTitles[j]+tableRowEnd;
  }
}

newHTML=tableStart+newHTML+tableEnd;
```

Now we add the completed menu to the page, inserting it into the empty table cell `menuCell`. Once again, we obtain a DOM reference to the desired element by using the `document.getElementById()` method and setting the resulting object's `innerHTML` property equal to the `newHTML` string. This property is actually not included in the W3C's DOM Level 1 or Level 2 specifications. It's a shortcut originally implemented by Microsoft for IE 4, but it was considered useful enough to be adopted in Mozilla and Netscape 6, so it may be thought of as a *de facto* standard.

```
    document.getElementById("menuCell").innerHTML=newHTML;
}
```

Now we write a function to perform all the tasks necessary to set up the page and create our menu correctly – first we attempt to retrieve the value of the `dynStyleCookie`; if it's been set, switch the stylesheet link to the saved style choice; then build the menu HTML and add it to the page. As our final step, we attach it to the window object's `onload` event handler so that these tasks will be performed as soon as the page has finished loading.

```
function initialise()
{
  selectedStyle=retrieveStyle();
  if(selectedStyle)
    document.getElementById("menuStyle"+selectedStyle).disabled=false;
  buildMenu();
}

window.onload=initialise;
```

One note before we move on: If you need to accommodate browsers that don't support JavaScript, it's relatively easy to do so. Just place a static version of the menu inside the element whose content is to be generated using the `innerHTML` property. (For example, we could place a static HTML table inside the `menuCell` table cell.) Advanced browsers will simply replace it with the dynamic content. For earlier browsers with JavaScript support (such as Netscape 4 and IE 3), we could use inline `document.write()` statements instead of `innerHTML` to generate the menu table. For Netscape 3 this in all likelihood wouldn't work, due to known issues with trying to use these statements inside table cells; the only sure workaround would be to generate the entire outermost table using JavaScript. If IE 4 support is needed, there is a workaround using its own proprietary DOM, which uses a `document.all` collection that was later superseded by the `document.getElementById()` method. Here's how we send the correct reference to the correct browser. First we write a function to test if the browser supports either of the necessary DOM objects.

```
function getElementReference(elementId)
{
  var value=false;

  if(document.getElementById)
    value=document.getElementById(elementId);
  else
    if(document.all)
      value=document.all[elementId];
  return value;
}
```

Then we replace the reference to `document.getElementById()` with one to our `getElementReference()` function, which we can also use to keep any other browsers from trying to evaluate the code, for example:

```
var myStyleEl=getElementReference("menuStyle");
if(selectedStyle&&myStyleEl)
  myStyleEl.disabled=false;
```

If you think this seems like a lot of work to accommodate different browsers, then you're starting to understand why developers are very grateful that browsers are converging on a single DOM standard, and that, within 2 or 3 years, such cross-browser "hacks" will (hopefully!) be largely a thing of the past. However, later in this chapter, we'll use a function very similar to this one to let us achieve some common DHTML functionality in Netscape 4+, IE 4+, and even (in some cases) Opera 5 and above.

We've covered quite a lot of ground in these first two examples, having discussed some of the basics of CSS and ways in which we can make use of advanced JavaScript and DHTML to create menus and tailor them both to current conditions and the user's preferences. We also showed how we can save those preferences between visits to our site through the use of cookies.

# Image Maps

The next few pages will provide a bit of a breather from a technical point of view, but they should still prove useful. We'll start out with a brief refresher on client-side image maps and how to create them, and talk a little about the pluses and minuses of using them.

Simply put, an image map is a way to place multiple links (also known as "hotspots") within a single image. They can serve as a very effective design technique because:

- The size, position, and shape (`circle` for circles, `rect` for rectangular shapes, and `poly` for anything else that can be drawn using straight lines) of these hotspots can be set by the designer.

- All browsers that support images support image maps.

Although there are two types of image maps, client-side and server-side, we'll use only the client-side variety here. (Server-side image maps are beyond the scope of this book, and are becoming very infrequently used in any case, since client-side image maps have been supported since Netscape 2 and IE 3.) These are constructed using an `<img>` tag that includes a `usemap` attribute, which points to a named `<map>` tag. The definitions for the hotspots go in `<area>` tags contained within the `<map>` element. Here's the HTML code for the example we'll be using first in this chapter:

```
<img src="images/menu.gif" width="325" height="85" border="0" usemap="#menuMap">

<map name="menuMap">
  <area shape="poly" coords="17,22,42,6,66,20,62,47,18,45" href="index.html"
        alt="Home" title="Home" onMouseOver="rollOn(0);" onMouseOut="rollOff();">
  <area shape="circle" coords="290,31,25" href="products.html" alt="Products"
        title="Products" onMouseOver="rollOn(1);" onMouseOut="rollOff();">
  <area shape="poly" coords="208,54,241,30,266,71,227,81" href="services.html"
        alt="Services" title="Services" onMouseOver="rollOn(2);"
        onMouseOut="rollOff();">
  <area shape="rect" coords="81,35,130,79" href="about.html" alt="About Us"
        title="About Us" onMouseOver="rollOn(3);" onMouseOut="rollOff();">
  <area shape="poly" coords="141,6,211,4,200,57,148,57" href="contact.html"
        alt="Contact" title="Contact" onMouseOver="rollOn(4);"
        onMouseOut="rollOff();">
</map>
```

And here's how it looks with the hotspots highlighted for easy viewing:

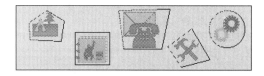

Note that we can (and should!) use both `alt` and `title` attributes in the area tags. This enhances usability for text-only browsers such as Lynx or screen readers employed by disabled persons. Most new browsers (Netscape and IE versions 4+) will display tooltips containing the text when the hotspots are moused over. Opera shows `title` tooltips in the same way as Netscape and IE 4+, and `alt` tooltips are also displayed in the Opera status bar. (Note that Netscape 4 is the only browser listed that does not support the `title` attribute at all.)

It's evident that coding anything but the most simple of image maps by hand is liable to be a complicated and tedious process. Fortunately, most (if not all) of the most common web design suites, including Macromedia Dreamweaver, Adobe GoLive, Macromedia HomeSite, and Microsoft FrontPage, provide built-in editors for the purpose (we used Dreamweaver to create the image maps used in this chapter). If you don't use one of these applications, there are a number of standalone tools available for creating image maps and editing existing ones, many of them available for free download from the Internet (a single search at Google.com on the phrase "image map editors" yielded in excess of 250,000 matches).

These include MapIt, LiveImage, GeoHTML, ImageMapper++, MapEdit, iMap, and many more. Several popular graphics programs can also produce image maps, including Corel PhotoPaint, Adobe ImageReady, and Macromedia FireWorks.

# Image Map Example 1

We can use event handlers on image map hotspots to trigger scripts in much the same way that we do using text or image links. The only difference is that when we use image maps, the event handlers are added to the appropriate `<area>` tags. Here's an example of a basic image rollover with a changing sidebar image, very similar in most ways to those we looked at in the previous chapter. Like our other image rollovers, this one's backward compatible with Netscape 3 and IE 4, and won't cause errors in incompatible user agents. In case our choice of symbols isn't obvious or the user misses the sidebar image, we've also supplied text links immediately below the image map. Furthermore, since it doesn't hurt us in the slightest, and enhances the visual effect of the menu a bit, we also use the text links to trigger the same image-swapping functions as the hotspots in the image map. When you view the file `ch4_ex3.html`, you'll notice that we can change the source file for the mapped image without disrupting the function of the image map in the slightest:

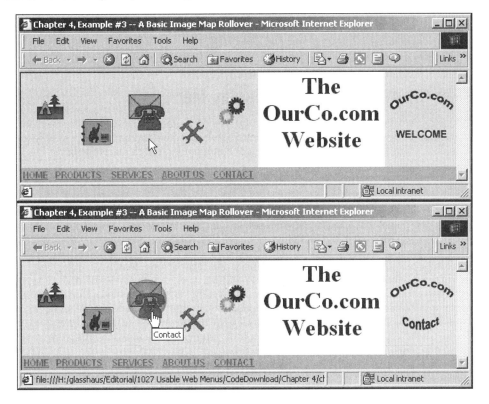

In terms of scripting techniques, there's not much else that's really new here; we create some arrays, populate them with `Image` objects, set their `src` properties, and write a couple of functions to swap the images. Let's take a look at the image map code after we've added the appropriate event handler and function calls to it:

```
<map name="menuMap">
  <area shape="poly" coords="3,16,20,8,38,16,32,39,8,39" href="index.html"
        alt="Home" title="Home" onmouseover="rollOn(0);" onmouseout="rollOff();">
  <area shape="circle" coords="68,60,20" href="products.html"
        alt="Products" title="Products" onmouseover="rollOn(1);"
        onmouseout="rollOff();">
  <area shape="poly" coords="88,10,133,10,158,45,113,45" href="services.html"
        alt="Services" title="Services" onmouseover="rollOn(2);"
        onmouseout="rollOff();">
  <area shape="rect" coords="176,38,204,73" href="about.html"
        alt="About Us" title="About Us" onmouseover="rollOn(3);"
        onmouseout="rollOff();">
  <area shape="poly" coords="271,8,313,8,252,75,210,75" href="contact.html"
        alt="Contact" title="Contact" onmouseover="rollOn(4);"
        onmouseout="rollOff();">
</map>
```

As you can see, we're doing exactly the same thing here with the `<area href>`s that we did with `<a href>`s in Chapter 3. It would be relatively simple, using the same sort of logic we've worked out before, to `document.write()` only the appropriate `<area>` and `<img>` tags in order to create an "intelligent" menu similar to what we've seen in that chapter or, for newer browsers, use the `innerHTML` property just as we did in the previous example.

Now let's combine some of these image maps with additional CSS attributes and scripting.

# Image Map Example 2: Tabbed Display Menu

Now we'll look at a very popular type of menu that's used on a great many sites – one that features a "tabbed" interface. This sort of menu features controls that resemble the tabs on a set of file folders, or that are sometimes used to mark the key sections of a ring binder, not unlike these here:

There are many different ways to program this sort of interface. We could use nothing but images in a table and a script to swap them, but lots of images means lots of bandwidth. It also makes it necessary to create new images whenever we need to update the content. We could get around this problem by using frames, but they bring about their own set of usability and other issues. Instead, we're going to employ CSS positioning and some cross-browser scripting that will work in both Netscape and IE 4+, and Opera 5+, using a pair of JavaScript functions that help to bridge the differences in how these browsers implement the DOM. We'll look at the code for these in a moment, but first let's talk about CSS positioning. This is very much as it sounds: using CSS to specify just where content appears on a web page. There are several different forms of it, but for this example, we'll use only **absolute** positioning, whereby we can tell the browser exactly where to display an element in terms of a fixed coordinate system. (Other CSS positioning types include **relative**, that is, relative to the parent element, and **fixed**, that is, relative to the browser window. For more about these consult the appropriate works cited in the Resources section.) Let's look at a very simple example. Suppose we write an ID selector in the style section of a page that looks like this:

```
#myDiv {position:absolute; left:100px; top:25px;}
```

Then in the body of the page we write a <div> element that looks like this:

```
<div id="myDiv">Hello there!</div>
```

When we load this page into a browser that supports CSS, we'll see the text "Hello there!" displayed at a point 100 pixels from the left edge of the page, and 25 pixels from the top, the zero point or origin always being the left-top corner of the document. Now change the left and top values to something different, say 50px and 200px, resave the file, and reload it in your browser. You'll see that the text has moved closer to the left edge, and further down from the top of the page. It's pretty simple, really. CSS positioning also permits us to include the third dimension, using the **z-index** property, by which we can determine the stacking order of elements that may overlap. This attribute is specified as an integer value, with 0 being the default z-index of the page itself. To place one element above another, so that it appears to overlap it or even cover it completely, we merely give its z-index a greater value. The latest browsers support CSS positioning on nearly all HTML elements, but for reasons of backwards compatibility (particularly where Netscape 4 is concerned), we're going to restrict ourselves to <div> tags for this example.

The other CSS property we'll be using here is **visibility**. This can take one of three values:

- visible: the element is visible unless obscured by another one with a higher z-index.

- hidden: the element is completely hidden from view and cannot be interacted with by the user.

- inherit: the element takes on the visibility attribute of its parent element. Since it's the default for all elements, you won't need to specify it very often, but we mention it here for completeness.

Elements are visible by default, and if enclosed within another element, inherit its visibility. Here however, we'll only be directly concerned with whether an element is visible or hidden.

Now let's talk a little more about the different versions of the DOM supported by different browsers. Before the DOM was standardized by the W3C, Netscape and Microsoft mapped HTML elements to scripting objects in radically different ways. Netscape 4 considers all positioned tags (those which it recognizes) to be "layers" – and elements of a document.layers collection. To access the positioned <div> above in that browser, we'd write document.layers["myDiv"]. IE 4 uses a different collection, document.all, so to be able to script the same <div> in that browser, we'd write document.all["myDiv"]. The W3C DOM-1 standard uses, not a collection, but rather a method of the Document object to access elements within the document as scripting objects. In DOM-compliant browsers, such as IE 5.5+, and Netscape 6 or Mozilla, we write document.getElementById("myDiv"). Fortunately, there is a way to access HTML elements from script in all three sorts of browsers without having to write completely different scripts or even pages for each one. We've created a function (and placed it in the xblayer.js file, see below) that does this. This function takes the id attribute of the HTML tag and returns either the correct object reference for the current browser, or a value of false if it doesn't support any of the three DOM implementations that we've discussed:

```
function getElementReference(elementId)
{
  var value=false;

  if(document.layers)
```

```
  value=document.layers[elementId];
else
{
  if(document.all)
    value=document.all[elementId];
  else
    if(document.getElementById)
      value=document.getElementById(elementId);
}

return value;
}
```

Using functions like this one can be an enormous help, but don't think for a minute that this solves all the problems of cross-browser DHTML, especially where it's necessary to be compatible with the version 4 browsers. Another big difference between them lies in the way that they handle scripting of styles. IE 4 and the standard DOM both employ a `style` object. This object's properties are those of the element's `style` attributes. To hide our `<div>` using the function we just showed you in Netscape 4 and IE 4, we could write the following:

```
getElementReference("myDiv").style.visibility="hidden";
```

However, Netscape 4 doesn't support this object, and doesn't actually support scripting of styles at all; instead, a limited number of properties are attached directly to the `Layer` object. To use our cross-browser function in this browser, we'd just write:

```
getElementReference("myDiv").visibility="hidden";
```

In order to bridge this additional gap between different browsers, we've defined a second function in the `xblayer.js` file:

```
function getStyleReference(elementId)
{
  var value=false;

  if(getElementReference(elementId))
  {
    value=getElementReference(elementId);
    if(!document.layers)
      value=value.style;
  }

  return value;
}
```

Basically, what this function does is to say, "If the current browser knows what `getElementReference()` does, but doesn't know what a `Layer` object is, we know it's not Netscape 4, and so we'll tack on a reference to the `style` object before trying to access any style properties." Now we can just write:

```
getStyleReference("myDiv").visibility="hidden";
```

The browser interprets this statement in terms of its native object model, and hides the <div> named "myDiv". Bear in mind that this doesn't solve all the problems encountered in cross-browser scripting – but it does allow us to access those style properties that are accessible in all three sorts of browsers with a minimum of fuss. These include the properties that we've mentioned already (left, top, and z-index co-ordinates and visibility) along with the background color, but that's about all. Lengthy script libraries have been written and published for emulating the DOM and style capabilities of one browser in the others, and we won't attempt to recreate all of that work here – only what's necessary to accomplish the task in hand.

Now that we've issued that *caveat*, let's move on to the example page, ch4_ex4.html. Let's walk through the complete source of the HTML file:

```
<html>
<head>
  <title>Chapter 4, Example 4 -- Tabbed Interface</title>
  <meta http-equiv="Content-Type" content="text/html; charset=iso-8859-1">
```

The tabs.css file referred to in the <link> tag contains all the style information necessary to position the elements of our menu correctly – we'll look at its contents below.

```
  <link rel="stylesheet" type="text/css" href="styles/tabs.css">
```

These refer to the script file containing the two cross-browser functions we discussed above, and another one containing the code that actually powers the menu, which we'll also look at shortly.

```
  <script type="text/javascript" language="JavaScript"
          src="scripts/xblayer.js">
  </script>
  <script type="text/javascript" language="JavaScript"
          src="scripts/tabs.js">
  </script>
</head>

<body bgcolor="#FFFFFF" leftmargin="0" topmargin="0" marginwidth="0"
      marginheight="0">
```

This <div> contains an outline of our tabs; if you look at the image tabs.gif by itself, you'll see that the tab areas themselves are transparent. That's because the coloured areas making up the tabs themselves are "under" this image.

```
<div id="tabOutline">
   <img src="images/tabs.gif" width="500" height="30" border="0"
usemap="#tabMap">
   </div>
```

Next, in order of descending z-index, we have the caption text for each tab:

```
<div id="tabText0" class="tabsText">HOME</div>
<div id="tabText1" class="tabsText">PRODUCTS</div>
<div id="tabText2" class="tabsText">SERVICES</div>
<div id="tabText3" class="tabsText">ABOUT US</div>
<div id="tabText4" class="tabsText">CONTACT</div>
```

**117**

All five of the following `<div>`s share the `tabsText` style class and thus have a `z-index` value of 3. Next, we have the selected tab backgrounds, which are in separate `<div>`s so that we can show and hide them one at a time to indicate the selected tab. All 5 of these are of the style class `tabsClicked` and so have a `z-index` of 2.

```
<div id="tabClicked0" class="tabsClicked">
  <img src="images/clicked_bg.gif" width="100" height="30">
</div>
<div id="tabClicked1" class="tabsClicked">
  <img src="images/clicked_bg.gif" width="100" height="30">
</div>
<div id="tabClicked2" class="tabsClicked">
  <img src="images/clicked_bg.gif" width="100" height="30">
</div>
<div id="tabClicked3" class="tabsClicked">
  <img src="images/clicked_bg.gif" width="100" height="30">
</div>
<div id="tabClicked4" class="tabsClicked">
  <img src="images/clicked_bg.gif" width="100" height="30">
</div>
```

In addition, here, the background for all the tabs shows the "off" colour:

```
<div id="defaultTabBg">
  <img src="images/default_bg.gif" width="500" height="30" border="0">
</div>
```

The `<div>`s below serve as our information display panels. Due to considerations of space, we've omitted the content of these, but you can see from viewing the source of this page that we can use practically any HTML we want in these, including images.

```
<div id="infoPane0" class="info"><!-- "HOME" INFO GOES HERE --></div>
<div id="infoPane1" class="info"><!-- "PRODUCTS" INFO GOES HERE --></div>
<div id="infoPane2" class="info"><!-- "SERVICES" INFO GOES HERE --></div>
<div id="infoPane3" class="info"><!-- "ABOUT US" INFO GOES HERE --></div>
<div id="infoPane4" class="info"><!-- "CONTACT US" INFO GOES HERE --></div>
```

*Warning: there are numerous and potentially severe issues with placing `<form>` elements affected by*
*`z-index` positioning in browsers below version 6. For instance, a `<select>` in an element with a*
*`z-index` of 2 may be visible through another element with a higher `z-index`, even though we'd expect the `<select>` to be hidden behind the other element. We recommend avoiding this if possible, or conducting very careful and exhaustive testing across all browsers and platforms that are expected to be used for viewing pages in which you intend to employ them!*

Finally, we have a `<div>` that serves as a background for the information display area:

```
<div id="infoBg"><img src="images/clicked_bg.gif" width="500"
height="250"></div>
```

plus the `<map>` element containing the definition of the image map that creates the hotspots, which the user clicks on to bring up the different information "panes":

```
    <map name="tabMap">
      <area shape="poly" coords="25,5,75,5,85,15,90,28,10,28,15,15"
            href="javascript:switchTabs(0);" alt="HOME" title="HOME">
      <area shape="poly" coords="125,5,175,5,185,15,190,28,110,28,115,15"
            href="javascript:switchTabs(1);" alt="PRODUCTS" title="PRODUCTS">
      <area shape="poly" coords="225,5,275,5,285,15,290,28,210,28,215,15"
            href="javascript:switchTabs(2);" alt="SERVICES" title="SERVICES ">
      <area shape="poly" coords="325,5,375,5,385,15,390,28,310,28,315,15"
            href="javascript:switchTabs(3);" alt="ABOUT US" title="ABOUT US">
      <area shape="poly" coords="425,5,475,5,485,15,490,28,410,28,415,15"
            href="javascript:switchTabs(4);" alt="CONTACT" title="CONTACT">
    </map>
  </body>
</html>
```

Now let's look at our CSS file, in which we make use of both style IDs and style classes. We use these to stack the elements for our tabs in the order described above, and we've organized them to be as economical as possible. The first style `id` applies to the outline for the tabs. Notice that a style ID name always corresponds to the unique `id` attribute of an HTML tag. This is followed by two style classes corresponding to, respectively, the `<div>`s containing the text labels for the tabs, and those containing the "selected" backgrounds; each holds the style information that's common to each set of five `<div>`s:

```
#tabOutline {position:absolute; left:0px; top:0px; z-index:4;}

.tabsText {position:absolute; top:15px; width:75px; z-index:3; visibility:visible;
           font:normal bold 11px Helvetica,Arial,sans-serif;}

.tabsClicked {position:absolute; top:0px; z-index:2; z-index:2; visibility:hidden;
              width:100px; height:30px;}
```

Here are the style IDs corresponding to the individual tab labels and backgrounds; note that each one contains only the style information that's unique to it. You'll also note that each identifier (and the `id` of the corresponding HTML tag) ends in a digit – there's a reason for this, which should become clear when we look at the function we use for "switching" the tabs:

```
#tabText0 {left:25px;}
#tabText1 {left:125px;}
#tabText2 {left:225px;}
#tabText3 {left:325px;}
#tabText4 {left:425px;}

#tabClicked0  {left:0px;}
#tabClicked1  {left:100px;}
#tabClicked2  {left:200px;}
#tabClicked3  {left:300px;}
#tabClicked4  {left:400px;}
```

Next, we have the style ID for the tab background:

```
#defaultTabBg {position:absolute: left:0px; top:0px; z-index:1;
visibility:visible;
              width:500px; height:30px;}
```

This is followed by the style definitions for the `<div>`s making up our display panels. Once again we place all the style information that's common to all of them into a single style class, and use style IDs for the style data that's unique to each panel:

```
.info {position:absolute; left:15px; top:50px; visibility:hidden;
       width:400px; height:175px;
       font: normal normal 10px Helvetica,Arial,sans-serif;}

infoPane0    {z-index:1;}
infoPane1    {z-index:2;}
infoPane2    {z-index:3;}
infoPane3    {z-index:4;}
infoPane4    {z-index:5;}
```

The final bit of positioning information necessary for building our tabbed interface is that for the panel background:

```
#infoBg   {position:absolute; left:0px; top:29px; z-index:0;
           width:500px; height:250px;}
```

We also define styles for some HTML tags that are used to format the panel content:

```
h1 {font:italic bold 18px Verdana,Arial,Helvetica,sans-serif; color:#330000;}

a {font-weight:bold; color:#FF6600; text-decoration:underline;}
a:hover {color:#CCFF00; text-decoration:none;}

p {font:normal normal 12px Helvetica,Arial,sans-serif; color:#330000;}
```

Now we're ready to write the function used to show and hide the appropriate `<div>`s when a tab is clicked, which is, as you'll recall, saved in the file `tabs.js`. We think of the tabs and the corresponding information display panels as being numbered from 0 to 4; each time the function is called, we pass it a value in this range:

```
function switchTabs(index)
{
```

Our objective here is to show the "selected" background element for the tab that's clicked, as well the corresponding panel. We accomplish this by looping through the integers from 0 to 4,

```
for(var i=0;i<5;i++)
{
```

and asking at each point, "is this the number for the tab that was clicked?" If it is, we set the visibility property of that tab and of the corresponding panel to "visible", using the `getStyleReference()` function discussed above to ensure that different browsers "see" the correct object reference.

```
if(i==index)
{
    getStyleReference("tabClicked"+i).visibility="visible";
    getStyleReference("infoPane"+i).visibility="visible";
}
```

Otherwise, we set the visibility of both to "`hidden`":

```
    else
    {
      getStyleReference("tabClicked"+i).visibility="hidden";
      getStyleReference("infoPane"+i).visibility="hidden";
    }
  }
}
```

Finally, the "HOME" tab is to be displayed by default when the page loads, so let's write a one-line function to do so and attach it to the pages `onload` event:

```
function initialise()
{
  switchTabs(0);
}

window.onload=initialise;
```

Here's a look at the finished product:

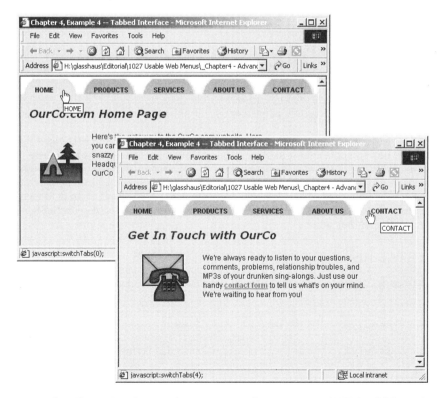

It may appear at first like we've thrown about a tremendous amount of HTML, CSS, and script code every which way in order to arrive at this result, and it may be difficult for you to take it all in at once. Just keep in mind that it's all there for a reason and that once you understand how it's all organized, it'll make perfect sense.

# Image Map Example 3: Floating Menu

"Floating" menus give rise to different reactions in different users. If you've not encountered one of these in your own Internet travels, it's a menu that remains stationary relative to the browser window when the page is scrolled (well, usually – if we look at http://www.ibizkit.se/, first encountered in Chapter 1, its menu stays put relative to the page, not the browser window, so can get lost if you scroll or resize!). Some find them convenient; others consider them a nuisance. Détente may be considered passé in some quarters, but we're going to show you a compromise solution to offer your users, one that allows them to minimize or even get rid of the menu altogether should they desire. Of course we'll make sure that they have a way to bring the menu back if they happen to change their minds! We'll employ the `<noscript>` element to provide an alternative means of navigation for visitors who aren't using JavaScript-capable browsers; we'll also provide this alternative menu to users of older browsers that don't support DHTML but do support JavaScript. In fact, we'll make this menu compatible all the way back to Netscape 2.

This menu has two visual components, corresponding to its maximized and minimized states:

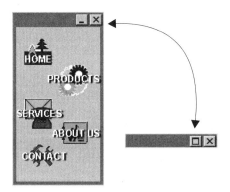

Each of these consists of an image map in a containing `<div>` (present for Netscape 4 compatibility). The "maximized" view has hotspots linking to other pages on our site. This view has a couple of additional hotspots as well, which it shares with the minimized one, corresponding to a couple of interface features that should look familiar to most computer users. The one on the left maximizes or minimizes the menu, depending on which state is currently displayed; the one on the right closes it (or at least appears to do so, as we'll see shortly). There are several different source files making up our example page – let's list them and describe what they do:

- **ch4_ex5.html**: the file that gets loaded into the browser.

- **xblayer.js**: contains the same cross-browser element and style object reference functions that we've used previously in this chapter, so we won't be repeating an explanation of it here.

- **create_menu.js**: writes the necessary HTML for the menu into the page at load time.

- **menu_driver.js**: contains the functions used for displaying the three different menu states (maximized, minimized, and closed) and for making the menu "float".

- **menus.css**: contains the style definitions for the menus.

- **content.css**: styles controlling the appearance of the page content; not strictly necessary for the functioning of the menu itself, so we won't look at the source here – feel free to look it up on the code download if you like.

- **menu_max.gif** and **menu_min.gif**: the images we use for the menu's maximized and minimized states, respectively (the other image files are just window dressing).

Let's dig into the code, starting with the HTML file:

```
<html>
<head>
  <title>Chapter 4, Example 5 -- Floating Menu</title>
  <meta http-equiv="Content-Type" content="text/html; charset=iso-8859-1">
```

Here are the links to the stylesheet files:

```
<link rel="stylesheet" type="text/css" href="styles/content.css">
<link rel="stylesheet" type="text/css" href="styles/menus.css">
```

Next come the JavaScript includes for the cross-browser object reference and menu driver script files:

```
<script type="text/javascript" language="JavaScript" src="scripts/xblayer.js">
</script>
<script type="text/javascript" language="JavaScript"
        src="scripts/menu_driver.js">
</script>
</head>

<body bgcolor="#FFFFFF" text="#000000" leftmargin="0" topmargin="0"
marginwidth="0"
        marginheight="0">
```

The JavaScript include for the menu creation script is as follows:

```
<script type="text/javascript" language="JavaScript" src="scripts/create_menu.js">
</script>
```

Content inside a `<noscript>` element is rendered by browsers that don't do JavaScript, and is ignored by those that do. (There is one rarely encountered exception to this rule, which we'll show you how to deal with a bit later, just in case it's ever an issue for you.) In this case, we've elected to show JavaScript-impaired user agents a horizontal table containing text links, but you can use any static content that suits your site and users.

```
<noscript>
  <table width="85%" align="center" border="1" bordercolor="#003366">
    <tr>
      <td align="center"><a href="index.html">HOME</a></td>
      <td align="center"><a href="products.html">PRODUCTS</a></td>
      <td align="center"><a href="services.html">SERVICES</a></td>
      <td align="center" nowrap><a href="about.html">ABOUT OURCO</a></td>
      <td align="center" nowrap><a href="contact.html">CONTACT US</a></td>
    </tr>
  </table><br clear="all">
</noscript>
```

In this example, we've placed all the page content in a fairly narrow table to ensure that the page will be long enough to force scrolling, so you can observe the menu's complete functionality. We omit the content itself here, since it's not really important otherwise.

```
<table width="45%" border="1" bordercolor="#003366" align="center">
  <tr>
    <td valign="middle">
      <!-- [CONTENT GOES HERE] -->
    </td>
  </tr>
</table>
</body>
</html>
```

Now let's take a look at the menu generation script file `create_menu.js`. First we declare three global variables. `myMenus` performs two functions: it holds the code we're going to assemble for the menu HTML, and later, in the menu driver script, we'll use it to test whether or not our menu's been created yet, before we try to manipulate it in script, which is why we initialize its value to `false`. The variable named `start` will be used when we initialize the menu; we'll show you how when we reach that point. The third is a convenient variable that saves us a little typing.

```
var myMenus=false;
var start=false;
var d=document;
```

Now we check for browser compatibility: if the browser recognizes one of the three DOM implementations that can handle DHTML, then we assemble the HTML for the `<div>`s that contain the two images representing the visible states of the menu, and the image maps that go along with them. We also write a text link to the function that redisplays the menu in the event that the user closes it.

```
if(d.layers||d.all||d.getElementById)
{
  myMenus="<div id=\"menuMax\" class=\"menu\">\n";
  myMenus+="<img src=\"images/menu_max.gif\" width=\"120\" height=\"220\"
          border=\"0\" usemap=\"#max\">\n";
  myMenus+="</div>\n";
  myMenus+="<div id=\"menuMin\" class=\"menu\">\n";
  myMenus+="<img src=\"images/menu_min.gif\" width=\"120\" height=\"18\"
          border=\"0\" usemap=\"#min\">\n";
  myMenus+="</div>\n";
  myMenus+="<p class=\"small\">Don\'t see the floating menu?<br>Want it back?<br>
          <a href=\"javascript:maxiMenu();\">Click here</a>.</p>";
  myMenus+="<map name=\"max\">\n";
```

To enhance usability and accessibility, we include appropriate `alt` and `title` attributes in the `<area>` tags:

```
myMenus+="<area shape=\"rect\" coords=\"81,2,99,16\"
        href=\";javascript:miniMenu();\" alt=\"MINIMISE MENU\"
        title=\"MINIMISE MENU\">\n";
myMenus+="<area shape=\"rect\" coords=\"101,2,117,16\"
        href=\"javascript:closeMenu();\" alt=\"CLOSE MENU\"
        title=\"CLOSE MENU\">\n";
myMenus+="<area shape=\"circle\" coords=\"37,57,27\"
        href=\"index.html\" alt=\"HOME\" title=\"HOME\">\n";
myMenus+="<area shape=\"circle\" coords=\"84,89,27\" href=\"products.html\"
        alt=\"PRODUCTS\" title=\"PRODUCTS\">\n";
myMenus+="<area shape=\"circle\" coords=\"41,188,24\" href=\"services.html\"
        alt=\"SERVICES\" title=\"SERVICES\">\n";
myMenus+="<area shape=\"rect\" coords=\"13,106,57,152\" href=\"contact.html\"
```

```
                 alt=\"CONTACT US\" title=\"CONTACT US\">\n";
   myMenus+="<area shape=\"rect\" coords=\"61,134,105,174\" href=\"about.html\"
                 alt=\"ABOUT US\" title=\"ABOUT US\">\n";
   myMenus+="</map>\n";
   myMenus+="<map name=\"min\">\n";
   myMenus+="<area shape=\"rect\" coords=\"82,2,100,16\"
                 href=\"javascript:maxiMenu();\" alt=\"MAXIMISE MENU\"
                 title=\"MAXIMISE MENU\">\n";
   myMenus+="<area shape=\"rect\" coords=\"100,2,118,16\"
                 href=\"javascript:closeMenu();\" alt=\"CLOSE MENU\"
                 title=\"CLOSE MENU\">\n";
   myMenus+="</map>\n";

   d.write(myMenus);
}
```

Otherwise we assemble, and then write to the page, the HTML for the table-based alternative menu described above:

```
else
{
```

It's debatable whether it's really necessary, but we include this in the interest of completeness – remember the exception in behavior regarding `<noscript>` content we mentioned above? Netscape 2 and IE 3 were released before this element became standardized, so it renders anything enclosed in it whether JavaScript is enabled or not. Therefore, we test to make sure the browser isn't one of these (or an earlier version of either) before writing the alternative menu, since the same code is already included in a `<noscript>` block and we don't want it to appear twice for Netscape 2 users. If compatibility with these browsers isn't a concern, the `if()` check can safely be omitted:

```
if( !(navigator.appName.indexOf("Netscape")!=-1 &&
      parseInt(navigator.appVersion)==2)
    &&
    !(navigator.appName.indexOf("Microsoft")!=-1 &&
      parseInt(navigator.appVersion)==3))
{
  var altMenu="     <table width=\"85%\" align=\"center\" border=\"1\"
              bordercolor=\"#003366\">\n";
  altMenu+="     <tr>\n";
  altMenu+="        <td align=\"center\"><a href=\"index.html\">HOME</a></td>\n";
  altMenu+="        <td align=\"center\">
            <a href=\"products.html\">PRODUCTS</a></td>\n";
  altMenu+="        <td align=\"center\">
            <a href=\"services.html\">SERVICES</a></td>\n";
  altMenu+="        <td align=\"center\" nowrap><a href=\"about.html\">ABOUT OURCO
            </a></td>\n";
  altMenu+="        <td align=\"center\" nowrap><a href=\"contact.html\">CONTACT
US
            </a></td>\n";
  altMenu+="     </tr>\n";
  altMenu+="  </table><br clear=\"all\">\n";

  d.write(altMenu);
  }
}
```

We'll step slightly out of order here to show you the CSS that provides the style information for the two <div>s we've called "menuMax" and "menuMin", which we've saved in the file menus.css. It's not a very large file.

First we define a style class named menu, which applies to the two <div>s. It establishes absolute positioning for both of them and sets their default visibility to hidden.

```
.menu {position:absolute; visibility:hidden;}
```

Then we use individual style IDs to set their z-index attributes. The values are large in order to (try to) insure that they'll remain above any other content in the page that might be absolutely positioned.

```
#menuMax  {z-index:10;}

#menuMin  {z-index:11;}
```

Finally, we write a selector for any <p> element of the small class – we apply this to the link that allows the user to restore the menu if it has been closed, and to the text that accompanies it.

```
p.small {font:italic normal 10px sans-serif;}
```

Now let's look at the menu_driver.js file, which contains the functions we need in order to perform two sets of tasks: first, to position the menu correctly and make it "float"; second, to allow the user to minimize, maximize, close, and reopen the menu.

First we define a new function to make it easier to position elements. It takes as its arguments the id attribute of the element, and the left and top coordinates where we wish to place it.

```
function setPos(elementId,newLeft,newTop)
{
```

Since we've included the xblayer.js file previous to this file in the page, we can use the functions defined there for obtaining cross-browser element and style object references. We set a variable equal to the correct style object reference:

```
var obj=getStyleReference(elementId);
```

Then we set this object's left and top properties to the desired values:

```
    obj.left=newLeft;
    obj.top=newTop;
}
```

You've probably noticed by now that, in general, it appears that we can set CSS attributes in script in the version 4 and newer browsers by using the attribute name as a property of an element's style object (except in Netscape 4, but our getStyleReference() function takes care of that for us). Suppose we'd like to change an element's z-index; it would reasonable to assume that we could do that by writing:

```
getStyleReference("myElement").z-index=4;
```

Right? Not quite. The – character is reserved for subtraction in JavaScript (and most, if not all other programming and scripting languages) and so this statement would cause an error. To get around this problem, observe the following rule when trying to set style attributes that have hyphenated names:

- Remove the hyphen(s)

- Capitalize the first letter of the second word (and of any subsequent words as well)

- Combine the result into a single property name

This is also known as intercap (or lower-camel-case) notation. So the correct way to set the z-index attribute using our custom function would be to write.

```
getStyleReference("myElement").zIndex=4;
```

which in standard DOM-1 syntax is:

```
document.getElementById("myElement").style.zIndex=4;
```

Let's get back to the task in hand. Now that we've a shortcut for positioning elements, we're ready for the next step, which is to position the menu so that it remains in the same location relative to the browser window rather than the document in that window. We want the menu to remain 15 pixels below the visible area of the page, and 15 pixels from the right edge. We'll write another function to do that for us:

```
function setMenus()
{
```

Netscape and IE have very different ways of determining measurements relating to the browser window. We set variable NS to true if the browser uses layers or W3C DOM and false if it can use document.all.

```
var NS=document.layers||(document.getElementById&&!document.all);
```

First we need to find out how much the user has scrolled the page, that is, the distance between the top of the document and the top of the browser viewing area. Netscape makes this distance available as window.pageYOffset; Microsoft browsers expose it as document.body.scrollTop. We add 15 pixels to the resulting value, the distance being measured from the top down, so the menu will be placed slightly below the top of the window.

```
var topPos=NS? window.pageYOffset:document.body.scrollTop;
topPos+=15;
```

We also need to get the width of the browser window. IE reports this as document.body.clientWidth. Netscape uses window.innerWidth, from which we subtract 15 pixels to allow for the scrollbar. We subtract 115 (the width of the menu) + 10 pixels so the menu's right edge is a bit to the right of the scrollbar if there is one.

```
var leftPos=NS?window.innerWidth-15:document.body.clientWidth;
leftPos-=125;
```

**127**

Using the `setPos()` function that was defined above, we position both of the menu `<div>`s at the resulting co-ordinates. This is so that, if either Maximize or Minimize are selected, the correct version of the menu can be displayed instantly in the correct place without the need to reposition it first.

```
setPos("menuMax",leftPos,topPos);
setPos("menuMin",leftPos,topPos);
```

Now we check the value of the `start` variable, which was declared and set to `false` at the beginning of the `create_menu.js` file. If it's still false, we show the `<div>` containing the maximized menu, then set its value to `true`. This ensures that the menu remains hidden until it's actually moved into the proper position for the first time. Once this is done, we don't need to repeat this step.

```
if(!start)
{
    maxiMenu();
    start=true;
}
}
```

This function is called once the page has loaded. We make sure that only compatible browsers attempt to execute the `setMenus()` function by checking to see if the menu HTML has been written to the page (otherwise, `myMenus` will still hold its original value of `false`).

```
function makeFloat()
{
    var myTimer;
    if(myMenus)
```

We use JavaScript's `setInterval()` method to force repeated execution of `setMenus()` every quarter-second, so that whenever the user scrolls the window, the menu will very quickly catch up and resume the proper position. This method repeats whatever script code is passed to it until it's halted by calling a `clearInterval()`. If you anticipate users spending a great deal of time on a single page using this menu, you may want to consider using a counter and halting the "floating" after a few minutes with a `clearInterval(myTimer);` statement – with some browsers and platforms. Allowing the loop to continue unabated may lead eventually to severe memory leaks and browser or even system crashes. However, we tested this page by leaving it running simultaneously in Netscape 4.77, IE 5.5, Netscape 6.2, and Opera 6.0 beta on a single Windows 95 PC with a 166 MHz Pentium processor and 64 MB RAM for upwards of 6 hours without any apparent ill effects, so perhaps our admonition is unfounded in his case.

```
myTimer=setInterval("setMenus()",250);
}
```

The `miniMenu()` function is called when the user clicks the Minimize hotspot – it hides the full-size menu and displays the minimized one. The `maxiMenu()` function does just the opposite when the Maximize hotspot is clicked on; the "Bring it back" link also calls this function. Clicking the Close hotspot calls `closeMenu()`, which doesn't actually destroy the menu; it merely hides both menu `<div>`s.

```
function miniMenu()
{
    getStyleReference("menuMax").visibility="hidden";
    getStyleReference("menuMin").visibility="visible";
}
```

```
function maxiMenu()
{
  getStyleReference("menuMin").visibility="hidden";
  getStyleReference("menuMax").visibility="visible";
}

function closeMenu()
{
  getStyleReference("menuMax").visibility="hidden";
  getStyleReference("menuMin").visibility="hidden";
}
```

Finally, we set the window's `onload` handler to fire the `makeFloat()` function:

```
window.onload=makeFloat;
```

You can customize this menu in a few different ways quite easily:

- By substituting your own images and image maps. Don't forget to make the images for the maximized and minimized menu the same width! You may need to adjust the values for leftPos and topPos if your menu is wider than the one we've used here.

- By adjusting leftPos and topPos to make the menu "float" somewhere else in the page; for instance, if you'd prefer to have your menu positioned in the upper left corner of the page, you can dispense with checking window.innerWidth and document.body.clientWidth, and just set leftPos and topPos to fixed values. By using other appropriate window or document properties, you can find the bottom of the browser window, and make the menu appear to float, for instance, in the lower-right corner of the page.

- Instead of using a large image map for the maximized menu, you could just use text links with an image above these containing only the top "slice" of the image we use here, which shows only the "minimize" and "close" buttons.

You're limited only by your imagination and your willingness to experiment! Don't worry if you make a mistake – you can always come back to the original version of the code we've provided here and start over if needs be.

# Expanding/Collapsing Menus

These are often requested, and can be very useful, because they can help reflect the organization of your site and take up much less room than a long, static list of links to every page on the site. For these last two examples, we've borrowed another bit of the Windows user interface paradigm: the opening (or closing) folder icon. Both of these menus will permit us to organize the pages in our site into sections, the heading for which will always be visible; each heading is accompanied by an image representing an open or closed folder. When the user clicks on a heading or the icon appearing next to it, that section – and the icon – will appear to open to reveal a list of links to pages in that section, or close if it's already open. Here are the folder icons we'll be using; of course, you can always substitute your own:

In addition, these will be intelligent menus that automatically provide cues to the user as to which page is currently being visited: when a page is loaded, the section of the menu to which it belongs will display as "open" by default. Additionally, the text title of the current page as shown in the menu will not be a link (since the user is already there), and will be displayed in a different style to emphasize this.

Both menus appear to work in a virtually identical fashion. The main difference is that the first one will use absolute positioning to redraw the menu whenever a section is opened or closed, and will be compatible with all Netscape and Microsoft browsers from version 4 upwards, as well as in Opera 5 and 6. The second will use only DOM-compliant CSS scripting, which, as we'll see, is actually much simpler since we won't have to do any tracking or recalculating of positions; however, this version will be usable **only** in IE5+ or Netscape 6+/Mozilla.

# Expanding/Collapsing Menu Example 1

This version of the expanding/collapsing menu uses CSS absolute positioning and the `visibility` style property, and is compatible with Netscape 4/IE 4 and above. We'll make use again of the cross-browser functions we've already developed in this chapter. Here's a view of what the menu looks like when first loaded (by clicking on `home.html`), and then when the OFFICES folder is opened, and the Kempsey option selected:

If you mouse over the text "Kempsey" in the menu while this page is loaded, you'll see that it's not a link, but the other items in that section are. By clicking on any of the section headings, the corresponding section appears to expand or collapse, the folder icon switches from the open to closed view to the other, and the sections below it are repositioned accordingly. Feel free to play with the heading and page links, and you'll see that it makes no difference what order they're clicked on – the menu always displays itself appropriately. Now let's dive into the code that makes this happen, starting with a list of the files used:

### ch4_ex6.html

This is the main page, and the prototype for all the other pages in the example folder, which are identical to this one; all we're lacking is content, which can easily be inserted into the correct pages once we've made copies of this template and named them appropriately. Note that the naming of these is not arbitrary; we'll explain this a little later. Here's the HTML:

```
<html>
<head>
  <title>Chapter 4, Example 6 -- Expanding/Collapsing Menu #1</title>
  <meta http-equiv="Content-Type" content="text/html; charset=iso-8859-1">
```

Links to the stylesheet files:

```
  <link rel="stylesheet" type="text/css" href="styles/content.css">
  <link rel="stylesheet" type="text/css" href="styles/menu.css">
```

The following `<script>` tags include the cross-browser and menu driver scripts. Note that the xblayer.js file comes first, because we use the functions that it contains in the other .js file.

```
  <script type="text/javascript" language="JavaScript"
          src="scripts/xblayer.js"></script>
  <script type="text/javascript" language="JavaScript"
          src="scripts/menu_driver.js"></script>
</head>
<body background="images/bluebg.gif" bgcolor="#000066" text="#000000"
      leftmargin="0" topmargin="0" marginwidth="0" marginheight="0">
```

The third JavaScript file dynamically writes the menu HTML to the page as it loads, so we include it immediately following the `<body>` tag:

```
<script type="text/javascript" language="JavaScript" src="scripts/create_menu.js">
</script>
  <table width="100%" cellpadding="0" cellspacing="0" border="0">
    <tr>
      <td width="275" bgcolor="#006699">
```

The image list.gif is a 1px-by-1px spacer we use to guarantee that the height of the document in Netscape 4 is sufficient to contain the fully expanded menu if the page content isn't enough to do so on its own. In adapting this menu to use in your own site projects – should Netscape 4-compatibility be an issue – you may need to adjust its height, or, should all of your pages have a sufficient amount of content, you may find that you can dispense with it altogether. You'll just have to experiment with Netscape 4 to see what works best.

```
                <img src="images/list.gif" width="1" height="800" border="0">
            </td>
            <td width="70%">
                <p> </p><p> </p><p> </p><p> </p>
                <p> </p><p> </p><p> </p>
            </td>
        </tr>
    </table>
</body>
</html>
```

### xblayer.js

This is the script file that contains our basic cross-browser functions. It's identical to the files of the same name we've used before in this chapter.

### create_menus.js

This script file contains the scripting that generates the HTML for the menu. Let's go through it and explain what each part of it does.

First we define a couple of variables. The first one holds the value (in pixels) for the top of the menu itself. You can adjust this to meet your needs – for instance, if you'd like the menu to start from the top of the page itself, or to make room for a header image or text. The second variable, named panelHeight, contains the height of each item in the menu. There are other ways in which we can control this, for instance by using CSS, but since there are problems in getting this approach to work identically in all the target browsers, we're going to take the easy way out and use a hack: this is exactly the same height as our folder (and other) icons.

```
var startHeight=50;
var panelHeight=20;
```

The text that's used for the section headings is stored in the elements of an array named sectionNames. When customizing this menu script for your own use, you can use any number of entries here – just make sure that you escape any quotes or other special characters with backslashes or use the HTML entity equivalents.

```
var sectionNames=new Array("MAIN","OFFICES","OURCO PRODUCTS","OURCO
SERVICES","ABOUT OURCO.COM","CONTACT US");
```

Next we get the number of section headings, and use that number to define another array.

```
var numSections=sectionNames.length;
var pages=new Array(numSections);
```

Each element in the pages array is itself an array that contains the titles for the corresponding section. (Advanced scripters will notice that we save ourselves some space by using array literals rather than the Array() object constructor function.) The same rules apply to the text used in these arrays as for that used in the sectionNames array. However, you shouldn't try to use any HTML tags in these unless you test **very** carefully, for reasons that will become apparent shortly.

```
pages[0]=["Home","Company News","Press Room","OurCo Opportunities"];
pages[1]=["Aurora","Birmingham","Buenos Aires","Cartagena","Kempsey","Mumbai",
          "Pune","Scottsdale","Stavanger"];
```

```
pages[2]=["Gizmoes","Somesuches","Thingoes","Whatsi","Widgets"];
pages[3]=["Deliveries","Estimates","Refunds and Exchanges","Specifications"];
pages[4]=["Company History","Corporate Profile","Management","Mission Statement"];
pages[5]=["Customer Service","Sales Enquiries","General Information","Telephone
          Numbers"];
```

Next we declare and initialize variables for the string of HTML that we're going to write to the page, and for holding the length of each of the `pages` arrays.

```
var output="";
var lastItem;
```

We mentioned above that the filenames for the pages used with this menu are not arbitrary; here's the function that reflects the rule we use for obtaining them. The rule is this: we take the link text, and check to see if it contains more than one word (that is, if it contains any whitespace). If it does, we use only the last word. In either case, we convert the word to lowercase. Further down in this script, we'll use this string to make a link by concatenating ".html" onto the end of it. (Now you can see why we warned you that trying to use any HTML tags in the page titles would be a bad idea.) For example, the "Birmingham" page would be `birmingham.html`, the "Corporate Profile" page would be `profile.html`, the "Refunds and Exchanges" page should be named `exchanges.html`, etc.

```
function getPageName(page)
{
  var value=page;
  var words;

  if(page.indexOf(" "))
  {
    words=page.split(" ");
    value=words[words.length-1].toLowerCase();
  }

  return value;
}
```

Now we're ready to put together the HTML that makes up the menu. For each of the section headings, we assemble the HTML for two `<div>` tags: the first of these will look like this after it's written to the page:

```
<div id="closed0" class="menuClosed">
  <a href="javascript:display(0);" class="section" title="Click here to open">
    <img src="images/closed.gif" width="20" height="20" border="0"
         alt="Click here to open.">
    MAIN
  </a>
</div>
```

The `<div>` contains a "closed" folder icon, and the name of the section inside a `javascript:` link that calls a function named `display()`. This function will "open" or "close" this section of the menu; it's defined in the `menu_driver.js` file, which we'll examine in due course.

```
for(var i=0;i<numSections;i++)
{
  output+="<div id=\"closed"+i+"\" class=\"menuClosed\">";
```

```
output+="<a href=\"javascript:display("+i+");\" class=\"section\"
        title=\"Click here to open.\">";
output+="<img src=\"images/closed.gif\" width=\"20\" height=\"20\" align=\"top\"
        border=\"0\" alt=\"Click here to open.\">";
output+=sectionNames[i]+"</a></div>\n";
```

The second `<div>` will look much the same, except that we'll use the "open" folder icon and corresponding `alt` and `title` text. Also, before we close it, we're going to insert the links to the pages in that section.

```
output+="<div id=\"open"+i+"\" class=\"menuOpen\">";
output+="<a href=\"javascript:display("+i+");\" class=\"section\"
        title=\"Click here to close.\">";
output+="<img src=\"images/open.gif\" width=\"20\" height=\""+panelHeight+"\"
        align=\"top\" border=\"0\" alt=\"Click here to close.\">";
output+=sectionNames[i]+"</a><br>\n";
```

We set `lastItem` to the number of pages in the current section, then execute the following loop that number of times:

```
lastItem=pages[i].length;

for(j=0;j<lastItem;j++)
{
```

We use the `getPageName()` function defined above to find out if the current page filename is the same as that of the page the menu's being loaded into, and set the variable `isCurrent` accordingly .

```
var isCurrent=self.location.href.indexOf(getPageName(pages[i][j]))!=-1;
```

If the current item is the last item in this section, we begin the current menu item with the image `item_last.gif`, which looks like this:

otherwise, we start it out with `item.gif`:

This will produce a look that's similar to the way in which directories are displayed in Windows Explorer – in a tree-like fashion. We also include an additional image in each row, an arrowhead pointing to the page title. This is optional, and you may remove or replace it safely as you desire if you want to adapt this menu to your own purposes.

```
output+="<img src=\"images/item";

if(j==lastItem-1)
  output+="_last";

output+=".gif\" width=\"20\" height=\""+panelHeight+"\" align=\"top\"
        border=\"0\">";
```

```
        output+="<img src=\"images/arrow.gif\" width=\"10\" height=\"20\"
align=\"top\"
                border=\"0\"> ";
```

If the current item refers to the page being loaded, we don't want to write a link; instead, we use a <b> element and assign it the style class `current` to make it stand out from the other items. Otherwise, we make the text a link to the corresponding page:

```
    if(isCurrent)
        output+="<b class=\"current\" title=\"You are here.\">";
    else
        output+="<a href=\""+getPageName(pages[i][j])+".html\" class=\"page\"
title=\""+pages[i][j]+"\">";

    output+=pages[i][j];

    if(isCurrent)
        output+="</b>";
    else
        output+="</a>";
```

If we've reached the last item in this section, we need to close the <div> that contains the items for the current section; otherwise, we write a line break, and then repeat the loop for the next item.

```
    if(j==lastItem-1)
        output+="</div>\n";
    else
        output+="<br>\n";
    }
}
```

Finally, once we've assembled all the <div>s that contain the "open" and "closed" sections of the menu, we place it in the page with a `document.write()` statement:

```
document.write(output);
```

Now that we've built our menu and placed it in the page, we're ready to make it do something.

### menu_driver.js

This script file contains the functions that make the menu sections appear to open and close. We need it to perform three functions for us:

- Hide a "closed" or "open" section when its heading is clicked.

- Show the corresponding "open" or "closed" section.

- Move the sections up and down when those above them are opened or closed.

So, before we do anything else, we'll define three functions that will make it easy for us to effect these functions. It should be easy to tell what they do from the way they're named. Each of them takes the id attribute of the element to be effected as an argument. The `setTop()` function takes a second argument as well – the new top coordinate for the element. Note that all three functions use the `getStyleReference()` function that's defined in the `xblayer.js` file.

```
function setTop(elementId,newTop)
{
  getStyleReference(elementId).top=newTop;
}

function showIt(elementId)
{
  getStyleReference(elementId).visibility="visible";
}

function hideIt(elementId)
{
  getStyleReference(elementId).visibility="hidden";
}
```

As we'll see in a moment, we also need a way to tell if an element is visible or hidden, so we define a function that tells us if it is. Part of the reason we do this is to take care of one of Netscape 4's idiosyncrasies: while we can **set** an element's visibility to `visible` or `hidden`, it actually reports it back to us as one of the Netscape 4.X-specific values `show` or `hide`.

```
function isVisible(elementId)
{
  var vis=getStyleReference(elementId).visibility;

  return vis=="visible"||vis=="show";
}
```

Now we're ready to update the menu display, using a function of that name. It takes a single parameter, `index`, which tells us which section's being clicked on and thus needs to be changed. We'll accomplish this in two steps: first we switch the visibility of the two sections whose identifiers contain this same index value, for example, if in our example we click on the heading "MAIN", the links call the function with a value of zero. If it's closed, we need to show the `<div>` `open0`, and hide the one with the id attribute `closed0`. Then we need to move all the sections below the current one up or down by a number of pixels that's equal to the number of items in that section plus one (to allow for the heading) times the height per item, that is, we need to move it by a distance of **(pages[index].length + 1) * panelHeight** pixels.

```
function display(index)
{
```

We define a variable to hold the `top` position to which we need to move each section in turn. The minimum possible value is the starting point of the menu.

```
  var currTop=startHeight;
```

What follows is possibly not representative of the most efficient algorithm for accomplishing our task, because we're redisplaying the entire menu each time it's executed, but it does work, and we don't have to store any values in between function calls. (Who knows, maybe you'll suggest an improvement that we can publish on glasshaus.com!) We loop through the indices for all the sections in the menu,

```
for(var i=0;i<sectionNames.length;i++)
{
```

and see if the section whose visibility we're going to check is the same as the section whose heading was clicked.

```
if(i!=index)
{
```

If it's not, we see if the "closed" version of this section is visible.

```
if(isVisible("closed"+i))
{
```

If the "closed" section is visible, we move it to the top coordinate value currently stored in currTop, and add its height to that variable.

```
setTop("closed"+i,currTop);
currTop+=panelHeight;
}
else
{
```

Otherwise, we know we need to move the "open" section to that point, and add its height to currTop:

```
setTop("open"+i,currTop);
currTop+=panelHeight*(pages[i].length+1);
}
}
else
{
```

If the section is the one that's been clicked (that is, if its index value is equal to that of index), we check to see whether it's currently open or closed.

```
if(isVisible("open"+i))
{
```

If it's open, we hide it, show the closed section in its place, and move it to a point currTop pixels from the top of the page. We then add the height of the heading to currTop.

```
hideIt("open"+i);
showIt("closed"+i);
setTop("closed"+i,currTop);
currTop+=panelHeight;
}
else
{
```

If the "open" section isn't visible, we know that the "closed" one must be, so we hide it, display the "open" one in its stead, move it to the `top` position stored in `currTop`, then increment that variable by the height of the "open" section, so we know where to place the next one:

```
            hideIt("closed"+i);
            showIt("open"+i);
            setTop("open"+i,currTop);
            currTop+=panelHeight*(pages[i].length+1);
        }
      }
    }
  }
```

The default visibility style for all the `<div>`s containing sections of our menu is `hidden`. When we load the page, we want to make sure the proper sections are in the proper positions before letting any of them be seen. This isn't absolutely necessary, but it looks better than to let our visitors see a jumble while the page is loading. Once it is loaded, we move the "closed" sections to their proper places – each spaced a distance equal to `panelHeight` below the preceding one – then display it:

```
function initialise()
{
  var currTop=startHeight;

  for(var i=0;i<sectionNames.length;i++)
  {
    setTop("closed"+i,currTop);
    showIt("closed"+i);
    currTop+=panelHeight;
  }
```

We could stop there, and our menu would be fully functional at that point – but we'd like this to be an intelligent menu that "knows" which page it's being used on, and provides the viewer with an appropriately modified display. We find out which section the current page belongs to (if any) by looping through the `pages` arrays and determining if its filename (less the `.html` extension) is part of one of the page titles for that set of pages (`pages[0]`, `pages[1]`, `pages[2]`, and so on). We start by obtaining the current page's filename,

```
  var URLbits=self.location.href.split("/");
  var currPage=URLbits[URLbits.length-1];
  var currPageName=currPage.split(".")[0];
```

and declaring and setting a `flag` variable to `false`:

```
  var flag=false;

  for(var i=0;i<sectionNames.length;i++)
  {
    for(var j=0;j<pages[i].length;j++)
    {
      if(pages[i][j].toLowerCase().indexOf(currPageName)!=-1)
      {
```

Once we've found which set of pages it's in (if any), we set `flag` to "`true`", and break out of the inner loop (where we iterate through each element in the array `pages[i]`):

```
        flag=true;
        break;
      }
   }
```

We use the flag to tell us that we've found which section of the site we're in, to (re)display the menu with that section in its "open" state, and to make it clear that it's time to break out of the outer loop as well:

```
      if(flag)
      {
        display(i);
        break;
      }
    }
  }
```

Finally, we tell the browser to execute the `initialise()` function as soon as the page has finished loading:

```
  window.onload=initialise;
```

### menu.css

This file contains stylesheet information controlling the positioning and other aspects of the menu's appearance.

First we define a style for the menu heading text. Since all the headings will be links, we use a `section` class to be applied just to those links. We also define a `:hover` pseudoclass that will cause the links to change colour when moused over, for the benefit of IE4+ and NS6/Mozilla users.

> *A CSS pseudoclass is used to describe an element in a given state. For instance, we can also assign* `:link`, `:visited`, *and* `:active` *pseudoclasses to an* `<a>` *element that controls how a link is displayed before and after it has been visited, and when the user is clicking on it. There are additional pseudoclasses that can be used with links as well as other HTML elements – see the W3C CSS-2 Specification (at http://www.w3.org/TR/REC-CSS2/) or check the Resources section for other resources with information about these.*

```
a.section { font:normal bold 16px Arial, Helvetica, sans-serif;
         color: #FF3333; text-decoration: underline }
a.section:hover {   color: #FFFF33;}
```

Next, we define a style class and `:hover` pseudoclass for the page links,

```
a.page { font:normal bold 12px Arial, Helvetica, sans-serif;
         color: #FFFFFF; text-decoration: none;}
a.page:hover {   color: #FFFF33;}
```

a selector for the `<b>` tag we use to indicate the current page,

```
b.current {font:italic bold 12px Arial,Helvetica,sans-serif; color:#00FFFF;}
```

and two classes, one each for the "closed" and "open" menu <div>s. This isn't strictly necessary, but we've done this to make it easy for you to apply additional styles separately to each of these if you desire:

```
.menuClosed {position:absolute; left:15px; visibility:hidden;}
.menuOpen   {position:absolute; left:15px; visibility:hidden;}
```

### content.css

This file sets the styles for the content of the page. So long as you don't try to reuse any of the names from the menu.css file in this one, you can do about anything you like with it.

# Expanding/Collapsing Menu Example 2

This is very similar to the previous example, but we've recast it for more advanced browsers – those that support the W3C's DOM standard, or most of it (NS 6 and MSIE 5.5+). It's much shorter and simpler to code because we don't have to worry about the positioning. Whereas in the previous example we scripted the left, top, and visibility properties, here we'll only have to deal with one, the display property, in order to change the appearance of our menu. This property is not, as some might think, just a synonym for visibility. It's much more powerful than that. Perhaps the best way to explain the difference is by way of an example. Let's build a very basic HTML page (vis_vs_display.html) that contains two paragraph elements, each containing some text, a span within one of the paragraphs, and five links, each of which is used to trigger a JavaScript statement via its onclick event handler:

```
<html>
<head>
  <meta http-equiv="Content-Type" content="text/html; charset=iso-8859-1">
  <title>Example -- Visibility vs. Display</title>
  <style type="text/css">

    p {font:normal normal 12px "Times New Roman",serif;}

    span  {font:italic bold 12px Arial,sans-serif;}

  </style>

</head>
<body bgcolor="#FFFFFF" text="#000000">
  <a href="#"
  onclick="document.getElementById('mySpan').style.visibility='visible';">
    visibility:visible
  </a><br />
  <a href="#"
  onclick="document.getElementById('mySpan').style.visibility='hidden';">
    visibility:hidden
  </a><br />
  <a href="#"onclick="document.getElementById('mySpan').style.display='block';">
    display:block
```

```
  </a><br />
  <a href="#" onclick="document.getElementById('mySpan').style.display='inline';">
    display:inline
  </a><br />
  <a href="#" onclick="document.getElementById('mySpan').style.display='none';">
    display:none
  </a><br />
  <p>
    This is some text in a paragraph. This the first paragraph. Watch the next
    paragraph closely! This is some text in a paragraph. This the first
    paragraph. This is some text in a paragraph. This the first of two
    paragraphs. This is some text in a paragraph. This the first paragraph.
    <span id="mySpan">
      This is some text in a span. This the only span. Watch this span closely!
      This is some text in a span. This the only span. This is some text in a
  span.
      This the one and only span. This is some text in a span. This the only span.
    </span>
  </p>
  <p>
    This is some text in a paragraph. This the second paragraph. Watch the
    previous paragraph closely! This is some text in a paragraph. This is the
    second of two paragraphs. This is some text in a paragraph. This the second
    paragraph. This is some text in a paragraph. This the second paragraph.
  </p>
</body>
</html>
```

The text of each of the links describes what happens when the link is clicked. (For example, clicking the first one sets the span's visibility to "visible".) You can see in the illustration overleaf what the page looks like when we first load it (*left*). We've included links to set the span's visibility to "visible" and "hidden", and its display property to "block", "inline", and "none" so you can play around with them a bit if you like, but what we're really interested in here is the difference between what happens when we change its visibility to "hidden" and what happens when we set its display property to "none". As you can see in the following illustration, when we do the former, the text in the <span> element is hidden from view (*centre*), but that's all – nothing else in the page that isn't contained in the span changes. Now reload the page and try the bottommost link; when we set the span's display property to "none" (*right*), something much more interesting happens: the remaining content reflows to take up the missing space, as if the <span> wasn't even there. This is but a small sample of the power given to us by the ability to script CSS styles.

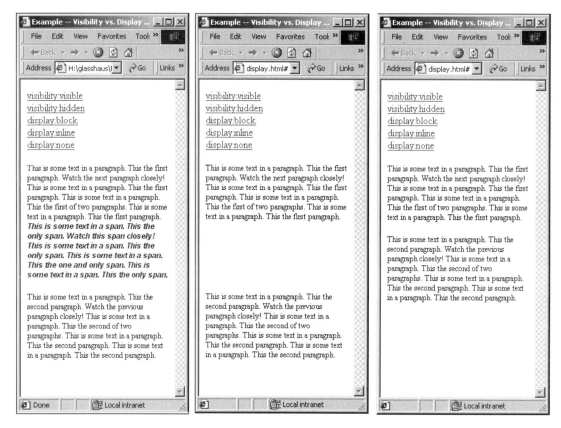

The only other styles influencing the appearance of the page and its content are the text styles we've applied to the `<p>` and `<span>` elements to make them distinct from one another – no CSS positioning is involved. The principle we've illustrated here is the same one that we'll apply in recoding our menu for the version 5 and 6 browsers. As we said above, the script code here will be a bit shorter than in the previous version. Once we've finished examining it, we'll offer a few suggestions on how you might deploy and customize these two menus. We'll take an additional step in this direction by generating a page heading and dynamically updating the contents of the page's `<title>` tag along with creating and displaying the menu itself.

The HTML page itself is not terribly interesting. It contains:

- A `<link>` to a stylesheet to control the appearance of the menu.

- Two included JavaScript files, one to generate the menu HTML and one for the functions and logic to control its behavior once it's been created and inserted into the page.

- a 2 x 2 table whose top-left cell contains a title image, the remaining three cells being empty at the start. The cell immediately below that containing the image has `id="menuCell"`, the cell immediately to the right of the title image has `id="pageHeading"`, and the last one is intended to be used for holding the (possibly static) content of the page.

Let's look at the `menu.css` file first. We can see that it provides a contextual selector for a class of hyperlinks, as well as for a class of `<b>` elements, very similar to what we've used before – we've just changed the color scheme a bit:

```
a.page {font:normal bold 12px Arial, Helvetica, sans-serif;
        color: #FFFFFF; text-decoration: none;}
a.page:hover {color:#FFCC66;}

b.current {font:italic bold 12px Arial,Helvetica,sans-serif; color:#CC6600;
           background-color:#EADFAE;  text-decoration:none;}
```

Next, we have two style classes, one of which we'll be applying to one set of `<spans>`s for our menu items, and the other one for the section headings. The panel class has only one style rule: all the spans containing the links will have `display:none` set by default. The heading class looks a bit strange, especially when we recall that we used links for the menu headings before, so why are we adding underlines and the `cursor:pointer` rule? As we'll see, there's really no need for our headings to be links at all, but since users are accustomed to the idea that only links can be clicked and have anything happen as a result, we'll give our headings the appearance of links, even though they aren't, as we'll see shortly. The "expected" way for a link to appear is as blue underlined text, as was discussed in Chapters 1 and 2. However, another thing that makes a link immediately recognizable is the change in appearance of the mouse pointer to a hand.

```
.heading {font:normal bold 16px Arial, Helvetica, sans-serif; color: #FFCC00;
          text-decoration: underline; cursor:pointer;}

.panel { display:none;}
```

In addition, we define selectors for the `<h1>` and `<h2>` elements that we'll generate for the `pageHeading` cell – notice that we give the former a top border, and the latter a bottom border. If you've guessed that we'll be placing `<h1>` content directly above `<h2>` content, then you've guessed correctly.

```
h1 {font:normal bold 24px Arial, Helvetica, sans-serif; color:#993300;
    text-align:center; border-top:4px solid #330000;}

h2 {font:italic bold 18px Arial, Helvetica, sans-serif; color:#993300;
    text-align:center; border-bottom:4px solid #330000;}
```

In the `create_menu.js` file, we use the same arrays to hold our section and page titles as we did previously, and instead of `document.write()`ing the generated HTML to the page during the loading process, we'll wait until it's finished, then set the `innerHTML` property of the `menuCell` table cell equal to that string value. The result for the first heading span will look like this:

```
<span class="heading" id="heading0" title="Click here to open."
      onclick="display(0);">
  <img height="20" alt="Click here to open." src="images/closed.gif"
       width="20" border="0" align="top">
  MAIN
</span>
```

Notice that we wrote the `onclick` event handler directly into the span – that's because in advanced browsers we can use nearly any event handler with any HTML tag, so there's really not much reason to use `javascript:`, #, or `void()`; links just to provide a way to trigger functions. Of course, the links in the menu panels really do take the user somewhere, so we do want those to remain actual hyperlinks. Also in the menu generation file we define an array:

143

```
var flags=new Array(numSections);
for(var i=0;i<numSections;i++)
  flags[i]=false;
```

This will be used to track what menus are "open", and which ones are "closed".

Now that we know how we're going to build our menus, let's look at the code that drives them. The file `menu_driver.js` contains two functions. The first one, called `display()`, is analogous to the function of the same name we used in our backwards-compatible version of the menu, but it's much simpler, as promised. When it's called, all it does is check to see if the links panel corresponding to the clicked heading is "open". The reason we don't check directly is that it's not possible to read style properties directly in IE 5.5+ (where we must use the proprietary `currentStyle` property instead) or Netscape 6.x. The latter requires a lengthy workaround, so it's easier just to use a true/false variable to do the job for us:

```
function display(index)
{
```

First we set some "shorthand" variables so we don't have to type long object references repeatedly, then we check the value of the flag corresponding to the clicked heading.

```
var currHeading=document.getElementById("heading"+index);
var currHeadingImg=currHeading.getElementsByTagName ("IMG")[0];
var currPanel=document.getElementById("panel"+index);
```

Above we've used another DOM method, `getElementsByTagName()`. This method can be used with any element to obtain an array of all its child elements of a certain type. It takes as its argument the name of an HTML tag in quotes; note that even though we normally write tags in lowercase, this method requires it all in capital letters. So what we've done is get a reference to one of the heading spans, for example, `document.getElementById("heading1")`, which we assign to the variable `currHeading`, then apply `getElementsByTagName("IMG")` to it in order to retrieve an array of all the `<img>` elements contained in that span – the folder image is the first (and only) image inside the span, so it's identified by the array index **0**.

```
if(flags[index])
{
```

If it's `true`, we know that the links panel is open, so we update the values for the heading's `title` attribute and the folder image's `source`, `alt`, and `title` attributes appropriately, set the panel's display property to "none", and set the corresponding flag to `false`.

```
    currHeading.title="Click here to open.";
    currHeadingImg.src="images/closed.gif";
    currHeadingImg.alt="Click here to open.";
    currHeadingImg.title="Click here to open.";
    currPanel.style.display="none";
    flags[index]=false;
}
else
{
```

Otherwise, we set the `alt` and `title` attributes to read `"Click here to close"`, the panel's display attribute to `none`, and the corresponding flag to `true`:

```
        currHeading.title="Click here to close.";
        currHeadingImg.src="images/open.gif";
        currHeadingImg.alt="Click here to close.";
        currHeadingImg.title="Click here to close.";
        currPanel.style.display="inline";
        flags[index]=true;
    }
}
```

There's no tacking or setting of coordinates here; we simply change the appropriate panel's display property, and what's known as **Incremental Reflow** does the work for us. Incremental reflow is another way of saying that the browser can update the display of any page element or group of elements in real time. If you've downloaded the code files from the glasshaus web site and played with the ch4_ex2 files, you may have noticed that when the menu text sizes were changed, the dimensions of the table and some of the buttons changed to accommodate this. That's an example of incremental reflow in action.

The rest of what we do here is, from a scripter's point of view, just window-dressing. However, from the standpoint of making our menu accessible, intuitive, and user-friendly it's quite important, so we hope that when you adapt this script for use in your own projects, you'll remember to do likewise!

We employ an initialization function very much like what we've used before to set the menu's appearance to correspond to the page that's currently loaded. We'll just discuss the differences here.

```
function initialise()
{
    document.getElementById("menuCell").innerHTML=output;
```

There's one little cross-browser hack we use in this script – Netscape 6 follows the CSS standard with regard to the `cursor` property, and when we set an element's style to include `cursor:pointer`, mousing over that element causes the mouse pointer to become a "hand" icon as though the element were a link. IE doesn't like `pointer` and instead prefers the non-standard `cursor:hand`. So, if IE is the browser (that is, if it understands what `document.all` means), we loop through all the elements whose id attributes are `heading0`, `heading1`, `heading2`, etc., and set their cursor properties dynamically to the value that it prefers:

```
    if(document.all)
      for(i=0;i<sectionNames.length;i++)
        document.getElementById("heading"+i).style.cursor="hand";
```

We employ the same process as we've used before in this chapter to get the section and page titles that correspond to the current page:

```
    var URLbits=self.location.href.split ("/");
    var currPage=URLbits[URLbits.length-1];
    var currPageName=currPage.split(".")[0];

    var pageTitle;

    var flag=false;
```

```
for(var i=0;i<sectionNames.length;i++)
{
   for(var j=0;j<pages[i].length;j++)
   {
      if(pages[i][j].toLowerCase().indexOf(currPageName)!=-1)
      {
         pageTitle=pages[i][j];
         flag=true;
         break;
      }
   }

   if(flag)
   {
```

Once we've found them, we add the page title onto the end of the document's `<title>` content (via the `document.title` property), then create a header for the page by assembling them inside of `<h1>` and `<h2>` elements and place that inside the `pageHeading` table cell using its `innerHTML` property. This is not unlike what some designers refer to as a "breadcrumb trail" (see Chapter 6 for more on these).

```
document.title+=" ("+pageTitle.toUpperCase()+")";

document.getElementById("pageHeading").innerHTML="<h1>"+sectionNames[i]+"</h1><h2>
"+pageTitle+"</h2>";
```

Finally, we call the `display()` function to display the menu appropriately for the current page, and then break from the outer loop just like we did with our previous example:

```
         display(i);
         break;
      }
   }

}

window.onload=initialise;
```

Let's take a look at the finished product. On the left side of the figure, we've loaded the Sales Enquiries page, and then clicked on the OFFICES menu section heading. On the right, we've done more or less the reverse – loaded the page containing information about OurCo's Scottsdale office, then clicked and opened the SERVICES section of the menu:

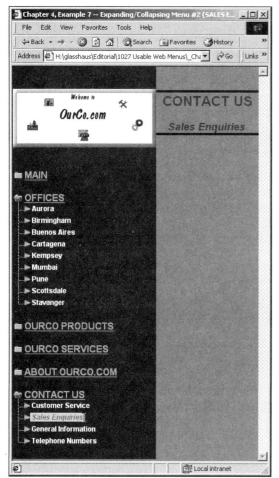 

Another way we could customize a menu such as this one, making it more responsive, would be to use the JavaScript `Date` object to find the day of the week or the month, and display only a related set of links or an image map, or to display an expanding and collapsing menu that's opened to an appropriate section with links to pages about Monday's events (if it happens to be a Monday). Or we could let users save a preference in a cookie so that whenever they visit the site, they see a menu that displays links to their favourite section of the site, or the pages that interest them the most from the site. This might also be adapted for use in an organizational chart.

# Summary

We've covered a wide range of material in this chapter, and shown you how you can use many different client-side techniques for building many different sorts of menus. Throughout its course, we've:

- Taken a look at CSS and how they can be used to enhance presentation, and to simplify the control of it both within a single page, and across an entire web site.

- Seen how cookies can be helpful in setting and preserving user preferences and thus making our sites more effective and appealing; we also demonstrated the basics of how to use them.

- Discussed image maps, how to create them, and how to use them by themselves and in conjunction with other techniques surveyed in this and the previous chapter.

- We also built further on some of the topics covered in Chapter 3, and demonstrated the use of some advanced client-side scripting techniques. We also showed how these can be combined to create highly dynamic menus that can respond both to our users' preferences and to the circumstances in which the menus are used.

Along the way, some aspects of modularity were also discussed, and we looked at some ways to use linked CSS and script files to ensure consistency of look and feel, and ease the work of maintenance on even a large site. Of course, usability and accessibility are paramount to good site design, and we demonstrated some ways to enhance presentation and to provide alternative content to users of browsers that might not support images, or CSS, or scripting.

# 5

- Flash usability issues

- Flash expanding menu

- Dynamic flash menu population using XML, PHP and MySQL

**Author: Andy Beaumont**

# Flash Menus

Now it's time to turn our attention to a possibly slightly less obvious, but still equally valid menu creation toolset – **Flash**. In this chapter, we will first be looking at Flash-specific usability issues, and how to overcome some of these, as well as having a brief discussion of standard Flash navigation concepts, such as the humble Flash button. Finally, we will go through a sprawling three-level menu system – the levels are as follows:

- Level 1 – A dynamic animated Flash menu, all contained within one `.fla` file.

- Level 2 – The same menu system, only the menu entries are pulled in from an XML file, so you only need to change the XML to update the menu.

- Level 3 – The same menu system again – this time however, the menu entries are stored in a MySQL database, dynamically pulled out and converted to XML using PHP, and imported into Flash.

*For more details on Flash, and to buy it, or obtain an evaluation copy, go to* http://www.macromedia.com/software/flash/. *For much more on XML/MySQL/PHP, including set-up information, go to* Chapter 6, *and check out the appropriate references in our* Resources *section.*

## Flash and Usability

Since its inception, there has been a lot of criticism levelled at Flash (indeed, "Web usability guru" Jakob Nielson once famously commented that 99% of all Flash is bad). A lot of these criticisms are fairly valid, such as Flash intros being obstructive to the user, Flash files becoming bloated and laborious to download and Flash sites being made overcomplicated for the sake of it.

However, a lot of these problems arise from the inexperience of the developer, rather than the software itself, and thankfully, as Flash matures it appears that Flash designers are maturing with it. Flash designers are becoming better at keeping file sizes down too, as it becomes more apparent that web users aren't actually happy to sit through a ten minute preload just because the content will look cool. Let's not forget that Flash is a relatively young technology, a few years ago it was common to find web pages with badly optimized images and bloated code.

There are a couple of Flash usability issues which still stand though, the most important of these is probably the plug-in. Whenever you are considering using Flash you have to take into account whether your target audience is going to have the Flash plug-in, and even if the answer is yes, what version of the plug-in they are likely to have. If the answer is no, is it reasonable to expect them to download it?

This really depends on your target audience (see *Chapter 2*, the *Understanding Your Target User* section, for more on this). The Flash plug-in, available from *http://www.macromedia.com/*, is only a few hundred kilobytes, so won't take an unacceptable amount of time to load, even with a 56K modem, as long as the user understands that you won't have to do it again. It is available for all browsers in this book's chosen browser set (IE 4+, Netscape 4+ and Opera 5+), and even auto-installs on some systems. At the time of writing, Macromedia stated, "Over 98.3% of all web users have the Macromedia Flash player".

It is possible to detect whether the user has Flash or not and redirect them to suitable content. Macromedia provide a sniffer script available from their web site, or alternatively Colin Moock has written the Flash Player Inspector, which you can download from
*http://www.moock.org/webdesign/flash/detection/moockfpi/*
There is also a very useful publish setting available with Flash 5 called Ad5Banner – if you select this option when publishing your movie, Flash will output all the necessary code to display an alternative image file if the user doesn't have the plug-in.

Flash also has its advantages – it is easy to program navigation links, or **Buttons**, to activate on release rather than on click ("second chance buttons" – on most desktop environments, like Windows, the user still has the option to roll off the button and then let go, in which case the button will not have any effect). A very basic usability issue but an important one nonetheless.

It is also easy to make a link button in Flash act like a real life button, appearing to push in when the user clicks on it (the same thing can be achieved with HTML and JavaScript rollover images). This isn't just a neat trick – it is a visual cue to the user that they can instantly relate to real-world experience even if they have never used a web site before. The original GUI on the Apple Lisa used metaphors of folders, desktops, and buttons to make the operating system feel less alien and more like the users traditional working environment. People are now very familiar with computer GUIs and so the metaphors have become less important. This frees up the designer a little to experiment with other ways of communicating to the user.

# Level 1: Dynamic Flash Menus

The easiest dynamic menu system to create in Flash keeps all the code inside the `.fla` file. We use the term "dynamic" here because we will not need to create every individual button for our menu separately. There will be a little bit of code from which our Flash movie can determine what is needed and create each button on the fly. The advantage of this system is that you don't need to know any technologies other than ActionScript.

The menu we are creating will be made up of two levels of navigation. The first, primary navigation level will contain the section headers, which in turn will activate the subnavigation:

# The Primary Navigation Button

We are going to create one instance of each button type in a way that will allow us to use that one symbol for all the buttons in our menu. Open up a new, blank document in Flash and save it as `flash_level1.fla`. Draw a basic, top-level navigation button onto the stage. Select it and then press *F8* (or choose *Insert*, then *Convert to symbol from the menus*) to turn it into a symbol, then choose *button* as the type and give it the symbol name "*Prime Button*". Select it again and press *F8* once more to create a movie clip containing the button – give this movie clip the symbol name "*primeMC*".

Next, double-click "primeMC" to edit it, and reposition the button so that the co-ordinates of its top left corner are 0x and 0y. Add a layer above the button called "title layer", and draw a dynamic textfield over the button, giving it the variable name "*title*". Turn on *HTML* and turn off *Selectable*. In terms of embedding the font there are two possible options open to us when creating our textfield. If we choose to embed the font, we cannot dynamically scale the width of the `movieClip` to fit the text. If we choose not to embed the font, then we have to use a font that is going to be on our end user's machine. In this example I'm not going to embed the font, but use Verdana as the typeface. Verdana is actually even more widespread than the Flash plug-in so the chances that the end user will have it are very high. Now, double-click the button to edit it and give it *over, down,* and *hit* states. Your display should now look something like the following:

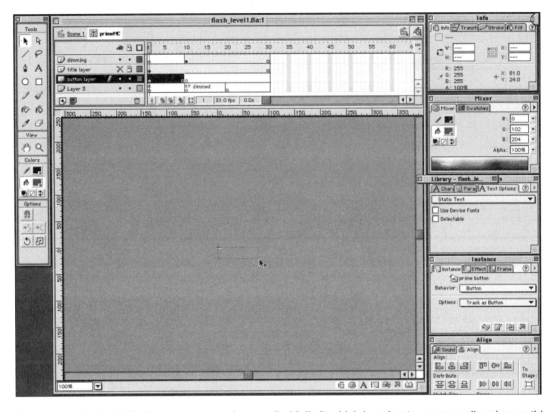

Back in the "*primeMC*" clip, create a new layer called "*dim*", which is going to serve as dimming on this button to show that it is active. Create frames for all layers up to frame 10. On the button layer, hit *F6* to create a new key frame, and select the button instance and press *Control-B* (*Apple-B on a Mac*) until your button is completely broken apart, but only on frame 10 – you don't want to lose the button instance on frame 1. Copy this broken button and place it on a key frame at frame 10 of the dim layer. Then, using the colour mixer panel, bring the alpha of the fill down to around 70%. Finally, give this frame the label "dimmed", and add a `stop()` command to frame 1 – our primary navigation button is now complete.

## Completing the Primary Navigation Element

Now we need to go back to the main stage and delete the instance of "*primeMC*" from it. Open the library and right click (*control-click* on a Mac) on the "*primeMC*", then go down to *linkage* – in the dialogue box that appears, check the *Export this symbol* option. In the *Identifier* box give it the name "*primeNav*". The menu and dialog box should appear to you something like this:

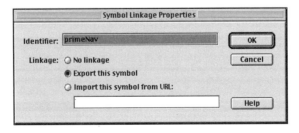

# Generating the Menu Entries

We now have our primary navigation element ready for use, so now let's set up the basis of the code from which our menu will be generated. On the first frame of the main timeline add the following code:

```
levelOneNav = new Array();
leveloneNav[0] = new Array ("home");
leveloneNav[1] = new Array ("the book","authors","chapters","buy");
leveloneNav[2] = new Array ("downloads","source files","screen
savers","desktops");
leveloneNav[3] = new Array ("support","help by email","forum","f.a.q.");
leveloneNav[4] = new Array ("contact","publishers","authors");
```

What we are doing here is creating an array, which holds other arrays. Each of the arrays it holds contains information necessary to build our menu – this is known as a **multidimensional array**.

> *To help you understand this better, let's look at what's going on in the last line – the array created contains three elements - "contact", "publishers" and "authors". The first element is going to be our primary navigation title, whilst the other elements will form the sub navigation for that section.*

# Building the Interface

Now that we have an information structure we can start coding the interface for it. Just below the previous code we're going to set up some variables that will be needed by the code later on:

```
// zIndex is the number at which depths are set
zIndex = 10;

// offsetY is our start position for the buttons to appear on the Y axis
offsetY = 5;

// offsetX is our start position for the buttons to appear on the X axis
offsetX = 85;
```

## Primary Navigation

Now we need to loop through the `levelOneNav` array, picking out the relevant information to build our initial interface:

```
// loop through the levelOneNav to build the initial interface
for(i=0;i<levelOneNav.length;i++)
  {
  // attach a ready-made button inside a MC for each nav section
  _root.attachMovie("primeNav","primeNav" + i, zIndex);
  // set myButton as a reference to the MC we have just created for easier coding
  myButton = _root["primeNav" + i];
  // set the button title to the first element in the subarray
  myButton.title = levelOneNav[i][0];
  // set the width of the button according to the length of the title string
  myButton._width = myButton.title.length * 10;
```

```
    // set the x position to the width of the button * i with the offsetX added on
    myButton._x = offsetX;
    // set the y position to offsetY so that all primeNav buttons line up from left
    // to right
    myButton._y = offsetY;
    // send info to button about its menuNo
    myButton.menuNo = i;
    // update the offsetX by adding on this buttons width
    offsetX += myButton._width + 1;
    // increment the necessary variables
    ++ zIndex;
}
```

These few lines will create our primary navigation. If you want, you can at this point test your movie to check that everything appears where you want it. One part of this block of code that you may not be familiar with is the following line:

```
myButton = _root["primeNav" + i];
```

This line simply creates a reference to the newly created movie clip, which we can use in the following code to make things easier to understand. For instance, if we didn't create this reference, the line:

```
myButton._x = offsetX;
```

would have to be written as:

```
_root["primeNav" + i]._x = offsetX;
```

It's not a big difference but it does make the script a lot easier to read back.

## Secondary Navigation

Now that the primary navigation is in place, we can think about the secondary navigation.
Duplicate both the "*primeMC*" and the "Prime Button" in your library, and name the duplicated versions "*subMC*" and "subButton". Also make sure that "*subMC*" contains the correct button – once again, open up the *linkage* dialog box and set the *identifier name* for "subMC" to *subNav*.

For our secondary navigation we want a way for our actions to affect all the buttons within one menu. The easiest way to do this is to create an empty movie clip that we can attach all the subbuttons to.

Create a new movie clip and call it "*subClip*". Set up its linkage as before, giving it the identifier name *emptyClip* (this acts as a container for the sub menus). Now we're ready to start adding the code for our secondary navigation so return to the first frame of the main timeline and open the actions panel.

Within the loop we created earlier, we'll add another loop to cycle through the array and generate our secondary navigation. Your loop should now look like this:

```
for(i=0;i<levelOneNav.length;i++)
{
    _root.attachMovie("primeNav","primeNav" + i, zIndex);
    myButton = _root["primeNav" + i];
```

```
myButton.title = levelOneNav[i][0];
myButton._width = myButton.title.length * 10;
myButton._x = offsetX;
myButton._y = offsetY;
myButton.menuNo = i;
offsetX += myButton._width + 1;
++ zIndex;
// attach the 'emptyClip movie clip we made to hold submenu buttons
if(levelOneNav[i].length > 1)
{
  myButton.attachMovie("emptyClip","submenu",10);
}
subYpos = myButton._height;
subXpos = 0;
// new index variable j in loop as we are still inside the main loop
for(j=1;j<levelOneNav[i].length;j++)
{
  // attach a button to the submenu clip
  myButton.submenu.attachMovie("subNav", "subButton" + j, j);
  // create reference object
  mySub = myButton.submenu["subButton"+j];
  // set the y position to just below the primary nav
  mySub._y = subYpos;
  // set the title
  mySub.title = levelOneNav[i][j];
  // set the width as before *Should be omitted if embedding font
  if(mySub.title.length < 8 )
  {
    widthVal = 12;
  }
  else
  {
    widthVal = 8;
  }
  mySub._width = mySub.title.length * widthVal;
  // temp set x
  mySub._x = subXpos;
  // update the offsetX by adding on this button's width
  subXpos += mySub._width;
  // send info to button about its pageNo and menuNo
  // this allows us to read the 'menus' array to find out what action
  // the button should have
  mySub.menuNo = i;
  mySub.pageNo = j;
}
}
```

If you test the movie at this point you should see all your subnavigation elements piled on top of each other just below the primary navigation (as seen below). Clearly our next task is to create a way to show and hide each of these menus.

# Behavior Clips

Rather than simply switching the visibility on and off, we are instead going to introduce a visual cue to the user about how the navigation works. By sliding the subnavigation on and off the screen, depending on whether it is currently active or not, we can indicate to the user that they are leaving one section of the site and entering another. We are now going to create a behavior clip to achieve this.

A behavior clip is a `movieClip` containing nothing but code, whose sole purpose is to cause an action to happen to its parent. For instance, you could create a "fade" behavior clip by having just two frames containing the code `_parent._alpha -= 5`: this would cause the parent `movieClip` to continuously fade out. Obviously you wouldn't want this script to continue running after the parent alpha reaches zero, so a little more code would be required to test whether or not the clip has done its job. Although not official Macromedia terminology, "behavior clip" seems to have become the commonly accepted term.

Our behavior clip is going to take x and y co-ordinate parameters from a function call and smoothly move its parent to the new position.

Create a new movie clip and call it "*moveTo*". On the first frame of this clip's timeline, you want a `stop()` command and a precision variable. The precision variable is simply a threshold to stop the clip from making unnecessary code operations. Add the following code to this first frame:

```
stop ();
precision = 1;
```

On frame two add:

```
// check that the parent has not reached its destination
// targetX, targetY, and speed will be sent to the clip from a function call
if (Math.abs(_parent._x - targetX) < precision && Math.abs(_parent._y - targetY) <
precision)
{
// if it has, get to frame 1 and stop playing
  _parent._x = targetX;
  _parent._y = targetY;
  this.gotoAndStop(1);
}
// otherwise, move parent clip towards destination
_parent._x -= (_parent._x - targetX)/speed;
_parent._y -= (_parent._y - targetY)/speed;
```

Copy frame two to frame three, and add the following line on to the bottom of frame three:

```
gotoAndPlay(2);
```

We now have a behavior clip capable of moving any other movie clip around the stage. To use it, simply drop it into the movie clip you want to move, send the new positions to it as the variables `targetX` and `targetY`, and then tell it to play. For our menu system this clip is going to move the submenus.

Double-click the "*subClip*" in your library to edit it and drop your behavior clip into the centre, giving it the instance name *motionClip*.

Now that we can send motion commands to our subnavigation we can add one final line to our original construction loop to make sure that all of the subnavigation elements start off the stage:

```
    }
      myButton.submenu._x = 2000;
    }
```

## Activating and Deactivating the Submenus

Now that we have built the submenus and included a behavior clip for moving them around, we need to create some functions to activate and deactivate them.

Back on our code frame of the main timeline, add the following function to activate a sub-menu.

```
    function dimButton(menu,page){
      unDim(_root.currentMenu, _root.currentPage);
      _root["primeNav" + menu].submenu.active = true;
      _root["primeNav" + menu].submenu.motionClip.targetX = 0;
      _root["primeNav" + menu].submenu.motionClip.speed = 3;
      _root["primeNav" + menu].submenu.motionClip.gotoAndPlay(2);
      _root["primeNav" + menu].gotoAndStop("dimmed");
      _root.currentMenu = menu;
      _root.currentPage = page;
    }
```

If we break down this function, we can see that the first line executed is another custom function – unDim – which we will create in a moment. Following on from that line, firstly we set a variable on the submenu that we are targeting, to flag it as active. We then send 2 variables to the *motionClip* and tell it to play. We also send our prime navigation button to it's dimmed label so that it becomes deactivated, and finally we reset the variables currentMenu and currentPage to reflect the fact that we have just activated a new menu.

At the moment, this function isn't getting executed from anywhere. We want it to function when the user clicks on one of the primary navigation buttons, so double click the "*primeMC*" clip in the library to edit it, and add some actions to the button on frame 1:

```
    on(release){
      _root.dimButton(this.menuNo, 1);
    }
```

You can test the movie again at this point – if you click on the primary buttons you should see the submenus come on to the screen from the right. You can play with the speed variable a little until you find a speed that you like. However, make sure that the menu comes onto the screen fast enough so that your user knows they have actually activated something.

At the moment, the submenus will just pile up on top of each other, which is why we need to code the unDim function. So, back on our code frame add the following function to the main time line:

```
    function unDim(menu,page){
      _root["primeNav" + menu].submenu.active = false;
      _root["primeNav" + menu].submenu.motionClip.targetX = 1000;
```

```
   _root["primeNav" + menu].submenu.motionClip.targetY = _root["primeNav" +
menu].submenu.motionClip._y;
    _root["primeNav" + menu].submenu.motionClip.speed = 8;
    _root["primeNav" + menu].submenu.motionClip.gotoAndPlay(2);
    _root["primeNav" + menu].gotoAndStop(1);
    _root["primeNav" + menu].submenu["subButton" + page].gotoAndStop(1);
  }
```

Test the movie again – the submenus should fly off screen as each new one arrives. Now we need to be able to dim the submenu buttons, but as we don't want this to activate the motion clip, we are going to create two simplified versions of the above functions:

```
function dimSubButton(menu,page)
{
  unDimSub (_root.currentMenu, _root.currentPage);
  _root["primeNav" + menu].gotoAndStop("dimmed");
  _root["primeNav" + menu].submenu["subButton" + page].gotoAndStop("dimmed");
  _root.currentMenu = menu;
  _root.currentPage = page;
}

function unDimSub(menu,page)
{
  _root["primeNav" + menu].gotoAndStop(1);
  _root["primeNav" + menu].submenu["subButton" + page].gotoAndStop(1);
}
```

Obviously these functions need to be called from somewhere, so double-click the "*subMC*" clip in the library and add the following actions to the button:

```
on(release)
{
    _root.dimSubButton(_parent._parent.menuNo, this.pageNo);
}
```

Test the movie again and you should find that clicking on one of the submenu buttons will dim it out.

We can go a little further on the usability front here. If you have more than three or four submenu items you'll find that they will start to hang off the right-hand side of the page. We can avoid this by having the submenus move in response to being passed over by the mouse button. Now that we have created our behavior clip we might as well get full use out of it, so add the following code into the buttons' actions:

```
on(rollOver)
{
  if(_parent.active == true)
  {
  pointx = this._x / 2;
    _parent.motionClip.targetX = pointx * -1;
    _parent.motionClip.speed = 20;
    _parent.motionClip.gotoAndPlay(2);
  }
}
```

You will notice here that we are using the active/inactive flag that we set up earlier. This makes sure that the rollover actions only affect an active menu. If this wasn't in here it would be possible for a user to roll over a menu as it was on its way off screen, resulting in that menu having a new destination set in its motion clip and leaving two submenus on screen at once. The rest of the code in the rollover is just sending new variables into the motion clip to smoothly move the rolled over button along the x-axis towards its parent in the primary navigation. This allows us to fit considerably more items into each submenu.

One more bit of usability code to add while we are here is to have the submenu item that is selected slide along to line up with its parent in the primary navigation when it is clicked on. Change the code in the `on(release)` handler to:

```
on(release){
  _root.dimSubButton(_parent._parent.menuNo, this.pageNo);
  pointx = this._x;
  _parent.motionClip.targetX = pointx * -1;
  _parent.motionClip.speed = 30;
  _parent.motionClip.gotoAndPlay(2);
}
```

This code only really makes a difference if you are going to use this menu in a Flash site or an HTML site with a separate frame for the Flash menu – if it is on an HTML page with no frames then the new page will start loading before the action takes place.

There is one thing left to do now to make this a fully functioning menu – we need to make the buttons actually do something, and for this example we are going to be opening new HTML pages. The first thing we need to do is create a storage system for the URLs. The simplest and most logical choice here is to create another two-dimensional array with a structure mimicking the original array. This way we can use the `menuNo` and `pageNo` values that we sent to each button to reference the new array and find out what action to take. This is often known as a parallel array.

Just below the original array add the following code (you'll need to construct the target pages yourself!):

```
menus = new Array();
menus[0] = new Array ("index.html");
menus[1] = new Array (null,"authors.html","chapters.html","buy.html");
menus[2] = new Array
(null,"source_files.html","screen_savers.html","desktops.html");
menus[3] = new Array(null,"email.html","forum.html","faq.html");
menus[4] = new Array(null,"contact_publishers.html","contact_authors.html");
```

You might be wondering why the first element of most of these arrays is `null` – If you refer back to the `levelOneNav` array, you'll notice that the first element of each subarray is the title of the primary navigation button. Usually, we are not going to want the primary navigation buttons to open a new page but occasionally, as is the case with our "*home*" button, we won't have a submenu attached, in which case the primary navigation button should be linked up. Alternatively you might want to have a section overview page activated when each primary navigation button is clicked, in which case you would simply insert the path to the relevant page.

Double-click the "*subMC*" clip in the library to edit it, select the button and open the *actions* panel. Inside the `on(release)` handler add in the code (seen below) that will check the relevant URL from the array, and then open it:

```
on(release)
{
    _root.dimSubButton(_parent._parent.menuNo, this.pageNo);
    pointx = this._x;
    _parent.motionClip.targetX = pointx * -1;
    _parent.motionClip.speed = 30;
    _parent.motionClip.gotoAndPlay(2);
    theURL = _root.menus[this.menuNo][this.pageNo];
    getURL(theURL);
}
```

That's our subnavigation linked up with those two simple lines. Optionally you might want to set a frame target up in the `getURL` command. Our final task with this version of the menu is to link up any primary navigation that doesn't have a submenu.

Open up the "*primeMC*" clip, select the button, and open the *actions* panel. Because we only want to open up a page if there is no submenu, we can check against the `null` value in our menu's array to see if any action should be taken. Insert the following conditional into the `on(release)` handler:

```
on(release)
{
    _root.dimButton(this.menuNo, 1);
    if(_root.menus[this.menuNo][0] != null)
    {
        theURL = _root.menus[this.menuNo][0];
        getURL(theURL);
    }
}
```

*Simply put, this equates to: "if the value in the menu's array for this button is not null, then open the returned value as a URL."*

Everything works now, but there is one minor improvement to add. Create a keyframe on frame 2 of the main timeline and enter a `stop()` command. The reason for this is to do with the functions we created on the first frame. When a Flash movie is stopped at a frame with function declarations on it, those functions will be declared at whatever frame rate the Flash movie is running at. Obviously, a function only needs to be declared once, and if it is getting declared 30 times per second you can end up with memory leaks causing the Flash player to slow down. If the Flash movie is running in a browser, after a time it can bring the browser to its knees.

This menu is now fully functional. The version I produced for this chapter weighs in at just 8k, and if you aim for around 60k for an entire web page so that your visitors aren't sat around waiting for the page to load for too long, you are left with 52k to play with for the content. There are two main reasons why we have managed to keep the file size so low. The first is our reuse of library items – if we had created each menu button individually including the text for each, we could have been looking at more like 20 to 25k. The second reason is our coded motion – if we had tweened all the motion within this menu that could have added a further 10k. You can see that using these techniques across an entire Flash site could save you a considerable amount of file size.

To check out the menu, go to the *ch5_ex1* folder in the code download.

# Level 2: Introducing XML

The menu we have produced so far is great for the end user, but what about the person who maintains the code? Do you really want to have to open up your `.fla` file and wade through all that code just to add a new menu item or change a URL? Of course not – this is where **XML** comes in. Although a similar system could be achieved using `loadVariables()` and a text/HTML file, you would have nowhere near the flexibility that XML brings – by the end of this example, we will be able to do all the updating we need, by updating a simple XML file.

When Flash 5 first came out, the leap from version 4 was a great one indeed. On top of the new ECMA standard version of ActionScript came all sorts of power features, and of all of them, XML is probably the most exciting. Although a text file containing a load of mark up tags may not seem like a very exciting technology, the use of XML as a separation of content from structure is spreading wildly. For Flash designers this means that there is a whole load of freely available content out there that, with a little practice, can be easily slotted into your Flash designs. When the XML is updated, so is your whole Flash site.

For those of you who haven't yet discovered XML here is a brief overview. XML stands for **Extensible Mark-up Language**, and has a similar look to HTML. The big difference between the two is that, while HTML describes the way content should look, XML just describes the content. At first this may sound like a step down from HTML, but that separation of content from structure is what gives XML its real power.

Imagine if you had a wholesale company and displayed all your products on your company web site, and all your retailers displayed your products on their sites. If each of these sites was hard coded in HTML and you wanted to change the description of a product, it would mean that somebody would have to make the same change on all of these sites. If all these sites used a single XML document to describe the content, they could all be designed to fit the relevant retailer and yet all be updated at the same time.

Let's have a quick look at the structure of an XML document. In many ways an XML document is very much like a database; it holds data in a structured and organized way. If we wanted to create a list of contacts for an address book we could structure it like this:

```
<contacts>
    <person firstname="Joe" secondname="Bloggs" email="joe@bloggs.com" />
    <person firstname="Andy" email="andy@eviltwin.co.uk" />
</contacts>
```

At first glance, the above example could be mistaken for HTML, until you look at the tag names. In XML you can make up your own tag names (also known as creating an **XML Vocabulary**): rather than having to describe the data to a bunch of standard browsers, you are required to describe it only to the users of that specific vocabulary, and custom applications that are built to parse the data. This means you can use nice descriptive tag names that anyone would be able to understand.

XML also allows us to make up our own attribute names. This means we can end up with a document that is almost as readable as if we had written it in plain English. Let's take our example a little further, introducing a new `<company>` element with `name` and `phone` attributes:

```
<contacts>
    <person firstname="Joe" secondname="Bloggs" email="joe@bloggs.com" />
    <person firstname="Andy" email="andy@eviltwin.co.uk" />
    <company name="The Pizza Place" phone="020 7777 8888" />
</contacts>
```

Here we see that we are not restricted to nesting one type of tag. Taking this example one step further, we could even nest a person within our company if there was a particular contact that we like to deal with: in this case we'll go for Luigi because he does the best toppings:

```
<contacts>
    <person firstname="Joe" secondname="Bloggs" email="joe@bloggs.com" />
    <person firstname="Andy" email="andy@eviltwin.co.uk" />
    <company name="The Pizza Place" phone="020 7777 8888">
        <person firstname="Luigi" position="topping meister" />
    </company>
</contacts>
```

Here I have highlighted the whole `<company>` element as new code, even though some of it existed in the last example – if you look closely you'll notice that `<company>` is no longer an empty element, but instead now fully encompasses Luigi's details. This makes the `<person>` tag containing Luigi a child of `<company>` – Luigi is now linked to that company, so if we were to search through our XML document as though it were a database, once we have found Luigi we can find out what company he works for by checking the parent element.

One last area to cover before we delve into using XML in a Flash project is use of elements over attributes for data representation. So far, we have been storing all our information in attributes, rather than elements – if you can get away with it, this is the best way to store the data if it is going to be interpreted by Flash; this is because:

- It makes going through the XML with ActionScript a little easier.

- It makes Flash's built-in `parseXML` routine considerably faster.

In some cases though, you will just have to use elements, particularly if you want to store some HTML in the XML:

```
<contacts>
    <person firstname="Joe" secondname="Bloggs" email="joe@bloggs.com" />
    <person firstname="Andy" email="andy@eviltwin.co.uk" />
    <company name="The Pizza Place" phone="020 7777 8888">
        <person firstname="Luigi" position="topping meister" />
        <details>The Pizza Place make some <b>very</b> fine pizzas. </details>
    </company>
</contacts>
```

Here you can see we have included an HTML `<b>` element in the `<details>`.

> As a general rule of thumb, when deciding on a structure for an XML document to be used with Flash, if it can go in an attribute, put it in an attribute.

# The Rules of XML

XML has its own set of rules to follow that must be adhered to, otherwise your XML will not be **valid**, and will fail, and produce some undesirable effects in your Flash movie:

- Close all tags: HTML tags within your document must also be properly closed; whereas a browser will often forgive you for not closing a couple of tags, in XML you even have to close a `<br />` tag!

- Nest properly: Your tags must be nested properly. For example, the following shows a line with correct nesting, followed by a line with incorrect nesting:

```
<p> This sentence contains some <b>bold</b> and <i>italics</i> </p>
<p> This <b>sentence <i>contains some bold</b> and italics</i> </p>
```

- Naming rules: there are some strict rules about what your tag names can and can't be:

- XML Names can only start with letters or an underscore, no other punctuation or numbers.

- XML Names can't start with the letters XML, in upper- or lowercase.

- XML names are case-sensitive, so the `<lastname>`, `<lastName>`, and `<LASTNAME>` tags are all different in XML terms.

- Names can't contain spaces.

Any HTML in your markup documents must also follow these rules (becoming XHTML) – Flash is not as forgiving about sloppy markup as a lot of web browsers (such as IE and Netscape).

*If you want to check that your markup is valid XML, you can simply parse your XML document in an XML-compliant browser, such as IE5.5/6, and see if any error messages are returned.*

# XML-based Menu

OK, now that we have the basic rules out of the way we can get on with using XML in our menu example. Open up the file that you produced in the first part of this chapter and resave it under a new name. The first thing we need to do is remove all the unnecessary code – all of the following code from frame 1 of the main timeline can go:

```
levelOneNav = new Array();
leveloneNav[0] = new Array ("home");
leveloneNav[1] = new Array ("the book","authors","chapters","buy");
leveloneNav[2] = new Array ("downloads","source files","screen
savers","desktops");
leveloneNav[3] = new Array ("support","help by email","forum","f.a.q.");
leveloneNav[4] = new Array ("contact","the publishers","the authors");

menus = new Array();
menus[0] = new Array ("index.html");
menus[1] = new Array (null,"authors.html","chapters.html","buy.html");
```

```
menus[2] = new Array
(null,"source_files.html","screen_savers.html","desktops.html");
menus[3] = new Array(null,"email.html","forum.html","faq.html");
menus[4] = new Array(null,"conatct_publishers.html","contact_authors.html");
for(i=0;i<levelOneNav.length;i++)
{
  _root.attachMovie("primeNav","primeNav" + i, zIndex);
  myButton = _root["primeNav" + i];
  myButton.title = levelOneNav[i][0];
  myButton._width = myButton.title.length * 10;
  myButton._x = offsetX;
  myButton._y = offsetY;
  myButton.menuNo = i;
  offsetX += myButton._width + 1;
  ++ zIndex;
  // attach a movie clip to hold sub menu buttons
  if(levelOneNav[i].length > 1)
  {
    myButton.attachMovie("emptyClip","submenu",10);
  }
  subYpos = myButton._height;
  subXpos = 0;
  for(j=1;j<levelOneNav[i].length;j++)
  {
    myButton.submenu.attachMovie("subNav", "subButton" + j, j);
    mySub = myButton.submenu["subButton"+j];
    mySub._y = subYpos;
    mySub.title = levelOneNav[i][j];
    if(mySub.title.length < 8 )
    {
      widthVal = 12;
    }
    else
    {
      widthVal = 8;
    }
    mySub._width = mySub.title.length * widthVal;
    mySub._x = subXpos;
    subXpos += mySub._width;
    mySub.menuNo = i;

    mySub.pageNo = j;
  }
  myButton.submenu._x = 2000;
}
```

Those two arrays are going to be replaced by one simple XML document that will hold all the information in a much more accessible way. The giant loop is going to be replaced by some slicker code.

# Creating our XML

The XML document we will use for this example has the following structure:

```
<menuData>
    <menu name="home" url="index.html" />
    <menu name="the book">
        <subItem name="authors" url="authors.html" />
```

```
            <subItem name="chapters" url="chapters.html" />

        <-- more subItem child elements -->

        </menu>

        <-- more menu elements here, with subItem child elements -->

    </menuData>
```

The complete file, `menus.xml`, along with all the other code files for this example, can be found in the *ch5_ex2* directory of this chapter's code download.

# Loading our XML into Flash

Now we've got our XML sorted out, it's a simple matter to tell Flash what we want to do with the information it finds in there. Firstly, we need to tell Flash to load the XML document – on frame 2 of the main timeline, add the following code before the `stop()` command:

```
menuXML = new XML();
menuXML.load("menus.xml");
menuXML.onLoad = buildMenu;
```

Line 1 creates the XML object for us to load the data into, line 2 loads the data, and line 3 executes the function `buildMenu` once the data has loaded. Don't get too excited – Flash doesn't have a built-in `buildMenu` function – we are going to create that next.

Double-click the first frame of your Flash menu to open the *frame actions* panel. Immediately below the variables that we initialized in the earlier version (where our loop was), we are going to create a function that will be executed when the XML is loaded. The first thing we are going to do in the function is create a new array that will hold everything between the opening and closing root tags:

```
function buildMenu()
{
    holder = new Array();
    holder =  menuXML.firstChild.childNodes;
    trace("holder = " + holder);
}
```

I have closed the function and added a `trace` command in there so that you can test the movie and see the results in the output window. When you are first learning XML, the `trace` command comes in extremely useful as you can use it while creating your function to see which part of the XML you are currently working with. I will add them in from time to time as we go through this code, and hopefully this will help you to visualize how the function steps through each section.

Next, we will create a loop, which will cycle through the elements of the holder array looking for ones named "`menu`".

```
function buildMenu()
    {
    holder = new Array();
    holder =  menuXML.firstChild.childNodes;
    for(i=0;i<holder.length;i++)
```

```
      {
        if(holder[i].nodeName == "menu")
        {
            trace("found menu: " + holder[i].attributes.name);
        }
      }
    }
```

Notice here that we can address sections of the holder array as though we were dealing directly with the menuXML XML object that we created. This is because the line holder = menuXML.firstChild.childNodes; doesn't actually populate the holder with the child nodes from our object – it simply creates references to them. The trace command here introduces the system for retrieving attributes from the XML. If you test the movie at this point, you should see the following in your output window:

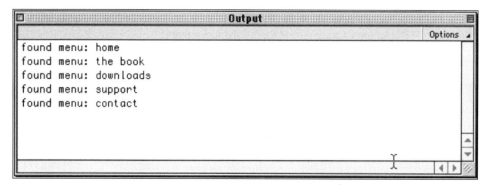

So far, our loop is working to plan – every time the loop finds a node called menu, we can do something with the information contained within that node. The first thing we want to do with this information is create the primary navigation buttons:

```
function buildMenu()
{
  holder = new Array();
  holder =  menuXML.firstChild.childNodes;
  for(i=0;i<holder.length;i++)
  {
    if(holder[i].nodeName == "menu")
    {
      _root.attachMovie("primeNav","primeNav" + i, zIndex);
      myButton = _root["primeNav" + i];
      myButton.title = holder[i].attributes.name;
      if(holder[i].attributes.url != null)
      {
        trace(holder[i].attributes.name + " url = " +  holder[i].attributes.url);
      }
      myButton._width = myButton.title.length * 10;
      myButton._x = offsetX;
      myButton._y = offsetY;
      myButton.menuNo = i;
      offsetX += myButton._width + 1;
```

```
      ++ zIndex;
    }
  }
}
```

You'll notice that this block of code is very similar to the code in the original version of this menu except for two points: we now use the attributes to get both the menu title and the URL. In addition, we also check to see if the `url` attribute exists, and if it does, send that value to the button itself.

Now that we have found a menu node and used its information, we can loop through the children of this node creating submenus as we go. First though, let's check to see if it has any child nodes and if so, attach our `emptyClip`.

```
function buildMenu()
{
  holder = new Array();
  holder =  menuXML.firstChild.childNodes;
  for(i=0;i<holder.length;i++)
  {
    if(holder[i].nodeName == "menu")
    {
      _root.attachMovie("primeNav","primeNav" + i, zIndex);
      myButton = _root["primeNav" + i];
      myButton.title = holder[i].attributes.name;
      if(holder[i].attributes.url != null)
      {
        myButton.url = holder[i].attributes.url;
      }
      myButton._width = myButton.title.length * 10;
      myButton._x = offsetX;
      myButton._y = offsetY;
      myButton.menuNo = i;
      offsetX += myButton._width + 1;
      ++ zIndex;
      subHolder = new Array();
      subHolder = holder[i].childNodes;
      if(subHolder.length > 0)
      {
        trace(holder[i].attributes.name + " has " + subHolder.length +" child
            nodes");
        myButton.attachMovie("emptyClip","submenu",10);
      }
      subYpos = myButton._height;
      subXpos = 0;
    }
  }
}
```

What we have done here is to create a new array, and assign the child nodes of `holder[i]` to that array. We can then check the length of the new `subHolder` array to see how many child nodes it has. Thanks to our friend the `trace` command, if you test the movie at this point you'll see something along the lines of the image overleaf:

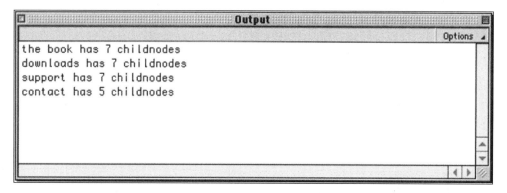

You might be wondering where it is getting those numbers from – after all, each submenu has no more than three items. This is a quirk of XML – every carriage return and tab in your XML document counts as a node. You can avoid this by having all your XML on one line, but this makes it a little difficult to read and update, so we are getting around it by simply checking the node name of each node before we perform any actions. Each of these "whitespace" nodes will have NULL as its node name.

To continue with our function, we can now loop through the elements of the subHolder array creating the submenu items. Once again, we use attributes to get the URL and title for each button:

```
function buildMenu()
{
  holder = new Array();
  holder =  menuXML.firstChild.childNodes;
  for(i=0;i<holder.length;i++)
  {
    if(holder[i].nodeName == "menu")
    {
      _root.attachMovie("primeNav","primeNav" + i, zIndex);
      myButton = _root["primeNav" + i];
      myButton.title = holder[i].attributes.name;
      if(holder[i].attributes.url != null)
      {
        myButton.url = holder[i].attributes.url;
      }
      myButton._width = myButton.title.length * 10;
      myButton._x = offsetX;
      myButton._y = offsetY;
      myButton.menuNo = i;
      offsetX += myButton._width + 1;
      ++ zIndex;
      subHolder = new Array();
      subHolder = holder[i].childNodes;
      if(subHolder.length > 0)
      {
        myButton.attachMovie("emptyClip","submenu",10);
      }
      subYpos = myButton._height;
      subXpos = 0;
      for (j=0;j<subHolder.length;j++)
      {
        if(subHolder[j].nodeName == "subItem")
        {
          myButton.submenu.attachMovie("subNav", "subButton" + j, j);
```

```
            mySub = myButton.submenu["subButton"+j];
            mySub._y = subYpos;
            mySub.title = subHolder[j].attributes.name;
            mySub.url = subHolder[j].attributes.url;
            if(mySub.title.length < 8 )
            {
              widthVal = 12;
            }
            else
            {
              widthVal = 8;
            }

            mySub._width = mySub.title.length * widthVal;
            mySub._x = subXpos;
            subXpos += mySub._width;
            mySub.menuNo = i;
            mySub.pageNo = j;
          }
        }
      MyButton.submenu._x = 2000;
    }
  }
}
```

And that is the completed function. All that is left to do now is change the way that the buttons work so that they look for a `url` variable on their own timeline, rather than retrieving it from an array on the root. Double-click the "*primeMC*" movie clip in your library, select the button and open the *actions* panel. In the `on(release)` handler, you need to change the code to the following:

```
on(release){
  _root.dimButton(this.menuNo, 1);
  if(this.url != null)
  {
    theURL = this.url;
    getURL(theURL);
  }
}
```

Obviously, we also need to change the code in the submenu buttons – double-click "subMC" in the library, select the button and open the *actions* panel if it's not already open. Change the `on(release)` code to:

```
on(release)
{
  _root.dimSubButton(_parent._parent.menuNo, this.pageNo);
  pointx = this._x;
  _parent.motionClip.targetX = pointx * -1;
  _parent.motionClip.speed = 30;
  _parent.motionClip.gotoAndPlay(2);
  theURL = this.url;
  getURL(theURL);
}
```

Publish the movie and test it in a browser, and you should find that everything works. The ActionScript for this version of the menu is only slightly more complex than the first version and the end result is identical. The real power of this version is in the simplicity of updating. Want to add a whole new menu? Just type the details into your XML file – you never need to open the `.fla` file again. Most Flash developers don't like to hand over the `.fla` to clients – using this method you can let a client make changes to the data without having to give them access to the source.

# Level 3: Databases, XML & Flash

For the ultimate in dynamic Flash menus, you'll want to hook up to a database. This is an area that many Flash designers shy away from, even more so than XML. Consequently, in this exercise, we are going to use both. I decided to go with MySQL for the database, and PHP for the middleware, not least because both of these technologies are free. PHP is also a good choice for Flash designers because the syntax is not overly dissimilar to ActionScript, which can make it a lot easier to pick up.

> Note that while I have used the PHP/MySQL combination, this does not limit you to the same. You could use any other database/middleware combination that takes your fancy – for example, the code download for this chapter, available at http://www.glasshaus.com/, includes an alternative version written in ASP, with MS Access for the database. For more on these, see the Resources section at the end of the book.

Our database is going to hold the information about the menus, our PHP is going to retrieve that information, turn it into XML, and send it to the Flash movie, and our Flash movie can then interpret it in a very similar way as in the previous exercise.

## Setting up our Database

We are going to create a table in a MySQL database with the following structure: The first column, `type`, is going to contain either "`prime`" or "`sub`", indicating whether the row data refers to a top-level or sub-level navigation item. The second column, `menuID`, exists so that we can re-associate submenus with prime menus once we get all our data back. The other two columns, `name` and `url`, are exactly what you would expect. So, our table needs to look like this:

| type | menuID | name | url |
|------|--------|------|-----|
| prime | 1 | home | `index.html` |
| prime | 2 | the book | |
| sub | 2 | authors | `authors.html` |
| sub | 2 | chapters | `chapters.html` |
| sub | 2 | buy | `buy.html` |
| prime | 3 | downloads | |
| sub | 3 | source files | `source_files.html` |

| type | menuID | name | url |
|---|---|---|---|
| sub | 3 | screen savers | screen_savers.html |
| sub | 3 | desktops | desktops.html |
| prime | 4 | support | |
| sub | 4 | help by email | email.html |
| sub | 4 | forum | forum.html |
| sub | 4 | f.a.q. | faq.html |
| prime | 5 | contact | |
| sub | 5 | the publishers | contact_publishers.html |
| sub | 5 | the authors | contact_authors.html |

There are a number of tools available for setting up your database; if you are on a PC you can use the MySQL Monitor utility, on a Mac it can be a little more tricky but there are many free MySQL admin tools available, most notably **phpMyAdmin**, available from *http://www.phpwizard.net/projects/phpMyAdmin/* – it's not the easiest software to configure, but once it's done it's pretty powerful (see *Chapter 6* for more on phpMyAdmin).

For the purposes of this exercise I have written a PHP script, which will connect to your database, create the table and the necessary columns and populate them with data all in one swift move (getMenus.php3). The only configuration required is to set up the username, password, and database name in the first few lines:

```
<?

$userName = "myUserName";
$pWord = "myPassWord";
$theDB = "myDatabaseName";


// end of user set up.


$menuData = array();
$menuData[0] = array("prime","1","home","index.html");
$menuData[1] = array("prime","2","the book");
$menuData[2] = array("sub","2","authors","authors.html");
$menuData[3] = array("sub","2","chapters","chapters.html");
$menuData[4] = array("sub","2","buy","buy.html");
$menuData[5] = array("prime","3","downloads");
$menuData[6] = array("sub","3","source files","source_files.html");
$menuData[7] = array("sub","3","screen savers","screen_savers.html");
$menuData[8] = array("sub","3","desktops","desktops.html");
$menuData[9] = array("prime","4","support");
$menuData[10] = array("sub","4","help by email","email.html");
$menuData[11] = array("sub","4","forum","forum.html");
$menuData[12] = array("sub","4","f.a.q.","faq.html");
$menuData[13] = array("prime","5","contact");
```

```php
$menuData[14] = array("sub","5","publishers","contact_publishers.html");
$menuData[15] = array("sub","5","authors","contact_authors.html");


$fields = array("type", "menuID", "name", "url");

// connect to database
$link = mysql_connect(localhost, $userName, $pWord);
if($link==1){
  $choose = mysql_select_db($theDB);
  if($choose != true){
    echo("failed to connect<br>");
    exit;
  }
}

echo ("connected<br><br>");

// create table

$query = "CREATE TABLE nav (type VARCHAR(10),menuID INTEGER,name VARCHAR(50),url
VARCHAR(255))";
$result = mysql_query ($query);
if ($result == false) {
  echo ("create table failed<br><br>");
  exit;
}

echo("created table<br><br>");

for ($index = 0; $index < count($menuData); $index++){
  // Build query
  $query = "INSERT INTO nav ($fields[0],$fields[1],$fields[2],$fields[3]) VALUES
('" . $menuData[$index][0] . "','" . $menuData[$index][1] . "','" .
$menuData[$index][2] . "','" . $menuData[$index][3] . "')" ;
  $result = mysql_query($query);
  if ($result == false) {
    echo ("query failed");
    echo("<br>the query was: $query <br><br>");
    exit;
  }
}

echo ("completed successfully!");

?>
```

# PHP Middleware

Now that our database is full of data, we need a way to retrieve that data – this is also a job for PHP. Don't worry if you are no PHP guru – neither am I – we are just going to cover what we need to know here. If you *are* a PHP guru please try not to laugh at my code! The full code can be found in *saveMenuData.php3*.

First up, let's create a connection to the database and then test it.

```
<?

// connect to database
$link = mysql_connect(localhost, "username", "password");
if($link==1){
  $choose = mysql_select_db("dbname");
  if($choose != true)
  {
    echo("failed to connect<br>");
    exit;
  }
  else
  {
    echo ("connection success<br>");
  }
}

?>
```

Note that the words in bold – username, password and dbname – should actually be replaced with the correct username, password and database name for your server. If you now save this file as connectTest.php3 and upload it to your server, you can test it by navigating to it in a browser.

If all your settings were correct, you should see the message "*connection success*" in the browser window. If your ActionScript is up to scratch, the PHP code so far shouldn't be too hard to follow. It basically sets up our connection and then sends back a message based on whether that connection was a success or not. The only really foreign thing in here is the "$" symbol before variable names, apparently a convention carried over from Perl, but nothing too much to worry about.

# Introducing the Database To the Middleware

Now let's try accessing some of our saved data. Firstly, we need to set up a query to perform on the database. We are going to send a very basic query to the database – SELECT * FROM nav – where the * symbol is a wild card. In plain English this query translates to give me everything from the table called nav:

```
<?

// connect to database
$link = mysql_connect(localhost, "username", "password");
if($link==1){
  $choose = mysql_select_db("dbname");
  if($choose != true)
  {
    echo("failed to connect<br>");
    exit;
  }
  else
  {
    echo ("connection success<br>");
```

```
        $query = "SELECT * FROM nav";
        $result = mysql_query($query);
        echo ($result);
    }
}

?>
```

Once again, save this script to the server for testing. At this stage you can think of the `echo` command as being akin to the `trace` command in ActionScript or `document.write` in JavaScript – it is simply sending information back out of the script. As an ActionScripter, you might expect this script to display all the variables retrieved from the database, but if you switch to your browser and hit *refresh* you will actually see something along the lines of:

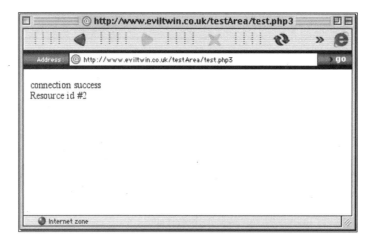

The variable `$result` is a resource within the PHP script that we can get our variables out of. To do this, we are going to create a little loop to go through the returned variables and store the values somewhere before sending them out with the echo command. Just before we do, I'm going to introduce another small difference between ActionScript syntax and PHP syntax – the "." operator.
In ActionScript you can concatenate two strings by using either + or `add` as in:

```
sentence = "hello " add "world";
```

or

```
sentence = "hello " + "world";
```

In both cases the variable `sentence` would equal "`hello world`". In PHP, you can achieve the same result using "." like this:

```
$sentence = "hello " . "world";
```

You can also use ".=" whereas in ActionScript you would use "+=". It's a small difference but a very important one. If you were unaware of it, the next block of code would make little sense:

```
<?

// connect to database
$link = mysql_connect(localhost, "username", "password");
if($link==1)
{
  $choose = mysql_select_db("dbname");
  if($choose != true)
  {
    echo("failed to connect<br>");
    exit;
  }
  else
  {
    echo ("connection success<br>");
    $query = "SELECT * FROM nav";
    $result = mysql_query($query);
    if ($result == false)
    {
      echo ("query failed");
    }
    else
    {
      $counter = 0;        $output = "";
      while ($row = mysql_fetch_array($result))
      {
        $type = stripslashes($row['type']);
        $menuID = stripslashes($row['menuID']);
        $name = stripslashes($row['name']);
        $url = stripslashes($row['url']);
        $output .= "row " . $counter . ": type=" . $type . " menuID=" .
                   $menuID . " name=" . $name . " url=" . $url . "<br>";
         $counter++;
      }
      echo ($output . "<br>");
    }
  }
}

?>
```

Save the file to the server once again and hit refresh in your browser – you should see all the information from our database laid out in a human readable way. This is fine if you want the information to be read by a human, but in our case it is going to read by our Flash movie. So, now we need to format the data as XML in our PHP script. This is not as difficult as it may sound. In the above example we formatted the data into a sentence – this time, we simply need to include some extra bits to make it into XML:

```
<?

// connect to database
$link = mysql_connect(localhost, "username", "password");
if($link==1)
{
```

```php
    $choose = mysql_select_db("dbname");
    if($choose != true)
    {
      echo("failed to connect<br>");
      exit;
    }
    else
    {
      // start with root element
      $menuXML = "<menudata>";
      $query = "SELECT * FROM nav";
      $result = mysql_query($query);
      $numrows = mysql_num_rows($result);
      if ($result == false)
      {
        echo ("query failed");
      }
      else
      {
        while ($row = mysql_fetch_array($result))
        {
          $type = stripslashes($row['type']);
          $menuID = stripslashes($row['menuID']);
          $name = stripslashes($row['name']);
          $url = stripslashes($row['url']);
          if($type == "prime")
          {
            $menuXML .= "<menu name=\"" . $name . "\" url=\"" . $url . "\"
menuID=\""
                        . $menuID . "\" />";
          }
          else if ($type = "sub")
          {
            $menuXML .= "<subItem name=\"" . $name . "\" url=\"" . $url . "\"
                        menuID=\"" . $menuID . "\" />";
          }
        }
      }
    }
    echo ($menuXML . "</menudata>");
    exit;
  }
  ?>
```

You'll notice a few changes to the code here, firstly we have started a variable called $menuXML with <menudata> as its content. If you remember from the earlier XML example, this was the root element in our XML document. We then cycle through the variables returned from the database on each loop through creating a new element, which is added onto the $menuXML variable. Eventually, once we are finished looping through, we echo the result, adding the close to our root element at the same time. If you save this file to the server again and hit *refresh* in your browser you should see nothing. Don't worry, view the source code and you'll see our XML data. Save this final version of the PHP script and upload to the server.

This is the XML created by the PHP script, with returns and tabs added for clarity:

```
<menudata>
  <menu name="home" url="index.html" menuID="1" />
  <menu name="the book" url="" menuID="2" />
  <subItem name="authors" url="authors.html" menuID="2" />
  <subItem name="chapters" url="chapters.html" menuID="2" />
  <subItem name="buy" url="buy.html" menuID="2" />
  <menu name="downloads" url="" menuID="3" />
  <subItem name="source files" url="source_files.html" menuID="3" />
  <subItem name="screen savers" url="screen_savers.html" menuID="3" />
  <subItem name="desktops" url="desktops.html" menuID="3" />
  <menu name="support" url="" menuID="4" />
  <subItem name="help by email" url="email.html" menuID="4" />
  <subItem name="forum" url="forum.html" menuID="4" />
  <subItem name="f.a.q." url="faq.html" menuID="4" />
  <menu name="contact" url="" menuID="5" />
  <subItem name="the publishers" url="contact_publishers.html" menuID="5" />
  <subItem name="the authors" url="contact_authors.html" menuID="5" />
</menudata>
```

The XML data returned by this PHP script is formatted differently from the version we created earlier – this is a much flatter format, where `<subItem>` nodes are siblings to `<menu>` nodes rather than children of them. Consequently, we are going to need to alter the ActionScript that parses the XML.

Open up the `.fla` file we created in the last version of the menu and save it under a new name. For the sake of making life easier, it's worth making a copy of the XML that was output by your script so that you can work on the Flash offline. Test the `getMenus.php3` script in the browser, view the source and copy the XML into your text editor. Save this file as `offline.xml` in the same directory as your Flash movie.

Make your way to the actions on frame 2 of the main timeline. Here, you should see the code that we used to load the XML document. Change the name of the XML file to be loaded to `offline.xml`, so your code now reads as follows:

```
menuXML = new XML();
menuXML.load("offline.xml");
menuXML.onLoad = buildMenu;
stop();
```

If you now go to our `buildMenu()` function on frame 1, we are going to have to change the way this walks through the XML. For a start, we can no longer check to see if a menu node has got child nodes to know if a menu has got a submenu. The simplest way to walk through the XML in this flatter structure is to go through it more than once. On the first run through, we'll create our primary navigation and at the same time, create a new array associated with this menu. Alter the first half of the function to reflect this, as follows:

```
function buildMenu()
{
  holder = new Array();
  holder = menuXML.firstChild.childNodes;
  for(i=0;i<holder.length;i++)
```

```
    {
      if(holder[i].nodeName == "menu")
      {
        _root.attachMovie("primeNav","primeNav" + holder[i].attributes.menuID,
                          zIndex);
        myButton = _root["primeNav" + holder[i].attributes.menuID];
        myButton.title = holder[i].attributes.name;
        if(holder[i].attributes.url != "")
        {
          myButton.url = holder[i].attributes.url;
        }
        myButton._width = myButton.title.length * 10;
        myButton._x = offsetX;
        myButton._y = offsetY;
        myButton.menuNo = holder[i].attributes.menuID;
        offsetX += myButton._width + 1;
        _root["subArray" + holder[i].attributes.menuID] = new Array();
        ++ arrayCount;
        ++ zIndex;
      }
    }
```

In the highlighted sections of code above are a number of changes:

- First, we have changed the way in which the `primeNav` movie clip is numbered, now taking its number from the `menuID` attribute.

- Next we have changed the way in which we check for a URL: instead of checking for a `null` value, we now check that we don't have an empty string (`""`).

- The third highlighted block is an addition – we create a new array for each menu element found and append its name with the `menuID` number. This allows us to populate each array with the relevant submenus and then check the length of that array is not zero before creating the submenu elements. We also increment a variable called `arrayCount` just to make life a little easier later on.

- Finally, we close the `if` and the `for` loop, as we are finished dealing with the primary navigation for now.

Still inside this function, we move on to our `subItem` nodes. The following block of code will start a new loop through the `holder` array – each time the loop encounters a `subItem` node, it will place it in the relevant `subArray`:

```
    for(i=0;i<holder.length;i++)
    {
      if(holder[i].nodeName == "subItem")
      {
        _root["subArray" + holder[i].attributes.menuID].push(holder[i]);
      }
    }
```

We now have a few subArrays, each containing the submenu data relevant to their particular primary navigation button. We also know how many of these subArrays there are because of our arrayCount variable set earlier. So, now we loop through each subArray in turn, pulling out the relevant data and building our submenus. Immediately below the last code we can add the rest of the function – I've included the function in full here so that the context will be more easily understood:

```
function buildMenu()
{
  holder = new Array();
  holder =  menuXML.firstChild.childNodes;
  for(i=0;i<holder.length;i++)
  {
    if(holder[i].nodeName == "menu")
    {
      _root.attachMovie("primeNav","primeNav" + holder[i].attributes.menuID,
                        zIndex);
      myButton = _root["primeNav" + holder[i].attributes.menuID];
      myButton.title = holder[i].attributes.name;
      if(holder[i].attributes.url != "")
      {
        myButton.url = holder[i].attributes.url;
      }
      myButton._width = myButton.title.length * 10;
      myButton._x = offsetX;
      myButton._y = offsetY;
      myButton.menuNo = holder[i].attributes.menuID;
      offsetX += myButton._width + 1;
      _root["subArray" + holder[i].attributes.menuID] = new Array();
      ++ arrayCount;
      ++ zIndex;
    }
  }
  for (i=0;i<holder.length;i++)
  {
    if(holder[i].nodeName == "subItem")
    {
      _root["subArray" + holder[i].attributes.menuID].push(holder[i]);
    }
  }
  for(i=1;i <= arrayCount;i++)
  {
    currentArray = _root["subArray" + i];
    if(currentArray.length > 0)
    {
    myMenu = _root["primeNav" + i];
    myMenu.attachMovie("emptyClip","submenu",10);
    subYpos = myMenu._height;
    subXpos = 0;
    for(j=0;j<currentArray.length;j++)
      {
        if(currentArray[j].nodeName == "subItem")
        {
          myMenu.submenu.attachMovie("subNav", "subButton" + j, j);
          mySub = myMenu.submenu["subButton"+j];
```

```
          mySub._y = subYpos;
          mySub.title = currentArray[j].attributes.name;
          mySub.url = currentArray[j].attributes.url;
          if(mySub.title.length < 8 )
          {
            widthVal = 12;
          }
          else
          {
            widthVal = 8;
          }
          mySub._width = mySub.title.length * widthVal;
          mySub._x = subXpos;
          subXpos += mySub._width;
          mySub.menuNo = i;
          mySub.pageNo = j;
        }
      }
    myMenu.submenu._x = -1000;
    }
  }
}
```

If you test the movie now, it should work exactly as the earlier versions did, but don't forget, it is still loading the data from our `offline.xml` file. Go back to frame 2 and change the code to load the XML from the PHP file we created, like so:

```
menuXML = new XML();
menuXML.load("getMenus.php3");
menuXML.onLoad = buildMenu;
stop();
```

You can now hit F12 to publish the movie, upload it and check it in a browser. It will still function in the same way as the earlier versions, but is now pulling all the information in from a database via PHP. If you are feeling adventurous and have developed a bit of a taste for this back-end stuff, you could try writing an admin application in Flash to add and edit menu items.

# Summary

In this chapter, we explored the use of Flash for creating navigation menus. First, we looked at some of Flash's usability issues and advantages. Then, we looked at our 3-level dynamic Flash menu example:

- Level 1 introduced functions, behavior clips, and attaching objects from the library.

- Level 2 introduced you to the power and simplicity of XML structured data.

- Level 3 brought you a taste of middleware and database integration.

This kind of dynamic Flash not only decreases your file sizes but also makes your life a bit easier. The behavior clip can be used in other projects without you ever having to write that motion code again, and the use of XML/databases means you can leave your clients to update their own content without having to call you!

In the next chapter we further explore dynamic server-side menus, building on some of the concepts we learned in this chapter, and applying them to our DHTML client-side menu functionality.

# 6

- Dynamically populating DHTML menus using middleware, databases and XML

- Breadcrumb Trails

- Includes ASP/SQL Server, ASP/XML, and PHP/MySQL

**Authors: Jon Stephens and Jody Kerr**

# Dynamic Server-Side Menus

In the last three chapters we've looked at a number of ways to create menus to allow users to navigate web sites. Many of these interacted with the user or changed in response to conditions such as the page they were used on, or the date viewed.

These menus (with the exception of the second and third levels, see *Chapter 5*) purely involved dynamism on the client. While there are some advantages to client-side dynamism (most notably response to user actions in real time), there are also some drawbacks. All of these are grounded in the fact that different users use different web browsers on different hardware and software platforms, that offer differing levels of support for scripting, stylesheets, and multimedia plugins, ranging from excellent to mediocre to none. Also, with purely client-side menus, you have to open up the code to update it. Yes, this sounds rather obvious, and not very troublesome to any developer. However, with a dynamic server-side menu, you can make updating the menu as easy as changing some values in a database or an XML file (perhaps via an HTML form).

In this chapter, you will see the following:

- First, we explore a simple breadcrumb trail example, fed from a datasource on the server using some middleware. The three scenarios looked at are:

- MySQL and PHP

- SQL Server and ASP

- XML and ASP

- Next, we look at an advanced example: We take the expanding/collapsing folder view menu from *Chapter 4* (*ch4_ex6*), and dynamically populate it from the server, again using MySQL/PHP, SQL Server/ASP, and XML/ASP

- Lastly, we say a few words about ASP.NET, and its implications on web development

In this chapter, the focus is on dynamism on the server. While we don't enjoy the benefits of direct, real-time interaction with our users, we do gain some benefits from using server-side programming, chief of which is that we control the processing of data and thus what content is sent to the user. We also can design and develop a site in a very modular fashion, especially when we employ a database to store and organize content, including information about how the site itself is organized.

# The Tools Available

There are a number of server-side programming languages and environments available on the Web today, including Perl-CGI, Python, Java and JSP (Java Server Pages), ASP (Active Server Pages), Cold Fusion, and ASP.NET, just to name a few. Methods of data storage range from simple flat text files to high-end, industrial-strength databases such as SQL Server 2000 and Oracle.

As we discussed above, for this chapter we're sticking to PHP/MySQL, ASP/SQL Server, and ASP/XML, because firstly, we don't have space to cover every possibility, and secondly, we feel that we have demonstrated the architecture of our examples well enough for you to go about adapting them for your preferred combination of middleware/database. We feel that the ones we have, represent the most prevalent technology combinations used on the Web today.

We know that this won't suit everybody, but to find out more on adapting these examples for use with other choices of datastore or server-side scripting language, see the appropriate references in the *Resources* section at the end of the book.

Now let's have a brief run-through of the languages and tools we employ during the course of the chapter.

## XML

As you will probably already know, XML allows you to create your own markup vocabularies, and provides a great way to store data separate from presentation. For a more complete introduction to and description of XML, check out the section of Chapter 5 entitled *Level 2 – Introducing XML*, which is where we encounter XML for the first time.

## PHP

PHP provides a server environment for creating dynamic web pages that comes equipped with its own scripting language. Unlike Perl and some others, PHP code can be inserted directly into an otherwise normal HTML page, so only the portions of it that the developer wants to be dynamic require any PHP programming. Its syntax is very similar to languages like C, Perl, Java, and JavaScript, so even if you've never written any PHP code before, you'll probably find that it looks quite familiar, and not too difficult to pick up. PHP supports both user-defined functions and classes, as well as a rich library of built-in functions for common web programming tasks such as working with strings, mathematical functions, regular expressions, images, PDFs, e-mail, and several of the more common databases. Additional libraries are available for a variety of less usual purposes, and new ones are being written all the time. Executable binaries are available for a great many operating systems and hardware platforms, and since PHP is open source, you can also obtain source code and compile your own if you desire.

The best place to obtain information about PHP is the PHP home page at *http://www.php.net/*. There, you can download PHP and get instructions on its installation as well as a copy of the PHP Manual (or search the online version, which features user-submitted comments). The site also features links to online tutorials and a listing of books and other resources, although in our experience, the best way to learn it is simply to download PHP and the PHP Manual and start using them.

PHP is constantly being updated and improved. As of this writing, the most recent stable version was PHP 4.1.1, and this is the version we've used in our examples, which were also tested with version 4.0.6. If you're using a different version and encounter problems with our examples, be sure to check the PHP Manual for any changes since your version was released.

# ASP

Microsoft® Active Server Pages (ASP) is a server-side scripting environment that may be used, like PHP, to create dynamically generated web pages. ASP files are executed on the server via either IIS, or ChiliAsp on UNIX. ASP has native support for two scripting languages: VBScript and JScript, the latter being Microsoft's implementation of JavaScript. There are also modules available for adding support for Perl, Python, and Tcl to ASP – if you program in one or more of these languages, you can obtain these modules from the ActiveState web site (*http://www.activestate.com/*).

# Databases

It's nearly impossible in today's development world to establish a web presence without some sort of database system delivering content and functionality. In developing navigation systems, we can leverage that database functionality to provide highly modular menus, that is, menus that reflect the organization of a site and which will respond to updates in that organization whenever changes are made. In addition to modularity, we are able to create menus that are customized for the user, security level, or content management systems. The general concept behind utilizing database content is the ability to pull menu information that is directly synchronized with the site's functionality.

In the database, each level of the menu is held in a table that contains the text to display, link, `title` attribute, and parent navigation item as a key. By running a query across these tables of navigation information we can create a recordset of information used to create the client-side HTML and JavaScript code used by the menu. In both the SQL Server and MySQL databases we will create tables reflecting the following structures:

*"menus" table: used in the breadcrumb examples*

| Field Name | Type | Description |
| --- | --- | --- |
| id | positive integer, unique, autonumber, not null | Provides a primary key for accessing menu item records |
| link_text | Text (up to 25 characters), not null | Text of menu link |
| link_url | Text (up to 25 characters), not null | URL to which menu link points |
| parent_id | positive integer, null value permitted | id of the section to which the menu link belongs |

*"sections" table: used in the expanding/collapsing menu examples*

| Field Name | Type | Description |
|---|---|---|
| id | positive integer, unique, autonumber, not null | Provides a primary key for accessing section records |
| name | Text (up to 20 characters), not null | Name of section |

*"pages" table: also used in the expanding/collapsing menu examples*

| Field Name | Type | Description |
|---|---|---|
| id | positive integer, unique, autonumber, not null | Provides a primary key for accessing pages records |
| name | Text (up to 25 characters), not null | Text of menu link |
| url | Text (up to 20 characters), not null | URL to which menu link points |
| title | Text (up to 50 characters), not null | Title attribute for the menu link |
| section_id | Positive integer, not null | Id of the section to which the menu link belongs |

Scripts for generating the database and tables, and for populating the tables for both SQL Server and MySQL are provided in the code download.

## MySQL

MySQL is another open source product, a database server developed by the Swedish company MySQL AB and available for download from its web site, *http://www.mysql.com/*, either in source code or precompiled, ready-to-use binary form for a number of platforms. While it is lacking in a few advanced features, such as views, and it's only recently added support for transactions and stored procedures, it can more than make up for this in many applications due to its speed, stability, and ease of setup and use. For the examples below, we tested using versions 3.23.21 and 3.23.39; the most recent stable release at this writing was 3.23.47, and MySQL 4.0.1 was under development.

Like PHP, MySQL is very well documented and a searchable version of the manual is available for use on the MySQL site; an HTML version can be downloaded for offline reference. You can also find links there to tutorials, books, and many applications for use with MySQL including administration tools.

PHP and MySQL seem to have a natural affinity for one another, or perhaps it's just because both are free, open source applications that are fast, have a light footprint on the server, and are relatively easy to install and use. Perhaps that's why so many sites use them in combination.

## Microsoft SQL Server (MS SQL)

Microsoft® SQL Server is a Relational Database Management System (RDBMS) available for the Microsoft Operating Systems. MS SQL supports both OLE and ODBC connections for retrieving data and is bridged to from ASP by ActiveX Data Objects (ADO). For more, see references in the *Resources* section at the end of the book.

# PHP+MySQL and phpMyAdmin

While it's perfectly possible to administer MySQL from the command line, it can be somewhat tedious (and error-prone) to do so. There is a tool that can simplify the job immensely, a browser-based tool known as **phpMyAdmin**. Not surprisingly, it's written in PHP. phpMyAdmin provides quick and dead-easy access to MySQL databases with a well-designed, DHTML-powered visual interface that's simple to understand, even if you're not a database expert. (We believe that it also provides some excellent examples of very usable menus in a Web application, and merits study for that reason as well as learning to use it for its intended purpose.) With it, you can create, drop, modify, import, and export tables, rows, columns, and even entire databases with a few clicks of the mouse, as well as run queries on your database, either by typing them in, or using the forms-based interface provided for the purpose. Another very useful feature is that it provides direct links to relevant portions of the MySQL documentation and download areas in appropriate places.

phpMyAdmin can be obtained most easily from one of two places on the Internet: the developers' site *http://www.phpwizard.net/*, or from its SourceForge project download page at *http://phpmyadmin.sourceforge.net/*. Installation is simply a matter of downloading and unarchiving the PHP files, making a few changes in a single configuration file, then uploading the files to a directory on the server where you wish to deploy it.

Here's a look at the phpMyAdmin main page on one of our development servers:

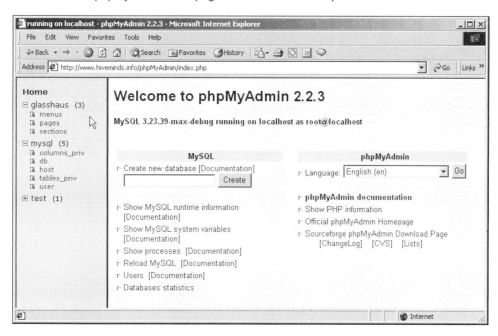

A basic installation of these three applications for development purposes on a PC can be accomplished in as little as one hour, depending on whether or not you already have a web server running on the machine. You may also wish to consider trying the **phpdev** package, an all-in-one installation of PHP 4.0.6 / Apache 1.3.20 / ActivePerl 5.6 / MySQL 3.23 for Windows platforms that's available from the FirePages web site at *http://www.firepages.com.au/phpdev4.htm*.

We won't go into the specifics of installing any of these – the documentation provided with each should take care of most situations that are likely to be encountered. Please note that while a quick setup is possible and perfectly all right for development purposes, it's **not** necessarily secure and you are urged to take the time to make sure that it is so before using it in a production environment! Again, your best course here is to consult the documentation.

## Setting Up the Database Tables and Running Queries

Setting up MySQL databases and tables using phpMyAdmin is almost too easy for words. Let's create a database named **glasshaus** – type the name into the textbox labelled *Create new database* and click the *Create* button. When the page reloads, you'll notice a new item in the left-hand navigation – click on it to bring up the glasshaus database page. Since we've not yet created any tables, you'll see the caption *No tables found in database*. Next, look for the area labelled *Create new table on database glasshaus*. Under *Names:* enter *menus*, and under *Fields:* type in **4**. Now click the *Go* button. You'll be presented with a form where you can enter the information necessary to define the database columns:

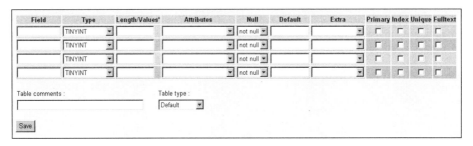

We need a unique ID, text fields to contain the text and `href` attributes of the links we'll be creating, and a parent ID field to contain the ID value of the current item's parent item. Fill in or select the appropriate options until your field creation screen looks like this:

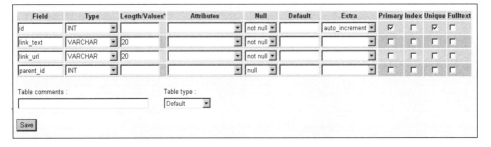

If you wish, you can enter a comment in the *Table comments* field for reference purposes. Hit the *Save* button. Next you'll need to do some data entry – click on the *Insert* link. To make things easier, we've included in the code download for this chapter a file called `menus.sql`, that will create the table and populate it as we've done for our example – in which case, you can skip setting the data types for the fields. Upload it by going to the main screen of your database – find the *Run Queries* area, and select the *Browse* option next to the *Location of the Textfile* textbox. You'll also find that we've included a simple PHP utility in the code package, which you can use to view a dump of all the tables in the database independently of phpMyAdmin, called `db_dump.php`.

To test your copy of the *menus* table, use the *Run Queries* feature we described above. To start with, let's make sure that we have only one record whose `parent_id` value is NULL. Type

```
SELECT * FROM menus WHERE parent_id IS NULL
```

in the indicated text area, and click *Go* to submit the query. You should get back a listing of a single record (the first one) – otherwise, browse through the table and make sure that only this record has a NULL value for `parent_id`. We'll use the **menus** table for our first example – you'll need to repeat these steps in order to set up and populate the two additional tables listed above, or, to save yourself some typing you can use the SQL files `sections.sql` and `pages.sql` that are also included in the download package.

## Accessing SQL Server with Enterprise Manager

While a command-line environment for accessing SQL Server does exist, most people use the *Enterprise Manager* that comes bundled with SQL Server. It is also available as part of the *Client Tools Package*. Since Enterprise Manager and SQL server are so widely documented and simple to use, we will not discuss them in the same detail as phpMyAdmin.

## Breadcrumb Trails

A common feature on large, complex sites is what's sometimes called a **Breadcrumb Trail**. This is basically a list of links that reflects a site's organisation. For example, in the figure below, taken from *macromedia.com*, the highlighted breadcrumb trail shows that the current page is the *Press Room*, which is a "child" of the *Company* page in the site hierarchy, which in turn is a "child" of the main home page:

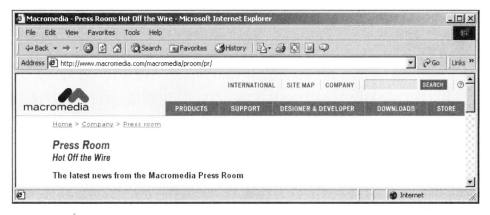

Now let's put the `menus` table to work for us, and build a simple breadcrumb trail example for our OurCo web site. First we will look at the PHP/MySQL scenario, then ASP/SQL Server, and last but not least ASP/XML. Whatever scenario you decide to utilize, the breadcrumb trail should end up looking something like this:

# Example 1: PHP/MySQL Breadcrumb Trail Header

We'll do this with a piece of reusable PHP code that determines which page it's currently loaded into, finds its parent page, and then the parent of that page, and so on until it's reached the main home page of the site. At this point, there are no more parents, so we'll build and output a horizontal list of links to the page, as shown above.

If you look at any of the PHP files in the *ch6_ex1* folder of the code download, you'll see only a single line of actual PHP code:

```
<?php include("includes/breadcrumb.inc"); ?>
```

All the rest is plain old HTML. Since the PHP we're going to use is identical on every page, we're going to place it in a **Server-Side Include** (**SSI**) and tell PHP to add this code to the page and execute it when the page is being served. (This is similar to what we did with `.js` and `.css` files in *Chapters 3* and *4*, except that they are parsed on the client-side, whereas the files that are included using an SSI are parsed on the server, and the result sent to the client.) There are other, language-independent ways of using SSI, but PHP has a convenient `include()` function just for this purpose, so that's what we will use in this, and the following example.

In a production setting, you should take steps to insure that visitors can't view the source of your includes, particularly if you store sensitive information such as passwords in them. Here are three things that can be done:

- Make sure the server's set so that `.inc` files are parsed as PHP; this prevents users from viewing the unprocessed source in a web browser.

- Use the `.php` file extension for your includes.

- Place the includes in a directory that can be accessed by your PHP pages, but not directly from the Web.

All that being said, let's jump into the code listing for `breadcrumb.inc`:

```
<?php
```

We mark the beginning of PHP code with this tag rather than `<?` (or the ASP-style `<%` which can be used if PHP is configured to allow it) because it's XML-compliant, and in these days of XHTML a good habit to get into. We connect to the MySQL server, and select the database; as you can see the first 4 lines tell the script the name of the MySQL server to connect to (in this case, "`localhost`"), the user ID to log on with ("`jon`"), this user's password ("" – that is, we've left this user's password blank), and the database to log in to ("`glasshaus`", which should be the same). You'll most likely need to edit the first 3 of these, since the MySQL setup on your own server will no doubt be different. Check the MySQL and phpMyAdmin documentation for information on how to set up database user accounts, or on how to use the default login.

```
$server="localhost";
$user="jon";
$password="";
$database="glasshaus";
```

We establish a connection to the MySQL server, and tell the server to which database we want to direct our queries. Note the use of `or die("...")` to alert us to any fatal errors in these operations.

```
$mydb=mysql_connect($server,$user,$password)
    or die("<p>User $user has failed to connect to MySQL server $server.</p>");
mysql_select_db($database,$mydb)
    or die("<p>Failed to select database $database.</p>");
```

We're going to put our links in a single-row table. We store the HTML for the beginning and end of the table in appropriately named variables:

```
$table_start="<table border=\"1\" bordercolor=\"#000033\" bgcolor=\"#CCCCCC\"";
$table_start.=" cellpadding=\"2\" cellspacing=\"1\">\n<tr>\n";
$table_end="</tr>\n</table>\n";
```

We then set an output variable to an empty string; we'll use this variable to store the HTML making up our table cells as we create them.

```
$output="";
```

Here's where we get the filename, less the `.php` extension.

```
$curr_url=explode(".",basename($PHP_SELF));
```

If we're not already on the home page, then we start to build a breadcrumb trail (if we are on the home page, we'll indicate that as well, as we'll see towards the end of this example).

```
if($curr_url[0]!="index")
{
```

If we're elsewhere on the site, we use the filename to build a query, which we use to obtain the appropriate text to write to the page, as well as the `id` of the current page's parent. Since we know the names of the fields whose values we wish to retrieve, we use the `mysql_fetch_assoc()` function, which returns the record in the form of an associative array or hash.

```
$query="SELECT link_text,link_url,parent_id FROM menus WHERE
        link_url='$curr_url[0]' LIMIT 1";
$result=mysql_query($query)
    or die("<p>Query $query failed to execute.</p>");
if($row=mysql_fetch_assoc($result))
{
  $text=$row["link_text"];
  $parent=$row["parent_id"];
```

We don't need a link to the current page, just a cell containing the text.

```
$output="<td align=\"center\" valign=\"middle\" title=\"YOU ARE
        HERE.\">$text</td>\n";
```

Now that we know the parent of the current page in the site hierarchy, we'll repeat a loop to make successive queries for the parent pages and write table cells containing links to them, starting with the current parent, and continuing until we run out of pages that have parents.

```
$flag=TRUE;
while($flag)
{
    $query="SELECT link_text,link_url,parent_id FROM menus WHERE id=$parent
            LIMIT 1";
    $result=mysql_query($query)
        or die("<p>Query $query failed to execute.</p>");
    if(mysql_num_rows($result)!=0)

    {
        $row=mysql_fetch_assoc($result);
        $text=$row["link_text"];
        $url=$row["link_url"];
```

We update the value of $parent here. We'll use it in the query at the top of the loop,

```
        $parent=$row["parent_id"];
```

unless, of course, it's a null value, in which case we can't go any higher in the chain. When we've reached that point, we set the flag variable to FALSE so that we'll break out of the loop:

```
        if(is_null($parent))
            $flag=FALSE;
```

Note that we concatenate the latest parent cell in front of the previous ones, so that when we've finished, the header cells will run from left to right, starting with the cell containing the *HOME* link, down to the cell containing the title of the current page:

```
        $output="<td align=\"center\" valign=\"middle\"><a href=\"$url.php\"
                title=\"$text\">$text</a></td>\n" . $output;
        }
    }
    }
}
```

If we're already on the home page, we need only a single cell containing an appropriate greeting:

```
else
    $output="<td> = WELCOME TO OURCO.COM = </td>";
echo $table_start . $output . $table_end;
?>
```

Now we have a simple yet useful component that we can easily deploy across a site. Anytime you add a new page to the site, just add a new record containing the appropriate information to the menus table, and the header's ready to go. Here's what it looks like when we load the 2002 Press Releases Page (y2002.php):

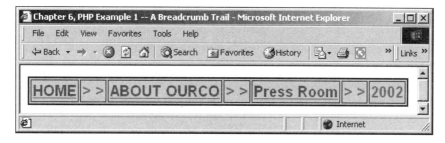

Note that it doesn't matter how the pages might actually be organized on the server, nor how many levels of organization we require, either for the site as a whole or within any given section or subsection: if we only need two levels for the *OFFICES* section and seven for the *ABOUT OURCO* section, our header component can handle it. If the site is particularly large and some pages are located in different directories, machines, subdomains, or even separate domains altogether, this shouldn't affect our breadcrumb header either, so long as the database tables and field values reflect the organisation we wish to present to users of the site.

Neither do we have any worries here about client scripting or plugin support. We've used a bit of CSS to dress up the header text; otherwise, it's completely self-contained and the desired organisation and functionality is available to any browser on any platform. For this reason, we've deliberately kept this example very simple, but we could change it or expand on it in a number of ways – for example, we could cause the links to be displayed vertically instead of horizontally by making a few changes in the HTML generated by the script. We could also use image links instead of text, just by altering a line or two to write an `<img>` tag pointing to (for instance) `images/y2002.gif`, and uploading the appropriate images (or by making use of PHP's own image-creation libraries); we could add a JavaScript rollover function to those images, or embed a set of Flash clips to provide more sophisticated effects. We can do all these things without having to change the structure of the database table that tells PHP how the site is organized, and without impairing its basic usefulness. When you visit the web site that accompanies this book, you'll be able to see and obtain client-side and server-side code for a DHTML "pulldown" or "flyout" menu generated using this same MySQL table and recursive methodology to trace the parent-child relationships and build the menu accordingly.

# Example 2: ASP/SQL Server Breadcrumb Trail Header

As in the preceding PHP example, we will now create a simple Breadcrumb Trail Header in ASP with Microsoft SQL Server providing our data. While these languages are similar, there are numerous syntactical differences between them.

Our ASP breadcrumb will also be contained within an include file. The ASP syntax is as follows:

```
<!--#include file="breadcrumb.asp"-->
```

Our ASP code file, `breadcrumb.asp` contains the entire ASP and VBScript programming necessary to generate the breadcrumb trail. The initial step involves connecting to the database and returning an ADO Recordset of information. Our example uses a DSN-based connection style. Note that in ASP code, `<%` indicates an ASP code block:

```
<%
  Dim dbConn  'As ADODB.Connection
  Dim rs      'As ADODB.RecordSet
  Dim strSQL  'As String
  Dim Flag    'As Boolean

  Set dbConn = Server.CreateObject("ADODB.Connection")
  dbConn.ConnectionString = "Provider=sqloledb;Data Source=serverName;
                            Initial Catalog=glasshaus;User Id=userName;
                            Password=password;"
  dbConn.Open
```

The three `Dim` statements declare and initialize the variables needed in this code. The information following the single quote is a comment in ASP. I have included what the variable types are as comments because VBScript doesn't support strongly typed variables thus all variables are treated as variants when declared. You'll note the connection string in the code listing above. For this to work on your machine you will need to add the serverName, userName, and password. Now that we have an active connection to the database, we need to generate the SQL statement necessary to return the information we need.

ASP handles system information differently from PHP. To determine our page we need to access the `ServerVariables` collection to determine the file path. From there, it is a matter of removing the unnecessary additional information:

```
  sPathInfo = Request.ServerVariables("Path_Info")
  arrPathInfo = Split(sPathInfo, "/")
  sPathInfo = arrPathInfo(UBound(arrPathInfo))
  arrPathInfo = Split(sPathInfo, ".")
  sPathInfo = arrPathInfo(Lbound(arrPathInfo))
```

This piece of code grabs the path to the current file and returns the part of the filename that precedes the period.

Next we create the table where the information will reside:

```
  sTableStart = "<table border=""1"" bordercolor=""#000033"" bgcolor=""#CCCCCC"""
  sTableStart = sTableStart & " cellpadding=""2"" cellspacing=""1""><tr>"
  sTableEnd ="</tr></table>")
```

We don't need to generate a breadcrumb trail if we are on the home page (index.html) so we initially test to make sure we're not on that page.

```
  If Lcase(sPathInfo) <> "index" Then
```

Now that we have the title of the page being loaded and we've determined that it isn't the index page, we can use that information to determine and build the breadcrumb trail through a successive series of recursive database calls. Before we do that, we need to begin constructing the HTML table that will contain the output.

```
strSQL = "SELECT link_text,link_url,parent_id FROM menus WHERE _
        link_url='" & sPathInfo & "'"
```

As the database information is queried ASP is used to dynamically create the HTML for the breadcrumb trail while inserting information returned by the queries.

```
Set rs = dbConn.Execute(strSQL)
 sPageContent = "<td align=""center"" valign=""middle"" title=""YOU ARE " &_
            "HERE.>"  & rs("link_text") & "</td>" & vbcrlf
Flag = True
Do while Flag = True
strSQL = "Select link_text, link_url, parent_id FROM menus WHERE id = " &_
        rs("parent_id")
Set rs = dbConn.Execute(strSQL)
sPageContent = "<td align=""center"" valign=""middle""><b>&gt; &gt;</b></td>" &
            vbsrlf & sPageContent
sPageContent = "<td align=""center"" valign=""middle""><a href=""" &
        rs("link_url")_ &            ".asp"">" & rs("link_text") &
            "</a></td>" & vbcrlf & sPageContent_
If rs("parent_id") = "" Then
  Flag = False

Loop
```

The loop structure used here traces the navigation structure back from its endpoint by using a Do ... While loop until the parent id reaches zero (the root navigation page).

```
Else
    SPageContent="<td> = WELCOME TO OURCO.COM = </td>"
End If
    Response.Write(sTableStart & sPageContent & sTableEnd)
%>
```

At this point our ASP has run and created the breadcrumb trail for us. While this does function well, there are a large number of database queries in this piece of code, particularly in our recursive function. In a heavy-usage production environment this may cause problems due to bandwidth, so it is suggested that you use the XML version in this kind of scenario.

# Example 3: ASP/XML Breadcrumb Trail Header

Because XML is based on nodes and positions within a tree structure, a different approach needs to be taken in processing the data. As it turns out, XML is perfectly suited for navigation-based systems as well as any system where information needs to be stored with a clearly defined hierarchy.

We will use the same basic include structure and file naming as the previous ASP example, except that we will have an additional XML file that stores our data. The XML file looks like this:

```
<root>
<menu link_text ="MAIN">
    <menu2 link_text="OurCo Home Page" link_url="index"
        title="Gateway to the OurCo Website" />
```

```
      <menu2 link_text ="Company News" url="news" title="Happenings Around OurCo" />
      <menu2 link_text ="Press Room" link_url ="press"
             title="Press Releases, and OurCo in the News" />
      <menu2 link_text ="Opportunities" link_url ="opp"
             title="Employment and Other Opportunities with OurCo" />
   </menu>
   <menu link_text ="OFFICES">
      <menu2 link_text ="Aurora" link_url ="aurora" title="Aurora, Colorado, USA" />
      <menu2 link_text ="Birmingham" link_url ="birm" title="Birmingham, UK" />
      <menu2 link_text ="Buenos Aires" link_url ="buen"
             title="Buenos Aires, Argentina" />
      <menu2 link_text ="Cartgagena" link_url ="carta" title="Cartagena, Colombia" />
      <menu2 link_text ="Kempsey" link_url ="kemps" title="Kempsey, NSW, Australia" />
      <menu2 link_text ="Mumbai" link_url ="mumb" title="Mumbai, India" />
      <menu2 link_text ="Scottsdale" link_url ="scotts"
             title="Scottsdale, Arizona, USA" />
      <menu2 link_text ="Oslo" link_url ="oslo" title="Oslo, Norway" />
      <menu2 link_text ="Kiev" link_url ="kiev" title="Kiev, Ukraine" />
   </menu>
   <menu title="PRODUCTS">
      <menu2 link_text ="Thingoes" link_url ="thing"
             title="Thingoes for Home and Industry" />
      <menu2 link_text ="Gizmoes" link_url ="giz"
             title="Every Gizmo You Can Think Of!" />
      <menu2 link_text ="Widgets" link_url ="widg"
             title="Widgets for Every Conceivable Use" />
      <menu2 link_text ="Whatsi" link_url ="what"
             title="Find a Whatsis Here, from Tiny to Humongous" />
   </menu>
   <menu link_text ="SERVICES">
      <menu2 link_text ="Estimates" link_url="estim"
             title="Know What You'll Spend, Before You Spend It" />
      <menu2 link_text ="Deliveries" link_url="deliver"
             title="Straight from OurCo to Your Front Door" />
      <menu2 link_text ="Refunds and Exchanges" link_url ="refetch"
             title="Wrong Size? Wrong Shape? No Worries!" />
      <menu2 link_text ="Specifications" link_url ="specs"
             title="Let Us Help You Figure Out Exactly What You Need" />
   </menu>
   <menu link_text ="ABOUT OURCO">
      <menu2 link_text ="Corporate Info" link_url ="corpinfo"
             title="Profile of OurCo: Who We Are, What We Do" />
      <menu2 link_text ="Mission Statement" link_url ="misstate"
             title="A Company with Purpose" />
      <menu2 link_text ="Management" link_url ="mgt" title="Management Profiles" />
      <menu2 link_text ="Company History" link_url ="cohist"
             title="OurCo's Story: Where We've Been, Where We're Going" />
   </menu>
   <menu title="CONTACT US">
      <menu2 link_text ="Customer Service" link_url ="cust"
             title="Ready and Able to Help!" />
      <menu2 link_text ="Sales Enquiries" link_url ="sales"
             title="Ready to Buy? We're Ready to Sell!" />
      <menu2 link_text ="Telephone and Fax Numbers" link_url ="telfax"
```

```
            title="Ring Us, Toll-Free, 24/7" />
  <menu2 link_text ="General Information" link_url="geninfo"
            title="Couldn't Find It Elsewhere? Try Looking Here..." />
</menu>
</root>
```

You'll notice that while the XML file stores relatively the same information as our database tables, it's held in a totally different fashion. While the data appears different, logically the concept is also similar: parse a data collection, determine the link hierarchy, and represent that as an HTML breadcrumb trail.

Instead of connecting to a database, we need to locate and load the XML data file. Since we're using a centrally located XML file, we already know where it is located and we can utilize the `Server.MapPath` directive to convert the relative web location to the true file path on the server. If you want to store your XML file where it cannot be easily loaded in a web browser, you would place the file outside of the web space and use the actual file path to load it. Next, an XML object is invoked, and used to load the XML file.

```
Dim sBreadcrumbTrail, sHolder
sSrcFile = Server.MapPath("menu.xml")
Set objXML = Server.CreateObject("Microsoft.XMLDOM")
objXML.async = False
objXML.Load (sSrcFile)
```

The `Set objXML = Server.CreateObject("Microsoft.XMLDOM")` line creates an instance of the XML object in our code for loading and manipulating the information in the XML file. Of special note is the `objXML.async = false` line. This sets the ability for asynchronous download to `false`, forcing the code to fully load the XML file before continuing. This is critical as it is quite difficult to parse a file that isn't already in memory. As was explained in the previous ASP example, we need to generate the file information using the `Request.ServerVariables` collection. To do this, we grab the path of the file and use the `Split` command to return the part of the filename that precedes the ".".

```
sPathInfo = Request.ServerVariables("Path_Info")
arrPathInfo = Split(sPathInfo, "/")
sPathInfo = arrPathInfo(UBound(arrPathInfo))
arrPathInfo = Split(sPathInfo, ".")
sPathInfo = arrPathInfo(Lbound(arrPathInfo))

GetPageNode(objXML.childNodes)
```

One thing that's different in this approach is that we are immediately utilizing a subprocedure (`GetPageNode()`) to perform the work. Because XML is a hierarchical data structure, rather than a row and column one, we can effectively utilize recursive procedures to perform analyses and HTML generation. When the XML document is loaded it is positioned at the root-level node in the menu. In our XML file, we are not using the root node for navigation or information purposes, but as a containing element for the entire menu.

When the subprocedure is run, we immediately declare two additional node objects, `objCurrentNode` and `objTempNode`, to be used later. `sBreadCrumbTrail` is a string variable to hold the HTML output of our procedures. We also initiate a counter to keep track of the node depth, or the depth within the XML document of our traversal so that we can tell how far we will need to back out once we have found our node.

```
Sub GetPageNode (ByVal objNodes)
Dim objCurrentNode, objTempNode
Dim sBreadCrumbTrail 'String
   iNodeIterator = iNodeIterator + 1
```

Next, a `for...` loop is initiated to iterate through the collection of nodes passed to the subprocedure.

```
For Each objCurrentNode In objNodes
```

We test to see if the current node is the node for the page. If it is, then we continue through the code block. If it isn't, we skip the code block.

```
If (sPathInfo = objCurrentNode.getAttribute("url")) Then
```

We set the node to a temporary node so that we can manipulate the temporary node without altering the position of the external looping structure. We also create a holder variable (`sHolder`), because we will be building our HTML backwards and cannot directly use `Response.Write` to output it. Finally we set the depth of the node so we know how far we need to traverse backwards in building the breadcrumb trail. We also create a `for...` loop that loops backwards (for example, 3,2,1) for looping back out of the XML tree.

```
iNodeDepth = iNodeIterator
sHolder = ""
Set objTempNode = objCurrentNode

For iReverseIterator = iNodeDepth to 0 Step -1
```

When our loop variable reaches one, we are at the final loop element, which is the outermost XML node. Because the main title for our breadcrumb trail is different from the other parts, we need to test for it and apply the appropriate formatting.

```
If iReverseIterator = 0 Then
    sHolder = "<td>" & objTempNode.getAttribute("title") & "</td>" & vbcrlf
```

If it is not the root element then we apply the formatting as above. The `getAttribute()` method allows us to pull the value of the attribute (either `link_url` or `link_text`) and insert it into the generated HTML.

```
Else
    sHolder = "<td align=""center"" valign=""middle""><b>&gt; &gt;</b></td>"_
            & vbsrlf & sPageContent & sBreadCrumbTrail
    sHolder = "<td><a href=""" & objTempNode.getAttribute("link__url") & _
            ".asp"">"_ & objTempNode.getAttribute("link_text") &
            "</a></td>"_ & vbcrlf
End If
sHolder = sHolder & sBreadcrumbTrail
sBreadcrumbTrail = sHolder
```

Here we maintain our HTML order by appending the new generated information in front of the old, and then reassigning that value to our global variable `sBreadcrumbTrail` that will eventually be used in the display.

Since we are looping back over the structure, we need to make sure that before the loop repeats itself we have a new node to work with, in this case, the parent node.

```
    If iReverseIterator >= 0 Then
      Set objTempNode = objTempNode.parentNode
    End If
```

In our initial loop, we needed to disregard a node if it wasn't the one we were looking for. It may, however, be the parent of the node we are looking for, so we need to then test its child nodes if it has any.

```
    Next
  ElseIf objCurrentNode.hasChildNodes Then
    GetPageNode(objCurrentNode.childNodes)
  End If
```

Finally, if it's not the node we want, we need to make sure that the depth is removed from our depth variable as we next test the node's sister node.

```
  Next
  iNodeIterator = iNodeIterator -1
End Sub
```

Now there are just a few last issues to wrap up. Once the subprocedure is done parsing and creating, we need to propend and append the HTML table formatting and finally `Response.Write()` the information into our page:

```
sBreadcrumbTrail = "<table border=1 bordercolor=""#000033"" bgcolor=""#CCCCCC"" _
                cellpadding=2 cellspacing=1><tr>" & sBreadcrumbTrail & _
                "</tr></table>"
Response.Write(sBreadcrumbTrail)
```

The final output is very similar to the screenshots we have already seen before, so refer to those for a visual idea of the output.

# Advanced Example – Populating a Client-side Script

Now we shall move on to show how to dynamically populate an advanced DHTML menu from a server-side data store, using our three by-now-familiar data store/middleware combinations. We'll reuse the DHTML expanding/collapsing "folder view" menu from *Chapter 4, Expanding/Collapsing Menu Example 1*, but with some changes. Here's what the menu looks like when the example site's "Refunds and Exchanges" page is loaded into the browser:

# Example 4: Advanced PHP/MySQL Example

First, we populate the menu with data from MySQL, using PHP. This time round, some of the JavaScript code for the expanding/collapsing menu has been rewritten using information stored in two database tables. This version of the site is organized a bit differently – we don't have actual pages corresponding to section headings, and we don't have the need to employ recursion to track parents and parents of parents and so on.

We'll use the **sections** table to store the section names, and the **pages** table to store the text, URLs, `title` attributes for the links, and the section to which each belongs. (**Note**: If you've not already created and populated the sections and pages tables, you'll need to do so, using the SQL scripts we've provided in the code download, before this example will work.) Since we already have stored filenames for pages that are independent of the page names, we make use of that information and adjust the client-side script accordingly.

We'll be using many of the same files as we did in the previous version of this example, so we'll try to omit any repetition and concentrate on what we've changed for this one. If it appears that anything's missing, be sure to check *Chapter 4* (*ch4_ex6*), where any of the JavaScript code that isn't covered here is explained in detail.

Let's start with the file `ch6_ex4.php`:

```
<html>
<head>
  <title>
    Chapter 6, Example 4 -- Expanding/Collapsing Menu #1 Redux (PHP/MySQL Version)
  </title>
  <meta http-equiv="Content-Type" content="text/html; charset=iso-8859-1">
```

If you're wondering where the closing `</head>` and opening `<body>` tags have gone, you'll find them in the `header.inc` file. It may seem odd at first if you've not used PHP includes or SSI before, but it's perfectly permissible, even common, to do this. The trick is to remember that the contents of the included file are inserted into the page before it's served up to users. In other words, the browser doesn't know that the include is there, seeing only the complete page that's assembled from the source file and any includes called from that file. So it's entirely possible for a page on the server to contain many included files, but from the browser's point of view, it's seamless.

```
<?php include("includes/header.inc"); ?>
<table width="100%" cellpadding="0" cellspacing="0" border="0">
  <tr>
    <td width="275" bgcolor="#006699">
      <img src="images/list.gif" width="5" height="800" border="0"></td>
    <td width="70%">
    <p> </p><p> </p><p> </p><p> </p>
    <p> </p><p> </p><p> </p></td>
  </tr>
</table>
</body>
</html>
```

Looks like there's quite a lot missing there – but if you've guessed already that the `header.inc` file is where all the action's really happening, then you're right on track – let's take a look:

```
<link rel="stylesheet" type="text/css" href="styles/content.css">
<link rel="stylesheet" type="text/css" href="styles/menu.css">
<script type="text/javascript" language="JavaScript" src="scripts/xblayer.js">
</script>
<script type="text/javascript" language="JavaScript"
        src="scripts/menu_driver.js">
</script>
</head>
<body background="images/bluebg.gif" bgcolor="#000066" text="#000000"
        leftmargin="0" topmargin="0" marginwidth="0" marginheight="0">
```

Everything thus far is exactly the same as it was before, and there's no need to re-examine the CSS or JavaScript files referenced above, because they're also identical to their counterparts from *Chapter 4*. Here's where things start looking different: gone is the reference to `create_menu.js`. Because we need to access the database on the server as the page is generated, we've moved that code into this server-side include where we can programmatically create those portions that require it.

As you might expect, we start out by connecting to the MySQL server and the database we'll be using. (As with the PHP version of the breadcrumb example, you'll probably need to edit the values in the first 3 lines below to match those needed for your MySQL installation.)

```
<?php
  $server="localhost";
  $user="jon";
  $password="";
  $database="glasshaus";

  $mydb=mysql_connect($server,$user,$password)
    or die("<p class=\"fatalError\">User $user has failed to connect to MySQL
            server $server.</p>");
  mysql_select_db($database,$mydb)
    or die("Failed to select database $database.");
?>
```

Since we're going to be generating JavaScript code in addition to HTML, we have to open a `<script>` block. We could do so with `echo` statements, but the browser doesn't care either way.

```
<script type="text/javascript" language="JavaScript">
<!--
  var startHeight=50;
  var panelHeight=20;
```

Now we send a query to MySQL to obtain all the records in the sections table and the number of records contained. We could have used the SQL `COUNT()` function to get the latter, but we'll need the records themselves shortly in any case, so we just use the equivalent PHP function on the result set. Note the closing `</script>` tag, which is necessary to permit the user to see the error message if the query fails.

```
<?php
  $query="SELECT * FROM sections ORDER BY id ASC";
  $result=mysql_query($query)
    or die("</script>The query $query has failed.");
  $num_sections=mysql_num_rows($result);
```

Now we use that value to `echo` a series of JavaScript statements, which declare and initialize a variable, as well as several JavaScript arrays:

```
echo "var numSections=$num_sections;\n";
echo "var sectionNames=new Array(numSections);\n";
echo "var pageNames=new Array(numSections);\n";
echo "var pageURLs=new Array(numSections);\n";
echo "var pageTitles=new Array(numSections);\n\n";
```

By way of comparison, here's the code that's seen by the client:

```
var numSections=6;
var sectionNames=new Array(numSections);
var pageNames=new Array(numSections);
var pageURLs=new Array(numSections);
var pageTitles=new Array(numSections);
```

Since JavaScript doesn't have built-in support for 2-dimensional arrays, we have to declare each sub-array explicitly using either array literals or successive calls to its `Array()` constructor function. When we were coding these by hand in *Chapter 4*, it was easier to use array literals. However, here we'd have to do quite a bit of juggling to assemble the elements of each subarray in the proper order, and it's necessary that all of these and the elements they contain bear the correct indices in order for the script to function as required. So we take the latter course:

```
for($i=0;$i<$num_sections;$i++)
{
    echo "pageNames[$i]=new Array();\n";
    echo "pageURLs[$i]=new Array();\n";
    echo "pageTitles[$i]=new Array();\n";
}
```

The client-side code we've generated looks like this:

```
pageNames[0]=new Array();
pageURLs[0]=new Array();
pageTitles[0]=new Array();
pageNames[1]=new Array();
pageURLs[1]=new Array();
pageTitles[1]=new Array();
pageNames[2]=new Array();
```

And so on. Were it being written by a human, this wouldn't be terribly efficient or easily maintainable. However, it's all the same to a web browser's JavaScript interpreter, which doesn't care about the order of the declarations, just as long as they're indexed or labelled properly. It will quite happily keep track of things for us, provided that we haven't left out anything.

Next we write variable assignments that the JavaScript uses for the section names. Note that we subtract one from the **id** values we get from the table because the auto number sequences we've defined for these begin with 1, while array indices in PHP begin with zero.

```
echo "\n\n";

while($row=mysql_fetch_assoc($result))
{
```

```
    $section=$row["id"]-1;
    $name=$row["name"];
    echo "sectionNames[$section]=\"$name\";\n";
}
echo "\n";
```

We've taken care of all the **sections** data. Now it's time to retrieve the **pages** data, and write it to the page in a form that the client-side script can use, which means we need to guarantee the ordering of two sets of indices. As you'll recall from *Chapter 4,* we use JavaScript arrays to build the `<div>` elements making up the menus, and to write their `id` attributes; the scheme by which the `id` attributes are created includes a numbering convention, and the function that opens and closes each section makes use of this "indexing".

In the outer loop of the next block of code, we iterate through all of the sections. We generate and then submit a query returning a recordset that contains all the pages belonging to that section, ordered by their names.

```
for ($section_count=0;$section_count<$num_sections;$section_count++)
{
  $curr_section=$section_count+1;
  $query="SELECT name,url,title FROM pages WHERE section_id=$curr_section ORDER
        BY name ASC";
```

Once again we precede the `die()` error message with a `</script>` tag so that the user will actually be able to see the error message in the event that the query fails.

```
  $result=mysql_query($query)
    or die("</script>The query $query has failed.");
  $page_count=0;
```

The inner loop fetches the records whose **section_id** field (which identifies a menu item's parent, as you'll recall) matches the current value as determined by the outer loop. Thanks to the ORDER BY clause, we know they'll be given to us in the order of their names. We fetch each record as an associative array, so that we can easily obtain the value of each column.

```
  while($row=mysql_fetch_assoc($result))
  {
    $name=$row["name"];
    $url=$row["url"];
```

Some of the `title` attributes contain apostrophes, and in order not to cause JavaScript errors when we `document.write()` them to the page, we need to escape these characters, that is, we replace each instance of an apostrophe or single quote mark with `\'`.

```
    $title=str_replace("'","\'",$row["title"]);
```

Now we can write the JavaScript assignment statements that populate the arrays.

```
    echo "pageNames[$section_count][$page_count]=\"$name\";\n";
    echo "pageURLs[$section_count][$page_count]=\"$url\";\n";
    echo "pageTitles[$section_count][$page_count]=\"$title\";\n";
```

The first index of each of these variables corresponds to a section; the second serves to identify each page within a given section. By way of example, for the third page in the second section, the text of the corresponding link will be `pageNames[1][2]`, the URL to which this link points is `pageURLs[1][2]`, and the `title` attribute given to the `<a>` element is `pageTitles[2][1]`.

Finally, we increment `$page_count` before fetching the next row from the result set. Note that once we've retrieved all the records from the current result set, and return to the outer loop, we reset the value of this variable to zero before control reverts to the inner loop again.

```
        $page_count++;
    }
  }
?>
```

This isn't the only way we could have accomplished our task. We could have retrieved all of the **names** records at once using

```
SELECT * FROM pages ORDER BY section_id ASC,name ASC
```

then tested each time through the **while** block for a change in the **section_id** value, and restarted the incrementing of `$page_count` at that point. For a very large number of sections and pages this might be preferable, in order to minimize the number of database queries. However, given the relatively small number of records we're dealing with here, it seemed simpler just to use the `for...` loop and a separate call to the database for each set of pages. We also could have written the `<div>` elements making up the menu using PHP instead of JavaScript, and eliminated much of the need for arrays at all. However, by using the code that already exists, we minimize possible errors in "translating" it into PHP. There is also the fact that, if the menu weren't generated using JavaScript, it would then be visible to JavaScript-incapable browsers, whereas by keeping the generation of the menu HTML client-side, we can easily drop in alternative content for such user agents using a `<noscript>` block.

The rest of the JavaScript is the same as for *Chapter 4*, except that we're pulling the links' `href` attributes from the database so they're no longer tied directly to the names of the pages, and we've added one small enhancement, a unique `title` attribute for each link that further describes the linked page. Here's the relevant portion of that code, with the part that's directly affected highlighted:

```
for(var i=0;i<numSections;i++)
{
  // ...omitted code; same as before...
  lastItem=pageNames[i].length;

  for(j=0;j<lastItem;j++)
  {
  // ...omitted code; same as before...
    if(isCurrent)
      output+="<b class=\"current\" title=\"You are here.\">";
    else
      output+="<a href=\""+pageURLs[i][j]+".php\" class=\"page\"
              title=\""+pageTitles[i][j]+"\">";

    output+=pageNames[i][j];

    if(isCurrent)
      output+="</b>";
    else
      output+="</a>";
```

```
      if(j==lastItem-1)
        output+="</div>\n";
      else
        output+="<br>\n";
    }
  }

  document.write(output);

  //-->
</script>
```

The end result is a site component that interacts with and helps to inform visitors, and which can be updated quickly and easily across a site without editing any of the code that generates it.

> *Note: We've included a "bonus" set of PHP files in the code download (in the* ch6_ex4b *folder), which are a reworking of* Example 7 *from* Chapter 4 *similar to what we've done above for* Example 6 *from that same chapter. Considerations of space prevent us from including a detailed explanation of them here. They were created during the development of material for this chapter and we've included them in the download package for your study and possible use.*

# Example 5: Advanced ASP/SQL Server Example

Now let's look at doing the same thing, except that this time we are using ASP to pull data from SQL Server to populate our menu. The approach is similar to the PHP one: determine what JavaScript code needs to be dynamically generated to support the menu, extract the data from the database, and format it appropriately. To ensure that our ASP processes correctly, all pages that need this functionality have the extension .asp.

Initially, we need to include our ASP menu file into the JavaScript within our page.

```
<script type="text/javascript" language="JavaScript">
<!--
var startHeight=50;
var panelHeight=20;
<!--#include file="menu.asp"-->
```

This means that we are recreating the variable declarations for the JavaScript with ASP and SQL Server rather than having them in the JavaScript code itself. Since all of our information is in the server, we need to start our include file (menu.asp) by declaring a few important variables and creating the connection to our database:

```
<%
  Dim dbConn        'As ADODB.Connection
  Dim rs            'As ADODB.Recordset
  Dim strSQL        'As String


  Set dbConn = Server.CreateObject("ADODB.Connection")
  dbConn.ConnectionString = "Provider=sqloledb;Data Source=serverName;
                            Initial Catalog=glasshaus;User Id=userName;
                            Password=password;"
  dbConn.Open
```

The first piece of information needed to create the menu is the number of sections within the menu. The count() directive in the SQL statement returns a count of the number of rows of data in the section table.

```
strSQL="SELECT COUNT (*) FROM sections"
```

In our first section of output we generate the variable declarations for the number of sections and the first set of arrays. You will note the vbcrlf at the end of each line. vbcrlf is a carriage return in VBScript. It has been added to help format the JavaScript for readability. (Note that we did the same thing using \n in the PHP version.)

```
Set rs = dbConn.Execute(strSQL)
numSections = rs(0)
rs.close
Response.Write("var numSections=" & numSections & ";" & vbcrlf)
Response.Write("var sectionNames=new Array(numSections);"& vbcrlf)
Response.Write("var pageNames=new Array(numSections);" & vbcrlf)
Response.Write("var pageURLs=new Array(numSections);" & vbcrlf)
Response.Write("var pageTitles=new Array(numSections);" & vbcrlf)
```

Next we have to output the declarations of the various arrays for each section:

```
For i = 0 to numSections
  Response.Write("pageNames[" & i & "]=new Array();" & vbcrlf)
  Response.Write("pageURLs[" & i & "]=new Array();" & vbcrlf)
  Response.Write("pageTitles[" & i & "]=new Array();" & vbcrlf)
Next
```

At this point, we need the menu information itself from the database. We will start by generating the information for the section headings. This section performs the SQL query and then uses a do...while...loop structure to iterate across the recordset to write out the sectionNames variable assignments.

```
Response.Write(vbcrlf & vbcrlf)
  strSQL="Select id, name From sections order by ID ASC"
  Set rs = dbConn.Execute(strSQL)
  Do While Not rs.EOF
    Response.Write ("sectionNames[" & (rs("id")-1) & "]=""" & rs("name") & """;" _
                 & vbcrlf)
    rs.MoveNext
  Loop
  rs.Close
```

With this complete, we now need all the information for the subnavigation as well:

```
Response.Write(vbcrlf & vbcrlf)

For i=0 to (numSections-1)
```

Now we need to query the database and get the exact values for all of our menu items.

```
strSQL = "SELECT name,url,title FROM pages WHERE section_id=" & (i+1) & _
         "ORDER BY name ASC"
Set rs = dbConn.Execute(strSQL)
```

Previously we have selected the name, URL and title from the `pages` table where it matches our section number.

```
    pageCount = 0
Do While Not rs.EOF
    Response.Write ("pageNames[" & i & "][" & pageCount & "]=""" & rs("name") & _
                    """;" & vbcrlf)
    Response.Write ("pageURLs[" & i & "][" & pageCount & "]=""" & rs("url") & _
                    """;" & vbcrlf)
    Response.Write ("pageTitles[" & i & "][" & pageCount & "]=""" & rs("title") _
                    & """;" & vbcrlf)
    pageCount = pageCount + 1
    rs.MoveNext
Loop
```

Since there are multiple pages within a section, we need to loop across the information returned from the database to create a variable declaration for each subnavigation item.

Finally, we clean up after ourselves by closing the recordset and the database connection – any time that a database is queried this needs to be done. Forgetting to close recordsets and database connections causes some potentially severe performance issues.

```
    rs.Close
dbConn.Close
    Next
```

Once this section of code has completed, we have successfully created our dynamic menu. The ASP is closed with the `%>` and the rest of the JavaScript resumes.

```
    %>
var output="";
var lastItem;

for(var i=0;i<numSections;i++)
    ...
```

Because of the number of database calls this particular method can cause problems on sites with heavy traffic or overly large menu systems. In that case it would be much more effective to use either a server-side component, a pregenerated include that is created when the database changes, or the XML example below.

# Example 6: Advanced ASP/XML Example

As with our earlier XML based example, we will take a slightly different programmatical approach. For this example, we will be using the same XML file as in the breadcrumb example – the node-tree-based nature of our XML file enables a simple approach to developing the script variable assignments. To begin, we need to open and read the XML file. The file we are creating (`XMLmenu.asp`) will be included into the JavaScript code, just as it was in the ASP/SQL Server example:

```
<%
    sSrcFile = Server.MapPath("menu.xml")
    Set objXML = Server.CreateObject("Microsoft.XMLDOM")
    objXML.async = False
    objXML.Load (sSrcFile)
```

As you will note, we are doing the same as we did with the breadcrumb trail example. Next we will create a looping structure to parse the entire XML file. You will note an extra `For...Each` loop wrapping the functionality – since our XML file uses a containing element to hold all others, we need to account for it, while not necessarily using it in context – this is the purpose of the extra loop.

```
iIterator = 0
sContent = ""
For each objRootNode in objXML.childNodes
For Each objCurrentNode In objRootNode.childNodes
sContent = sContent & "sectionNames[" & iIterator & "]="""" & _
          objCurrentNode.getAttribute("title") & """;" & vbcrlf
Dim objSubCurrentNode, iIterator2
iIterator2 = 0
  For Each objSubCurrentNode in objCurrentNode.childNodes
     sContent = sContent & "pageNames[" & iIterator & "][" & iIterator2 & "]="""_
               & objSubCurrentNode.getAttribute("name") & """;" & vbcrlf
     sContent = sContent & "pageURLs[" & iIterator & "][" & iIterator2 & "]="""_
               & objSubCurrentNode.getAttribute("url") & """;" & vbcrlf
     sContent = sContent & "pageTitles[" & iIterator & "][" & iIterator2 &
"]="""_
               & objSubCurrentNode.getAttribute("title") & """;" & vbcrlf
     iIterator2 = iIterator2 + 1
  Next
  iIterator = iIterator + 1
Next
Next
```

Because of the XML file structure, we know that the first level of `childNodes` that we parse is the section headings. Immediately inside the second `For...Each` loop the JavaScript code is created, then, providing that the section has `childNodes`, or subnavigation, its `childNodes` are parsed to create the next level of navigation variable assignments. Finally, as we walk through the XML data we are collecting the number of sections in the accumulator `iIterator`. Using the section count, we can then write out the initial variable assignments as in the previous ASP example.

```
Response.Write("var numSections=" & iIterator & ";" & vbcrlf)
Response.Write("var sectionNames=new Array(numSections);"& vbcrlf)
Response.Write("var pageNames=new Array(numSections);" & vbcrlf)
Response.Write("var pageURLs=new Array(numSections);" & vbcrlf)
Response.Write("var pageTitles=new Array(numSections);" & vbcrlf)
For i = 0 to numSections
   Response.Write("pageNames[" & i & "]=new Array();" & vbcrlf)
   Response.Write("pageURLs[" & i & "]=new Array();" & vbcrlf)
   Response.Write("pageTitles[" & i & "]=new Array();" & vbcrlf)
Next
Response.Write (sContent)
```

What is interesting about this XML example, as opposed to the database ones, is that all of the JavaScript is generated in a different order. In the earlier examples all of the section names are declared in a block, and then the page names are declared in a block. By performing the same task with XML we have these two sections merged, which helps to improve code readability. The output of the XML appears as such:

```
sectionNames[0]="MAIN";
pageNames[0][0]="OurCo Home Page";
pageURLs[0][0]="index";
pageTitles[0][0]="Gateway to the OurCo Website";
pageNames[0][1]="Company News";
pageURLs[0][1]="news";
pageTitles[0][1]="Happenings Around OurCo";
pageNames[0][2]="Press Room";
pageURLs[0][2]="press";
pageTitles[0][2]="Press Releases, and OurCo in the News";
pageNames[0][3]="Opportunities";
pageURLs[0][3]="opp";
pageTitles[0][3]="Employment and Other Opportunities with OurCo";
sectionNames[1]="OFFICES";
pageNames[1][0]="Aurora";
pageURLs[1][0]="aur";
pageTitles[1][0]="Aurora, Colorado, USA";
```

Now, by quickly scanning the output JavaScript we can tell which navigation sections contain which links.

# Future Work – ASP.NET

There probably isn't a developer on the planet that has managed to completely ignore the noise about Microsoft's .NET Framework. It is set to revolutionize Microsoft application development, and will give ASP web developers a lot of powerful new tools to play with, so we thought we'd better give it a mention here.

ASP.NET, like ASP, is a server-side framework that delivers dynamic content to web pages, but it has many advantages over its predecessor, such as better performance, due to the compiled, rather than interpreted nature of its code, and the seamless integration it has with other parts of the .NET framework, as well as other MS products.

So what would this mean for our menus? Well, with ASP.NET, we can build custom server controls that can contain all our menu functionality, and be included on a page using a simple `runat="server"` attribute in a declarative tag. This hides the code that implements the menu and allows menu functionality to be flexibly reused.

Database connectivity is also improved – by encapsulating database access in components, we gain the benefits of better performance and a simplification of our page code. XML handling gains similar benefits; transforms, in particular, are blisteringly fast with .NET.

Due to space, we will not expand further on this vast topic here – check out the references in our *Resources* section for more, and check out the code download for some examples, including a reworking of some of the examples we have seen in this chapter.

# Summary

And so we conclude not only this chapter, but also our journey into the varied and exciting world of navigation menus. This chapter has covered the most complicated area of menu design – dynamic population of menus from server-side datastores using middleware. The three middleware/datastore combinations we looked at were:

- PHP/MySQL

- ASP/SQL Server

- ASP/XML

We used these to accomplish two tasks: first we created a simple breadcrumb trail, and then we populated one of our client-side JavaScript examples, first seen in *Chapter 4*. This should allow you to create intelligent, dynamic, modular menus that are more easily maintainable – because we've separated the data from the client-side logic and presentation, we can modify these menus simply by updating the datastore, rather than editing client-side code.

We also said a few words about ASP.NET, and what the future holds for Microsoft web development.

# Resources

## ASP

ActiveState (Provider of largely Open Source resources for programmers, including lots of cool ASP tools): *http://www.activestate.com/*.

ASPToday (Subscription resource site packed with useful ASP articles, tutorials, and more): *http://www.ASPToday.com/*.

ASPFree (Another ASP resource site, featuring samples, tutorials etc.): *http://www.aspfree.com/*.

Beginning Active Server Pages 3.0: *Chris Ullman et al, Wrox Press, ISBN: 1861003382*.

## ASP.NET

Microsoft ASP.NET Quickstart Tutorial (comprehensive beginner's tutorials on ASP.NET): *http://www.aspfree.com/quickstart/aspplus/*.

The Microsoft ASP.NET Homepage: *http://www.asp.net/*.

Professional ASP.NET Website Programming: *Marco Bellinaso et al, Wrox Press, ISBN: 1861006934*.

## Cookies

Official cookie specification: *http://www.netscape.com/newsref/std/cookie_spec.html*.

Cookie Central: *http://www.cookiecentral.com/*.

# CSS

WebReview.com's "Style Sheet Reference Guide & Browser Compatibility Charts": *http://www.webreview.com/style/index.shtml*.

Glish's CSS Layout techniques: *http://www.glish.com/css/*.

W3C Schools – CSS. Very basic introductory tutorials on CSS: *http://www.w3schools.com/css/*.

# Document Object Model/Dynamic HTML

Document Object Cross Reference: *http://developer.netscape.com/evangelism/docs/technotes/xref/document-object/*.

DOM CSS 2 Property Cross Reference: *http://developer.netscape.com/evangelism/docs/technotes/xref/dom-css-style-object/*.

The W3C DOM homepage: *http://www.w3.org/DOM/*.

Microsoft DHTML reference (summarizes what is standard in DHTML and what are MS proprietary additions): *http://msdn.microsoft.com/library/default.asp?url=/workshop/author/dhtml/reference/dhtml_reference _entry.asp*.

# Flash/ActionScript

Colin Moock's Flash Player Inspector: *http://www.moock.org/webdesign/flash/detection/moockfpi/*.

Flash developer sites:

- *http://www.ultrashock.com*

- *http://www.were-here.com*

- *http://flashguru.co.uk*

New Masters of Flash: *Joel Baumann et al, Friends of ED, ISBN: 1903450039*.

Foundation ActionScript: *Sham Bhangal, Friends of ED, ISBN: 1903450322*.

Article – "How to detect the presence of the Flash Player": *http://www.macromedia.com/support/flash/ts/documents/uber_detection.htm*.

# JavaScript

The ECMAScript specification (ECMA-262): *http://www.ecma.ch/*.

Beginning JavaScript: *Sing Li et al, Wrox Press, ISBN: 1861004060*.

Instant JavaScript: *Nigel McFarlane et al, Wrox Press, ISBN: 1861001274*.

JavaScript References, code snippets and news: *http://www.javascript.com/*.

# PHP

PHP Home Page (Development and related news, downloads, the PHP Manual, links to tutorials): *http://www.php.net/*.

PHPBuilder (Good source of articles, with searchable help forums): *http://www.phpbuilder.com/*.

phpWizard (Home to several PHP applications including phpMyAdmin, phpPolls, and phpEasyMail; several tutorials; links to other resources): *http://www.phpwizard.net/*.

Instant no-hassle set-up for an open-source development on Windows (sets up PHP, MySQL, Apache, Perl, etc on your machine, instantly): *http://www.firepages.com.au/devindex.htm*.

# Usability

Don't Make me Think!: A Common Sense Approach to Web Usability: *Steve Krug, New Riders, ISBN: 0789723107*.

Article: "Users decide first, move second" (explores the idea that web users prefer simple menus where they can see all the options before they make a navigation choice, rather than fancy flyouts etc): *http://world.std.com/~uieweb/Articles/whatTheyWantArticle.htm*.

Web Sites That Suck (Vincent Flanders' site, dedicated to bad web design – what to avoid doing): *http://www.webpagesthatsuck.com/*.

Information Architecture for the World Wide Web: *Louis Rosenfeld and Peter Morville, O'Reilly, ISBN: 1565922824*.

# SQL/MySQL/SQL Server

SQL In A Nutshell (Survey of SQL in its 4 most widespread implementations; especially useful if you've worked with postgreSQL, MS SQL Server, or Oracle before, and need to get up to speed on MySQL in particular or need to port a database between it and one of the other three): *Kevin Kline, O'Reilly, ISBN: 1565927443*.

MySQL AB Website (The company that develops MySQL): *http://www.mysql.com/*.

Microsoft SQL Server Homepage: *http://msdn.microsoft.com/library/default.asp?url=/nhp/default.asp?contentid=28000409*.

MySQL: *Michael Kofler, APress, ISBN: 1893115577.*

Microsoft ADO Homepage: *http://www.microsoft.com/data/ado/default.htm.*

# XML

Beginning XML 2nd edition: *Jonathan Pinnock et al, Wrox Press, ISBN: 1861005598.*

XML Developer resources:

- *http://www.xml.com*
- *http://www.xml101.com*

# Index

## A Guide to the Index

The index is arranged hierarchically, in alphabetical order, with symbols preceding the letter A. Most second-level entries and many third-level entries also occur as first-level entries. This is to ensure that users will find the information they require however they choose to search for it.

**wrox**
Programmer to Programmer

# p2p.wrox.com
### The programmer's resource centre

## A unique free service from Wrox Press
### With the aim of helping programmers to help each other

Wrox Press aims to provide timely and practical information to today's programmer. P2P is a list server offering a host of targeted mailing lists where you can share knowledge with four fellow programmers and find solutions to your problems. Whatever the level of your programming knowledge, and whatever technology you use P2P can provide you with the information you need.

**ASP** Support for beginners and professionals, including a resource page with hundreds of links, and a popular ASP.NET mailing list.

**DATABASES** For database programmers, offering support on SQL Server, mySQL, and Oracle.

**MOBILE** Software development for the mobile market is growing rapidly. We provide lists for the several current standards, including WAP, Windows CE, and Symbian.

**JAVA** A complete set of Java lists, covering beginners, professionals, and server-side programmers (including JSP, servlets and EJBs)

**.NET** Microsoft's new OS platform, covering topics such as ASP.NET, C#, and general .NET discussion.

**VISUAL BASIC** Covers all aspects of VB programming, from programming Office macros to creating components for the .NET platform.

**WEB DESIGN** As web page requirements become more complex, programmer's are taking a more important role in creating web sites. For these programmers, we offer lists covering technologies such as Flash, Coldfusion, and JavaScript.

**XML** Covering all aspects of XML, including XSLT and schemas.

**OPEN SOURCE** Many Open Source topics covered including PHP, Apache, Perl, Linux, Python and more.

**FOREIGN LANGUAGE** Several lists dedicated to Spanish and German speaking programmers, categories include. NET, Java, XML, PHP and XML

### How to subscribe
**Simply visit the P2P site, at http://p2p.wrox.com/**